Praise for [ ] Moms

Kim Newell, MD,
I love it!—the writi. . . . . ks directly to the questions that many new parents ask me.

Lissa Rankin, MD, OB/GYN physician, founder of OwningPink.com and proud Mama

The Survival Guide for Rookie Moms serves up a much-needed dose of comfort, reassurance, humor and wisdom. Lorraine and Erica, who survived the first year and lived to write about it, hold your hand as you walk down your own unique, uncharted path of motherhood. With humor, candor and accurate information, this book reads like a girlfriend's guide but serves up the wisdom of a medical manual. As an OB/GYN physician, I wish I had this book to swaddle into the baby blankets when I pass off a newborn to the anxious new mother. And as a mommy, I wish I'd had this book to guide me through what they don't teach you in medical school.

The Survival Guide for Rookie Moms provides new moms with the best support of all: the knowledge that others—MANY others—have experienced the same trials, conundrums, confusion and loneliness that often accompanies the first year of motherhood. Think of it as the best friend, adoring mother, mentor, medical adviser, entertaining comedian and wise sage you wish you had sitting on your shoulder during every moment of your baby's first year.

Brigitte Schulte, RN

As a certified nurse responsible for the care of infants and their new mothers, I really connected with the content of this book. I found the information to be humorous, accurate and, most importantly, relevant. I would recommend this book to any of my patients and, as a mom myself, I can't wait to get a copy for my own enjoyment.

Melanie Osmack, Director/Instructor of Fit 4 Two Pre and Postnatal Fitness Inc.

Finally! A book that is as funny as it is accurate. New moms will tone their tummies from laughing as much as from exercising. I applaud Lorraine and Erica for encouraging women to ease back into fitness rather than jump back in—postpartum moms need to hear this message. I love all the core exercise ideas. They are simple, realistic and you can do them anywhere. Best of all, they produce results. Also, thank you for talking about *diastasis recti*! I get so many questions about this in class and it's great to see it covered in this fantastic book for new moms.

Melanie Berezan, mom of 4

I wish I'd had *The Survival Guide for Rookie Moms* when I had my first baby! Even after my fourth child I still appreciated the humorous insight and accurate information. The book is a great gift idea for any new mom.

Paula Vanni, mom of 2

Having a new baby can make an overachieving, competent and confident mom a total mess in a matter of seconds. Why?—because you are a rookie. Everything is new and confusing and you want to make the best possible decision in every area from what to feed, when to sleep to which shoes to put on your baby. *The Survival Guide for Rookie Moms* is the resource I wished I had when my babies were born—both of them—because it helps you navigate all the choices and priorities in a way that brings back some of the competence and confidence you need to be the best mom you can. It is a roadmap for the rookie mom that will make it so much easier to enjoy your baby rather than worry through the best years of your life.

Auntie Debbie

Being an Auntie I watched what my sisters went through during the first year of mommyhood, and truthful, honest advice, like what's in this book, is really what a new mother needs to be successful . . . and sane.

Erica's mom

Back in my day we didn't talk about "nether regions" and other body parts, so I am glad there has been an evolvement with mothers and am entirely sure that all the new moms out there are going to benefit from the helpful information in this book.

Susan Barclay, mom

I love this book! It's been my bible; every new mom should have a copy!

Martine Spinks, mom of 2

The Survival Guide for Rookie Moms helped me realize that I am not alone out there. It was so comforting to know that other moms struggled as much as I did and faced the same challenges in their first year of mommyhood. I really appreciate the advice and will pass this book on to other new moms.

Vicky Beaney, mum

As a new mum you are constantly bombarded with advice and directed to "great" sources of information. None were as useful, frank, and therefore funny, as *The Survival Guide for Rookie Moms* and I wouldn't have "survived" without it. A must read for all first time mothers.

The Survival Guide for Rookie Moms

THINGS YOU NEED TO KNOW THAT NO ONE EVER TELLS YOU

ERICA WELLS & LORRAINE REGEL

John Wiley & Sons Canada, Ltd.

Library and Archives Canada Cataloguing in Publication

Wells, Erica
    The survival guide for rookie moms / Erica Wells, Lorraine Regel.

Includes bibliographical references and index.
ISBN 978-0-470-73642-5

   1. Infants—Care.   2. Mothers—Health and hygiene.   3. Mother and infant.
4. Parenting. I.   Regel, Lorraine II.   Title.

HQ774.W44 2009   649'.122   C2009-906219-4

Production Credits
Interior Design: Michael Chan
Typesetter: Thomson
Illustrator: Jared Barber, Polar Animation
Printer: Friesens Printing Ltd.

Editorial Credits
Editor: Leah Fairbank
Project Coordinator: Pamela Vokey

John Wiley & Sons Canada, Ltd.
6045 Freemont Blvd.
Mississauga, Ontario
L5R 4J3

Printed in Canada

1 2 3 4 5 FP 14 13 12 11 10

ENVIRONMENTAL BENEFITS STATEMENT

John Wiley & Sons - Canada saved the following resources by printing the pages of this book on chlorine free paper made with 100% post-consumer waste.

TREES	WATER	SOLID WASTE	GREENHOUSE GASES
43	19,702	1,196	4,091
FULLY GROWN	GALLONS	POUNDS	POUNDS

Calculations based on research by Environmental Defense and the Paper Task Force.
Manufactured at Friesens Corporation

Dedications

Erica
For my two wonderful children, Mackenzie and Parker

Lorraine
For Pickle and Bowser—my two little inspirations

Contents

Foreword

By Lissa Rankin, MD, OB/GYN physician

You've navigated the fertility journey, survived nine months of gestation and successfully achieved your goal—Baby is here! Now what? I hear the postpartum whispers that echo around the exam rooms of my OB/GYN practice: *Why do I still look pregnant after giving birth? What do you mean I can have SEX again? Will my baby still get into college if my breasts don't make enough milk? How can I prevent getting knocked up again right away? Will my body ever be the same? Will I ever get my life back?*

It's easy to lose your mojo when you're a new mother. Before you became a mom, chances are you felt some element of control over your life, received positive validation for the hard work you do and found some measure of acceptance—if not love—for the skin you live in. Giving birth can change all that. You find yourself suddenly thrown into what is arguably the most important task of your life, with little to no education to prepare you. You struggle to succeed at your new job, only to discover that there are no benchmarks to define success and nobody to validate the job you're doing. It's enough to make a woman feel rootless, insecure and lonely.

Sound familiar? *You are not alone.* We mothers all experience swirling, confusing emotions in the aftermath of childbirth, but too few people talk about it. We're led to believe that having a baby should be the happiest time of our lives, but most of us feel overwhelmed, out of sorts and frumpy after we give birth. What does it mean to feel this way? It means you're *perfectly normal.* Sleep deprivation, body image issues, disruptions in your relationship, time constraints, changes in your sexual life, career stressors and your evolving role threaten to rob you of your identity, your peace of mind, your joie de vivre and your mojo.

Don't despair, Mommies! *The Survival Guide for Rookie Moms* serves up a much-needed dose of comfort, reassurance, humor and wisdom. Lorraine Regel and Erica Wells, who survived the first year and lived to write about it, hold your hand as you walk down your own unique, uncharted path of motherhood. With humor, candor and accurate information, this book reads like a girlfriend's guide but serves up the wisdom of a medical manual. As an OB/GYN physician, I wish I had this book to swaddle into the baby blankets when I pass off a newborn to the anxious new mother. And as a mommy, I wish I'd had this book to guide me through what they don't teach you in medical school.

The Survival Guide for Rookie Moms provides new moms with the best support of all: the knowledge that others—MANY others—have experienced the same trials, conundrums, confusion and loneliness that often accompanies the first year of motherhood. Think of it as the best friend, adoring mother, mentor, medical adviser, entertaining comedian and wise sage you wish you had sitting on your shoulder during every moment of your baby's first year.

Lissa Rankin, MD, OB/GYN physician, author of *What's Up Down There? Questions You'd Only Ask Your Gynecologist If She Was Your Best Friend* (St. Martin's Press, 2010), founder of OwningPink.com and proud Mama.

Foreword

By Kim Newell, MD, pediatrician

"I'm going to break my baby!" At some point, these words have been on the lips of every rookie mom who comes to my pediatric practice.

Being a mom in our generation is not easy. Women used to be surrounded by wise experienced grandmothers, aunties and neighbors who showed them the ropes. It is rare for us to have such communities these days. But in this information age, surely there is no lack of resources to help new moms navigate the ins and outs of raising their child: with countless how-to books, parent-centered websites, mothers' groups and mommy blogs to turn to, the answer to all of your questions and needs should be easy to find, right?

In spite of all this information, the moms I see in my practice are still full of questions, anxieties and fears about every aspect of caring for their newborn baby. As a physician, I can help them to prioritize what is—and is not—important to worry about. Does Baby's goopy eye need urgent care? Is green poop something to panic about? What is that scary looking rash? It gives me great joy to be able to help ease these fears, but I have long wondered why there is no book that can guide rookie moms through the early days of the toughest job they'll ever get, a job for which they have had no training. Well, that book is finally here. And it is not like other parenting books.

When I first read *The Survival Guide for Rookie Moms*, I was amazed to see how perfectly Lorraine Regel and Erica Wells have zeroed in on all of the top issues that parents come to ask me about.

As moms, they know best what aspects of raising a little one are confusing or anxiety provoking. And they get the answers right. With chapters on all the parts of your babies' little bodies that seem so familiar and yet so confusing, the authors have given top-notch information to help you feel confident and competent in caring for your baby. Their accessible style is authoritative but not preachy; they impart knowledge based on experience and backed up by research; and most importantly, they do so with a sense of humor that adds levity to the dark moments of parenting.

Their survival guide gives plenty of answers about caring for infants by the book, but with their **Comrades' Recommendations, Survival Secrets** and **Tips from the Trenches** the authors add a dose of parenting realism that is comforting and refreshing. As they put it, "Oh, blah blah blah—every now and again I catch myself regurgitating advice and overlooking what happens in the real world. Before we start to sound just like every other baby book out there, let's step back and be honest: babies don't like lumps."

Many of the moms in my practice use my office as a confessional, guiltily admitting to all of the parenting rules they have not followed. The authors make sure to use their own "failings" as mothers to help new moms laugh at the times they think they're being a terrible mommy, reminding us that we're all human: "Oh crap, I just put my son to bed forgetting to clean his teeth once again. Well, it takes time to remember it should be a part of the bedtime routine."

Being a new mom is full of joys and also many anxieties. I hate to see rookie moms reduced to tears by worries when I can so easily reassure them. Unfortunately I cannot be at home with parents day and night. But you now have the perfect companion to accompany you on this exciting journey. Armed with this book, you too will be able to accept the fact that your wardrobe is "one big burp cloth" and—"accustomed to eau de vomit as your new perfume"—cruise through the early days of constipation, feeding difficulties, spit ups, diaper rashes and sleepless nights. *The Survival Guide for Rookie Moms* is now required reading for all the new moms in my practice. And after Mom is done, please pass it on to Dad too.

Kim Newell, MD, pediatrician and
blogger at drkimmd.com

Introduction

First of all, no one told me that giving birth was like trying to have a huge poo. Sure, there was a lot of talk at prenatal classes of pushing and bearing down, but no one actually told me the whole down-and-dirty truth. Why the big secret, I wonder. Okay, it's not a very romantic analogy for the wondrous process of bringing a new life into the world, but I wish I had known. And that was only the first of many half-truths, untruths and pieces of parenting advice wrapped in cotton wool that I received prior to having my baby.

If you're anything like me, you probably spent a lot of your pregnancy eating chocolate as you diligently read your pregnancy manual. At any given week you knew exactly what to expect from your body and delighted in knowing the current food analogy for Baby's size. You'd go over the labor section several times, even though it was like reading a horror story and it put you off your chocolate. You'd go to prenatal classes and—when you finished eyeing up the other women, thinking, "I don't look that big, do I? Maybe she eats too much chocolate,"—you'd listen intently and take notes. It all led up to that momentous day when you gave birth, as if it all ended there. Then suddenly you're less informed and—dare I say it?—clueless. You may know a little about babies, but do you have the faintest idea what disasters might befall your body and mind in the coming months? There's one sure thing: you're going to have to cut back on the chocolate consumption.

A baby is a pretty complicated piece of machinery when you think about it. What other hi-tech device would you bring home without instructions? Sure, you might manage to get the new, top-of-the-line DVD player functioning, but could you get the most out of all the extra, exciting features? More importantly, where would you be without the don't-do-this-or-it-will-break warning list? The afterbirth shouldn't be a gelatinous mass that you don't even want to look at; it should be the instruction manual, or at the very least be inscribed with a few helpful hints. "Oh look," the nurse would say as she handed you the baby and its accompanying booklet. "You have the 2010 early-walker, late-talker model with the big appetite function. Congratulations!"

An experienced mommy friend is bound to tell you, "Call me any time you need to," but after the tenth call of the day you may start to wear out your welcome and find yourself talking to the answering machine. Would you really call her at 2 a.m. with a question? Because that's inevitably the time when you find yourself at your wit's end, pacing the floor with a screaming baby, not having a clue what to do.

Having a baby is probably the biggest lifestyle change you will ever experience. As a friend put it, "Having a baby doesn't change your life; it becomes your life." For me, embarking on motherhood was like entering a whole new world—without a map, guidebook or phrasebook. Luckily, after only a few weeks adrift in Baby World, I was fortunate enough to find some fellow castaways and soon built up a lifesaving band of mommy friends. Chatting with this group, I discovered more truthful and helpful info than I ever did reading the typical baby book. We were soon discussing the nitty-gritty facts about how difficult breastfeeding really is and how explosive baby poo can be, sharing tales of vaporized sex drives, and admitting that it's fairly common to pee your pants at this postpartum stage. Quite often it wasn't an answer to a problem that brought relief, but simply the knowledge that what was happening to me was normal, and that other moms have been there. It made me feel a whole heap better to have comrades, and, with the chance to laugh about my woes thrown into the bargain, they might well have saved my sanity.

The Survival Guide for Rookie Moms was conceived one night over a fabulous curry when fellow new mom Erica suggested we collaborate on a baby book. Why not make a down-to-earth, practical, helpful and humorous survival guide and get these "I wish I had known" topics out in the open? Let's try to help rookie moms raise a smile through the pain of chafed nipples, regardless of the fact that they can't sit down except on a doughnut cushion, and even when they haven't slept more than four hours in the last 48. It's our chance to reassure them: "You may think you are going insane and your body is falling apart, but actually you're perfectly normal." Once we mentioned the idea to our mommy friends, there was unanimous agreement that this fresh approach would be gratefully received by rookie moms, and the suggestions of topics to be included in the book came flooding in.

Our survival guide is aimed primarily at new moms rather than dads because that's where our expertise lies and, let's face it ladies, we do bear the brunt of the new-parent experience. For a start, giving birth and breastfeeding are obviously up to us. It's our bodies (and minds) that change, change again, then refuse to change back the way we want them to. It's we who develop the hearing of bats, the sense of smell of a bloodhound, eyes in the backs of our heads and as many arms as an octopus (we wish). In most cases it's also we who will provide the lion's (sorry, lioness's) share of the caregiving, at least for the first year. As hard as dads might try, they can't fight nature, and it is Mom whose "spidey senses" will be on full alert for the foreseeable future to nurture and protect the baby no matter what. So forgive us for poking fun at dads just a little; no offense is intended. That said, we hope this guide is a help to all new parents. Dads will undoubtedly benefit from hearing some mommy water-cooler talk to get insight into what is making Mom tick these days and learning how to avoid getting their heads bitten off quite so often.

We're not medically trained and don't have letters after our names (well Erica does, but unfortunately nothing that qualifies her to give advice on sick babies), so although we may touch on common baby and new mom ailments, we're not going into medical detail. Those books have been done to death and done very well already. We don't presume to be experts in our field, but between ourselves and our learned friends, we believe we have a few words of wisdom to share. Nobody has all the answers, because there are no "answers." Having been through pregnancy, you now know that nothing happens at exactly this time, lasts this long, is precisely this big or hurts this much. There is no "normal" with babies either. No two babies are the same. We can vouch for that fact because Erica and I both have an elder daughter and younger son of almost identical ages, but our parenting experiences have been vastly different. We have taken these experiences and consolidated them into one voice to provide you with a helpful (and, we hope, humorous) survival guide to life during the first year of motherhood.

Since Mom and Baby are both embarking on new life journeys, we decided to divide our book into two. In the first half, the **Baby Map** concentrates on the new addition to the family. In the second half, the **Mommy Map** is dedicated to the issues a postpartum mom might encounter as she adjusts to her new body and lifestyle. These are the truths we wish we had been armed with on our initial expeditions to Baby World. We wish you happy travels.

Lorraine

THE BABY MAP—
AN INTRODUCTION

Most baby books tend to follow a chronological format, with chapters dedicated to "the first month at home with baby," "two to three months," and so on. One thing you quickly learn as a rookie mom is that babies don't follow any timetable but their own, so we saw no sense in formatting our book this way. Instead, we've organized our information around a map of your baby's body. Each chapter zooms in on a body part. We tackle the trouble zones and attempt to navigate a way through them. The intention is that even the most sleep-deprived or distraught mom can easily locate the section of the book where she might find relevant advice on a problem.

Join us on our quest to understand the complexities of Baby World. **Comrades' Recommendations, Survival Secrets** and **Tips from the Trenches** gathered from our band of mommy friends will aid us on our journey, starting at the top of Baby's sweet-smelling head and working our way down to the less fragrant regions.

CHAPTER 1

Baby Map—Hair and Head

HAIR GROWTH—OR NOT

We are hairy parents. I'm the sort of woman whose legs get a five o'clock shadow. My little girl refers to Daddy's forearms and chest as "furry." Consequently, we are still in amazement that our baby girl was born with a bald, shiny pate and not a hair in sight. By age one she had barely more than a dusting of fuzz. The only glimmer of hope was her lovely long eyelashes and shapely brows. At two and a half, we just managed to scrape together enough hair to make pigtails, and boy, was she proud—it was worth waiting for.

Some babies are born with a full head of hair, others are born with peach fuzz, and some are bald until they turn one—or two. Don't despair if you can't put your little girl in beautiful ponytails. There are always cute headbands to fill the gap while you wait for her hair to grow in, provided you don't mind your kid looking like a fancy Easter egg. At least people will stop calling her a boy. Actually, they might not. It seems that in most people's minds, long hair equals girl, and short or no hair equals boy. You can dress your baldy gal in pink from head to toe and adorn her noggin with all manner of accessories, and the old biddy in the elevator will still marvel at your "cute little guy." As the mother of a follicularly challenged baby, you will inevitably encounter someone who knows someone who was similarly hairless until age two, three or even four. "Yet look at her now," they'll say. I even heard of one mom sewing some of her own hair into her infant daughter's hat.

Until it grows, enjoy the low maintenance and fresh look of your baby's bald head, and be glad that you don't have to comb out all those tangles after bath time. Think of the savings on baby shampoo and haircuts alone. Don't be tempted to shave Baby's head to promote growth—there is no scientific evidence to prove this works. If your child's hair doesn't appear to be growing in *at all* by the time she turns two, then you may want to consult your doctor.

HAIR LOSS

You may be gloating because your baby was born with a beautiful, full head of hair, but you'll be disappointed to discover it's not necessarily here to stay. Don't worry, it's not a sign of early balding. Baby's not following in Dad's footsteps just yet. It's a phase that most babies will go through (providing they are born with hair in the first place). From the time that you bring your sweet bundle of joy home from the hospital until she is about one month old, she will lose hair due to a drop in hormone levels, just like postpartum moms. It will thin out rather than come out in chunks, and some babies will lose more than others. You'll notice the downy strands on Baby's bedding. The good news is that the hair will begin to grow back again immediately after it's gone. Unfortunately, the same is not true for Dad.

BALD SPOTS

Just when you think that Baby is finally in the stages of hair growth rather than hair loss, you might notice he is developing a bald spot. (So he is taking after Dad after all!) This peculiar bald spot, patch or line is due to hair rubbing off the back of the head where it is almost constantly in contact with the mattress, car seat, stroller, bouncy chair or rug. We are all aware of the reduced risk of sudden infant death syndrome (SIDS) if Baby sleeps on his back, so that's 15 hours a day spent horizontal straight off the bat. Newborns also spend most of their waking hours just lying around on a blanket;

after all, what else is there to do when you can't support the weight of your own head? There is really no way to avoid this type of baby baldness since tummy time is limited to short phases in the first few months, although changing Baby's sleep position from one end of the crib to the other may help. Once Baby is spending more time on his tummy and is starting to sit and crawl, the hair will start to fill in. In the meantime, don't worry: the monk look is all the rage at baby groups.

HAIR COLOR

Don't let Dad start a row over true paternity in the delivery room if Baby is born with dark hair while the two of you are blonde. Babies are kind of like chameleons; the color of their hair when they are born is not necessarily the color it will be a year or two later. As your baby gets older, the pigment in her hair will mature to what her permanent color will be. Often the changes are sudden: when Baby loses her birth tresses in the first month, the new growth may appear in a different shade. In other babies, color change is more gradual. For instance, a friend's daughter was born with a thick head of jet-black hair. Her husband has black hair, so it all made sense, but by three years old their daughter had gorgeous blonde hair, just like Mom. And no, Mom didn't take her along to the salon for highlights, as some friends have suggested.

HAIR CARE—WASHING

To the fastidious groomers out there this may sound gross, but you actually don't need to wash your baby's hair every day, or even every second day—or every third day, for that matter. A newborn baby often has greasy-looking hair due to the overactive oil glands on his head, but unless you are trying to combat cradle cap, a hair wash with a twice-weekly bath is ample. Too much washing can dry a baby's scalp.

Comrades' Recommendations

- You don't need to use shampoo to wash your baby's hair; you can use the same baby body wash you use on his sensitive skin.
- Ensure that the shampoo or body wash is specifically designed for newborns. Suds will inevitably get in your baby's eyes, so you'll want to make sure that it's the "no tears" kind—you don't want to put Baby off bath time with stinging soap.

- Two arms never seem enough for the novice mom when washing a baby's hair. Here are two recommended hair-washing methods:
  - ○ Wash his hair before you put Baby in the tub. Keep him diapered (for obvious reasons) and wrapped in a towel while you hold his head over the tub to shampoo and rinse. Dry off his head, then bathe the rest of him.
  - ○ Recline Baby in the bathtub, support his head with one hand and rinse it with a washcloth. Or, the gentle flow of water from a toy watering can may be effective for rinsing out the shampoo.
- Use a pump-action shampoo dispenser that you can work with one hand, or squirt the shampoo onto the side of the bath before you start.
- Don't over-lather—a pea-sized serving of baby shampoo is ample, otherwise you will never be rid of the suds.
- Use a calm voice to talk your baby through the process, or sing a song.
- Have a dry washcloth on hand to wipe away drips from his eyes.
- If you have any hands left, try distracting a fussy baby with a toy as you wash.
- Try to make hair washing a fun part of bath time or you'll have a battle on your hands in toddlerhood, when kids typically get scared of water in their faces.
- Make fun shapes out of your older baby's soapy hair and get him laughing with you. Give him a countdown to the rinsing so it doesn't take him by surprise.
- Wash hair last if Baby doesn't enjoy it to avoid tears through the rest of bath time.

CRADLE CAP

Cradle cap—that unsightly scabby head that prevents your little angel from looking her best for visitors—is not caused by poor hygiene, and is neither contagious nor harmful to your baby in any way. But to the vain, doting new parents among us it can be distressing, and we certainly don't want it spoiling the baby pictures. The exact cause of cradle cap isn't known, but it is likely a result of hyperactive oil glands due to a hormonal imbalance. This gives Baby greasy hair just like a teenager. The excreted grease acts like glue, adhering old skin cells to the scalp and creating a flaky, yellow/orange/brown crust on the head and often around the eyebrows and behind the ears. Most babies have it to some degree in their first year, usually during the first few months.

Tips from the Trenches

- There's no need to do anything about cradle cap. It will right itself soon enough, usually by six to 12 months. The good news is that once it is entirely gone, the chances of it returning are slim.
- If you do want to tackle it, wash Baby's hair and scalp more frequently with mild baby shampoo.
- A surefire way to get rid of cradle cap is to gently massage baby oil (almond or olive work well also) into your baby's scalp, avoiding the eyes. After a few minutes, brush her head lightly with a soft baby brush to loosen the flakes, then rinse off the oil with mild baby soap or shampoo.
- If the cradle cap is severe, itchy or not responding to treatment, see your doctor for advice.

HAIR CARE—CUTTING

Ah, Baby's first haircut. What a milestone; what a disaster! "Nothing to it," we amateurs assume as we rev up the clippers or move in for the first snip—then Baby squirms and there go the straight bangs. You'll be lucky if she's left with any bangs at all as you try to improve on your wonky efforts. There are also other minor considerations, such as earlobes, which you would rather remained untrimmed and attached to Baby's head.

Comrades' Recommendations

- Relax; this model can't complain if you do a bad job. Have fun and make the most of it if you want to practice your hairdressing skills. It will be the only time in your child's life that she lets you near her hair with a pair of scissors.
- If you want a more professional look and you're somewhat challenged in the hairdressing department, it might be safer to let a competent, skilled friend do the job. It's probably not worth splashing out on a salon visit just yet.
- Unless Dad is John Frieda, don't let him assume control of any kiddy haircut. While my husband's first attack with the clippers left our baby's head resembling a pet prepped for an operation, I know one dad who had the bright idea of putting a hat on his toddler and cutting around. Needless to say, Mom—who was not too keen on her little one modeling a Jim Carrey *Dumb and Dumber* cut—had to step in and salvage the situation.

CONE HEADS AND MORE

Beauty is in the eye of the beholder, and unless the beholder is a smitten grandma, new babies aren't really that beautiful. To be perfectly frank, they can be somewhat aesthetically challenged and they often have certain alien qualities. Okay, E.T. is cute, but not a stunner. We nicknamed our newborn Gollum.

It's not surprising that they aren't looking their best, having been squeezed through your nether regions for hours on end. The journey can take a toll and leave babies looking a little misshapen. Cone heads, swollen faces, squashed noses, folded ears and squinty, puffy eyes are common battle scars that your baby can emerge with, but all will settle down and ping into place within days, if not hours. C-section newborns have a distinct advantage in the looks department, but all babies look a bit strange initially, with their oversized heads and nonexistent necks. Add to this the various skin blemishes and complaints new babies are prone to, such as milk spots, birth marks and baby acne (see the **Skin** chapter) and you might want to avoid using the zoom lens for the early photos. Rest assured, she'll be gorgeous a month or so down the line.

FREAKY FONTANELS

I think most new parents are nervous about the fontanel, or "soft spot," on Baby's head. We all know it's going to be there, but the sight of this spongy diamond, especially when it pulses, just screams, "Vulnerable vital organ here!" It's true there is no bone protecting the brain, but this tough, fibrous membrane is more than enough to guard from all but the freakiest of accidents.

At birth a baby actually has more than one area of the skull where the bones are not fused together, but we usually only notice the biggest fontanel on top of the head. It will close gradually starting around six months, and the bones are usually fused together by 18 months.

The fontanels actually made childbirth easier for you. (That was the easy version? Could have fooled me.) The soft spots allowed the head to mold as it moved along the birth canal. If babies' skulls were fixed, women would need wider hips to be able to give birth—not a popular alternative. The skull also needs to be flexible to allow for massive brain growth in the first year. Since the bones of the skull are able to flex around the soft spots, the spots actually function as a safety mechanism to protect Baby's noggin from the multitude of bumps and bangs it will get in early mobility.

The fontanel can even serve as a health indicator. A markedly sunken fontanel is a sign of dehydration, and a persistently bulging fontanel can be a symptom of a serious ailment and should be checked immediately by a doctor. So although the fontanel may make you a little squeamish, you have to admit it is a pretty useful feature.

FLAT HEAD SYNDROME

As one parenting dilemma is tackled, so another comes along to top up the worry tank. In an effort to reduce the risk of SIDS—easily the number one worry of all new parents—we ensure Baby sleeps on her back. (Whatever you do, don't stop being fanatical about "back to sleep.") However, so much time spent putting pressure on one part of the head while Baby's skull is still soft and pliable is increasing a phenomenon known as positional plagiocephaly, in which babies' heads develop flat spots at the back. In severe cases, it can lead to uneven eyes and ears. Happily, flat spots will normally round out once Baby masters sitting and crawling and is not spending so much time lying around.

Tips from the Trenches

- One way to help eliminate flat head syndrome is to have your baby spend significant time on her tummy during the day. See **Head Control and Neck Strength** (below) for tips on safe tummy time.
- Alternate Baby's position in the crib. Some nights, put her head at the other end of the crib. She will naturally turn to look out of the crib rather than at the wall, thus lying on a different part of her head.
- If you don't notice any improvement from these home remedies, see your doctor to assess the severity of the flattening. There are helmets and bands available that Baby can wear to prevent her from putting pressure on the flat spot.

HEAD CONTROL AND NECK STRENGTH

Second only to the pulsing fontanel, the most tricky and alarming part of a new baby for novice parents to handle has to be his weak neck. You have to constantly support Baby's head and neck as you hold or carry him for the first couple of months—a fact you can't help reminding everyone of as you pass them your precious cargo. By a month old, Baby should be able to lift his head and turn it from side to side while lying on his tummy. Encourage these neck-strengthening exercises by giving your baby lots of supervised tummy time, and by three months old he should be able to lift his head somewhere between 45 and 90 degrees from horizontal. What a relief when Baby is robust enough that you aren't afraid he will snap whenever you pick him up. By the time they are about four months old, most babies build neck muscles adequate to hold their head up unsupported, but they may still have an amusing bobblehead quality until around six months.

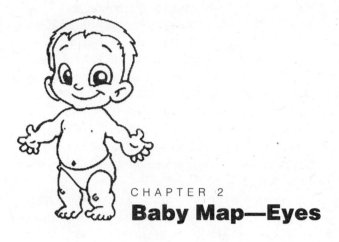

CHAPTER 2
Baby Map—Eyes

VISION

Until a baby is two months old, her sight is limited and hearing is her primary sense. Her sight will develop gradually, until by about eight months she sees as well as you can. Studies show that a newborn can focus 8 to 14 inches (20 to 35 centimeters) in front of her, so she can see the important things in life: Mommy's boobies at feeding time, Daddy's big nose as he leans in to plant a kiss on her cheek and, most fascinating to Baby, the smiling face of whoever is holding her. A new baby can detect images further away, like shapes, movement and light from a window, but these are blurry; so, if you have any sneaky chocolate eating to do, you can do so far away and Baby won't see. (But remember, her ears work well, so she may hear the rustling of the wrapper and tell on you anyway.)

A new baby has no depth perception because her eyes aren't even working together at this point. Experts also say that a new baby has limited color vision. How on earth they know a one-month-old can't see the color blue is a mystery to me—who did they ask? This is a great reason to carefully choose the toys you put in front of your baby. No sense in spending a lot of money on toys she can't or doesn't want to look at. Toys with contrasting colors are always a hit, especially black and white, or bright colored patterns like stripes, checks and polka dots. Mobiles or toys hanging from the baby gym should be 8 to 12 inches (20 to 30 centimeters) from Baby, or she's not going to get much out of them.

As Baby grows, a human face will remain the most appealing view, and by three months she will be able to recognize a familiar face. Interestingly, studies say that baby girls are much more interested in facial expressions than boys are, and are more likely to make eye contact in the first three months—it's all in the brain wiring.

At four months old, your baby's color vision is improving. She will still enjoy brightness and contrast, and will watch moving objects and people. A friend's baby used to go into rapture at the sunlight twinkling through leaves on the park trees, and would babble so loudly as to make passersby turn and stare. (Which was very sweet—except that at least one member of the mommy gathering would likely be breastfeeding and wouldn't particularly want attention drawn her way.)

By six months, a baby has more control over her eyes and is developing depth perception and fine detail vision. She's hungry for anything new to look at, and Mother Nature has it all worked out: Baby will likely start to crawl around this time, so she can go see interesting sights on her own instead of waiting for Mom to bring stuff. Pretty soon she'll be spotting the tiniest bits and bobs on the carpet and presenting them to you (or eating them), so it's time to get your housework in order.

EYE COLOR

"Ah, doesn't he have beautiful blue eyes," has to be the most common compliment visitors bestow on a new baby. They are likely clutching at straws given that newborns can be sadly lacking in the looks department, but it's a pretty meaningless comment as almost all Caucasian babies are born with blue eyes, and it's not necessarily their permanent color. The eyes may remain that beautiful shade of blue or gray, but as Baby grows he can develop more pigment in his eyes (melanin), which changes the color to brown or green. At eight months, eyes are close to their final color, although the shade may change subtly. By the time Baby turns one year old, the eye color that he has will be permanent—unless, of course, he is lured by colored contacts in adulthood.

Babies who have dark skin pigmentation, such as those of Asian, African American, Hispanic or Native American descent, will usually be brown-eyed at birth and will stay that way.

If you are playing a betting game and want to predict your child's eye color, you shouldn't necessarily risk your stake on your own or Dad's eye color. While two blue-eyed parents are most likely to have blue-eyed children, brown-eyed parents also commonly have blue-eyed children. If the parents are a combo, it's best to keep your money in your pocket and wait to see what nature delivers.

BLOCKED TEAR DUCTS

A brand new baby may do plenty of crying, but she won't initially produce any tears. Tears start to fall after a couple of weeks, which is when symptoms of a blocked tear duct might show. If your baby's eyes are getting excessively watery, even when she is not crying, it is probably due to a blocked tear duct. This happens when the tear drainage system into the nose is obstructed or fails to break open properly at birth, causing the eye to flood. It is fairly common for a baby to be born with one or two blocked tear ducts, but it usually rights itself as Baby grows. In the meantime, Baby may experience a swollen or infected tear duct sac resulting in a mucous discharge around the eyelid.

Tips from the Trenches

- Try to keep Baby's eyes clean at all times to help prevent infection. Wipe them with saline solution on a cotton ball. Use a fresh cotton ball for each eye to prevent spread of infection.
- Consult your doctor or community health nurse on your next visit to determine whether a blockage is severe. They will tell you if massaging the inner corner of the eye might help clear it up, or if antibiotic eye ointment is necessary.

CRYING

The million dollar question: how do you know what a baby's cry means? I have no idea, and I've tried my hardest to understand the reasons behind my son's constant griping. I honestly don't remember learning to decode different cries for my first child. I now know we were lucky—she didn't complain much. It's pretty obvious if Baby cries every time you change his diaper or give him a bath that he dislikes that particular activity, but if he's sitting seemingly happy and suddenly dissolves into tears, it's less easy to work out why. We know babies cry to tell you they need something, but determining exactly *what* they need involves a little detective work. According to baby language expert Priscilla Dunstan, babies have a language they use to tell us the reason for their cry just before they start bawling. Hmmm, no joy there for me; my baby didn't give cues. He just launched from sleep into a full-blown squawk. All newborns like to dedicate more than two hours a day to crying, so we have plenty of opportunities to learn—and some babies give us more learning opportunities than others.

Babies fit roughly into three categories: the contented baby (or just "the baby"), the high-needs baby and the colicky baby. If you have the first, thank your lucky stars; commiserations if yours falls into one of the other two groups. You're going to have plenty of opportunities to learn to decode those cries. I was worried that my son's cranky, miserable demeanor was due to some failing on my part. Was he lacking attention, since he was sharing me with my three-year-old? However, a mom of fraternal twins admitted that while one of her girls was a contented baby, the other was as miserable as sin. This confirms it: it can't be anything you are doing (or not doing) as a mom; it's just your baby's nature, which was set at birth. So don't take it personally if yours is less content than others.

The following is a list of common reasons for Baby to be unhappy, and some suggestions of how to try to remedy the situation, although most of the time your instinct will guide you. Take it as slowly and calmly as possible, rather than frantically trying three things at once, or Baby might get more agitated. Besides, if you try more than one strategy at once, you'll never know which one worked.

- Most of the time he'll cry when he's hungry. A little tummy doesn't hold much food, and breast milk in particular is quickly and easily digested. If a newborn didn't cry to order food, there would be no way he would get back to the boob every two hours. It's Baby's way of teaching Mom the feeding schedule. Hunger cries can start as fussiness and build in intensity, especially if Baby sees Mom passing by.
- Grumpiness is often brought on by being overtired. We imagine babies are experts at falling asleep, but frequently they find it hard to switch off. Calming them with rocking or singing can help.
- Pain cries are more piercing and urgent, or more like a scream. Gas pains are common for babies, and they often just need a good burp. To release the trapped gas, you can try the typical winding methods: patting or rubbing his back, rubbing his tummy or laying him on his back and bicycling his legs. Excess gas in a breastfed baby could be a response to a gas-producing food that

you have eaten (see **Breastfeeding Diet** in the **Boobs** chapter of the **Mommy Map**).

- Some babies complain about a dirty diaper, others couldn't care less and some even find the warm squishiness comforting. A baby is more likely to protest if wetness is irritating a diaper rash.

- Baby might be too hot or too cold. Ideally your room temperature should be about 71.6° Fahrenheit (22° Celsius), and Baby's normal body temperature is 98.6° Fahrenheit (37° Celsius). Don't be guided by how warm a baby's hands and feet seem—feel his body and neck to see if he feels cold or sweaty.

- Other discomforts, like a diaper that's too tight, uncomfortable clothing or a scratchy clothing label, could be the problem. Strip a layer off to see if Baby is happier unbundled. Or try a new outfit— maybe the other one was stiff, had itchy fabric or wasn't breathable. Maybe he just didn't like the color.

- Some babies find being swaddled in a blanket comforting, as if freedom of movement outside the womb is disturbing. If you mastered the swaddle technique while in the maternity ward, try it out.

- Often a baby wants to be on the move. Whether he is trying to fall asleep or just fussy, some movement might help. Each baby has a preferred move, which you will soon learn by experimenting with rocking, patting, jiggling or swaying. Our particular favorite was a hand under the bum giving a gentle bounce. A relative admitted that he spent so much time standing and swaying with his babies that for years after he would catch himself swaying oddly from side to side while in conversation with someone. A baby swing or a vibrating bassinet or chair could create the desired effect while saving your back and lessening the chance you'll develop a peculiar parental tick.

- What nicer reason to cry than just needing a cuddle? Sometimes babies crave contact or simply some company in the form of a smiling face and a soothing voice.

- A baby often has a preferred holding position, just like he has a favorite movement. Try over your shoulder or turned towards you with a full view of your face. The football hold with tummy down on your forearm is often a winner. My arms were always too spindly for this; Dad's were much more substantial and satisfying. If you don't have the muscles for the football hold, try tummy down across your lap.

- Feeling anxious about the new environment is also a cause for a newborn's crying. Soothing, rhythmic sounds that mimic Mom's heartbeat, like a ticking clock, or white noise, such as the hum of the washing machine or vacuum cleaner, can help baby feel more at home. Familiar rhythmic music can also be calming.
- It is possible that Baby is just a miserable soul. If you've tried all the above (and more) and nothing works, it might be time to accept that Baby isn't enjoying his new life just yet. Maybe he liked it in the dark, warm, comfy womb and isn't keen on the outside world.
- A miserable baby is one thing, but a colicky baby is a whole other story. Persistent crying for hours, often at the same time of day, every day, is likely colic (see later in this chapter).

Sad to say, but things are likely to get worse before they get better. Often a newborn will lull you into a false sense of security for the first couple of weeks. It's almost as if he is born with a wrapper protecting him from the big bad world that he sheds at two weeks, leaving him fully exposed and vulnerable. Universally there is a recognized peak in crankiness around six to eight weeks for unknown reasons. So it's important to set your expectations. Once Baby reaches about the three-month mark, he'll likely chill out a bit and reduce crying to an hour or less a day. Maybe we do start to recognize the cries, or maybe by now we are in tune with the feeding and changing schedule and are anticipating some of Baby's needs. However, it's not all free sailing from here on; there are some new causes of baby misery on the horizon to keep you on your toes.

- **Teething pain:** See **Teething** in the **Mouth** chapter.
- **Boredom:** Keep the toys rotating and the entertainment fresh. It's time to polish up your song-and-dance routines. Don't worry if you're not Beyoncé. Your audience is not discerning, although Baby may heckle and throw things all the same.
- **Frustration:** With limited mobility and motor control, it's often hard for a baby to achieve what he's set his heart on. Once he is mobile and into everything, there will be lots of frustration arising from not being allowed to do certain things and go certain places.

HIGH-NEEDS BABY

If my son had been my firstborn, he would have been an only child. "Miserable toad," "rat bag" and other less printable monikers were being used to describe his crabbiness until I heard the term "high-needs."

The arrival of this highly unreasonable human being made me realize that my daughter had been a happy baby (although I didn't fully appreciate it at the time). With her, full-blown crying was reserved for hunger or overtiredness. From early on she would lie happily kicking at the toys in the activity gym, and if she was fussing and we weren't able to hold her, she could be soothed by the swinging chair. My son viewed the swinging chair as a torture device. He would scream blue murder if left unattended, so we would assume he must be starving, excessively tired or in serious pain, yet we'd pick him up and suddenly he was happy. I use the term "happy" loosely—it just meant he stopped complaining; we weren't rewarded with heartwarming grins or chuckles for our efforts. And he soon started squirming and protesting again once this particular comforter became stale. What next?

Admittedly, all babies are needy; but the high-needs baby can't lie or sit unattended for more than a few minutes without moaning or wailing. The crying can sound serious, but rather than being in pain, her crying is related to temperament. She needs constant holding, talking to, entertainment or movement. If Baby's screaming stops immediately once you pay attention to her, she is high-needs rather than colicky. While it is a relief to know your baby isn't in pain, her unreasonable behavior can wear on your nerves, and it will be quite a challenge to get anything done while Baby is awake. Looking on the plus side (if we dig deep, we can find one), dealing with a high-needs baby transforms tasks like emptying the dishwasher into light relief.

A high-needs baby may exhibit other demanding traits too, like expecting to be fed the instant she feels the first pang of hunger, needing to feed often, being hypersensitive, having low sleep needs or experiencing separation anxiety.

Survival Secrets

- Carrying Baby in a carrier or sling around the house will likely keep her from complaining, although there are limits to this from a safety point of view (stir-fry and a baby do not mix well) and for the sake of your back.
- If you're not napping with Baby, use the time to do things like preparing meals early.

- Give up trying to do anything else. It's less frustrating to just accept your baby needs you and go with the flow, letting her call the shots. It won't be forever. Just ensure you get regular breaks and be sure to dedicate that time to yourself.
- Don't take it personally. It's highly frustrating when you can't make your baby happy, but it's not your fault. It's just Baby's personality. Keep trying to find the key to unlocking Baby's misery mystery—it's the best you can do.

For me, there is a happy ending to this topic. I am ecstatic to report that at seven months my son emerged from his misery as a new and improved baby, having apparently undergone a personality transplant. I don't know whether it was because he was well rested (suddenly he was sleeping 11 hours a night) or because sitting, crawling and standing gave him a new perspective on the world that suited him a whole lot better. It was as if the limitations of his baby body frustrated the hell out of him for the first six months. So for parents of high-needs babies, there is a light at the end of the tunnel—although no way of knowing how long that tunnel is. Baby may chill out somewhere in this first year, but it's also possible your high-needs baby may turn into a high-needs toddler and a high-needs child. Either way, they can be lots of fun when kept engaged.

COLIC

I used to think colic was a stomach disorder—I think I was getting confused with horses. Horse colic is defined in the Oxford English Dictionary as "a pain in the gut." Infant colic is a pain in the neck for Mom and Dad, but no one is sure where the pain is for the baby, if anywhere. Parents worldwide will be eternally grateful to the expert who discovers the cause; babies might welcome the advance too.

Did you know babies can tell time? Colicky babies can: they glance at the clock, note that it's time to start work (usually in the late afternoon) and proceed to cry inconsolably for several hours. Some colicky babies are fussy and cranky all day, with a misery escalation in late afternoon. The onset of colic usually occurs around three weeks of age, and it will typically occur daily, or at least three times a week. Fortunately, colic will disappear as quickly as it arrived; possibly from a remedy, but more likely because Baby has outgrown it, usually at about three months.

Theories for the cause of the crying are usually linked to some kind of digestion issue, such as intolerance to wheat or dairy in a breastfeeding mom's diet, or to cow's milk protein in formula. My mom swears that my colic was cured by making a bigger hole in the nipple with a knitting needle. This is not a recommendation, especially if you are breastfeeding. (My mom wasn't, in case you were worried.) But why these things should upset Baby at a certain time of day and not, say, after every feed is a mystery. The digestion-related theories are backed up by the fact that babies often appear to be in pain, drawing their knees up to their chests, arching their backs and going red in the face as if trying to pass gas, often succeeding. However, as a baby cries he gulps in lots of air, so the gas pains could just as easily be self-inflicted. Other experts say colic is a sensitivity issue caused by an immature nervous system and an inability to stop crying once started.

The most frustrating problem with colic is that, as hard as you try, there is probably nothing you can do to ease Baby's discomfort. If you've exhausted your repertoire of comforts yet the crying continues, it will grate on your nerves, leave you feeling stressed and inadequate, and of course cause you to worry, even if you've confirmed there is nothing physically wrong. A baby's excessive crying can take a toll on new parents to the point where they wonder why they embarked on parenthood. It's particularly hard for Mom: crying triggers a hormonal response to tend to Baby's needs, so it's harder for her to tune out even if there is nothing she can do about it. Time will move at a snail's pace, and 10 minutes of crying will seem like an hour; hours of crying like an eternity. A friend woefully recalls the day her colicky daughter cried nonstop from 11 a.m. until 2 a.m. the next day; the exact date is imprinted in her memory. With a newborn, it is particularly depressing because he doesn't have the endearing smiles, coos or babbling of an older baby to offer in contrast. Accepting that you have a high-maintenance baby is important. Knowing that it won't last forever helps too.

Comrades' Recommendations—What To Do for Baby

- Try the rocking, holding, moving, rubbing and burping comforters suggested in the **Crying** section earlier in this chapter.
- Learn baby massage techniques, which you can pick up from a book or class.

- If you are breastfeeding, try removing dairy from your diet as an experiment. Some babies have a lactose intolerance that improves with age. If there is no improvement, try eliminating wheat. If these don't appear to be the culprits, you can work your way through the list of other possible offending foods in the **Breastfeeding Diet** section in the **Boobs** chapter of the **Mommy Map**. If an allergy is behind colic, there are usually other signs of the irritant, such as a runny nose, a rash, diarrhea or wheezing.
- If bottle-feeding, try using a different brand of bottle, such as one with a collapsible bag or vents that reduce the amount of air intake as Baby feeds.
- If formula-feeding, try a different brand.
- Try feeding Baby little and often.
- Carry Baby in a carrier or sling for the crying period.
- Try a soother. However you feel about soothers, it must be worth a try in these circumstances.
- Go out for a walk. While it would be nice to do this alone, I actually mean with Baby in the stroller. Stroller movement often improves a baby's mood, as do fresh air, a change of scenery and a big wide world of distractions.
- A drive in the car is not so eco-friendly, but these are desperate times. The motion of the vehicle is also a hit with most babies.
- Don't behave like a deer caught in the headlights; keep experimenting. After all, it can't get any worse, and you may luck out and discover the magic move/hold/position that offers some comfort.
- While colic isn't a medical problem, it is worth consulting your doctor just to set your mind at rest that there is no underlying physical problem.

Tips from the Trenches—What To Do for Yourself

- It's a tall order, but your best bet is to try to calm down and accept the colic as a character trait of your baby. Your tense and anxious disposition will tip Baby off—"Hey, Mom doesn't know what to do to make me feel better. Help!"—and will exacerbate the situation.

- Once you accept that anything you do isn't going to help, try to ignore the crying to whatever extent you can. Put the miserable mite in the baby swing, turn on some music and have a relaxing bath while he wails alongside. It sounds heartless, but if there is nothing you can do for Baby, you may as well use the time to nurture yourself.
- If the colic hours fall in the evening, beg Dad to be home on time if he possibly can. This phase is also rough on him, but it's a huge relief to share your grief.
- Share the misery with any willing volunteers or, failing that, bribe someone to come and help you out for part of the colic period while you take a break.
- Get help with other chores that are piling up because all your time is being spent caring for your baby. Or, if you'd prefer doing those chores to looking after Baby, get someone to help with him instead.
- Incessant crying can lead moms to "lose it" briefly. If you feel your stress rising to disturbing levels, leave your baby as comfortable as possible and spend time alone in another part of the house to cool off.

SLEEPING

Babies sleep a lot, right? Right. Newborns sleep on average 15 hours a day. So why is it that most new parents have complete sets of luggage under their eyes and all they seem to do day and night is try to get the baby to sleep? Babies are unreasonable, that's why. They don't take a nice 15-hour rest at 5 p.m. and leave you to eat a relaxed meal, bathe, watch TV, turn in yourself and get your eight hours of beauty sleep. Actually, they can't. At best, their little tummies can hold enough milk to keep them content for three hours; at worst, they will enter the world with a skewed concept of day and night, keeping you up all night while they snooze peacefully during the day.

Funnily enough (although I am not laughing), I am currently suffering through a bout of insomnia. My little one was sick recently and I am still consumed by futile Mommy Worry, serving as a poignant reminder of what it's like to have a newborn in the house and get much less than a five-hour stretch of unbroken sleep a night. I feel physically unwell and mentally deranged. So while I can write this section with empathy, it might not be the most intelligent prose in the book.

Baby sleep (leading to parent sleep) is a topic close to every new parent's heart; there are entire books dedicated to the subject. You should invest in one if you are having specific troubles with your baby's sleep patterns or lack of them. To tide you over and set realistic expectations, here are just a few sleep-related topics.

How Much Sleep?

There is a lot of contradictory information out there on how much sleep your baby will need within her first year of life. Of course, you would like Baby to enjoy an infinite quantity of sleep so that Mommy and Daddy can too; however, your baby will have her own idea of how much is enough and when she's going to get it. Some babies' sleep needs are relatively low; others barely last 90 minutes before conking out again, and enjoy naps around the clock. There are catnappers and sleepyheads who nap contentedly for hours. I know; I've had one of each. Since each baby's sleep needs are different, the figures we quote are only ballpark to give you an idea of what to expect.

In the first month, Baby will sleep about 15 hours out of every 24. With any luck she'll do half or more of this sleeping at night, but not necessarily; sleep can be very erratic at this stage. Sometimes Baby's body clock is out of sync initially, making life especially difficult for new parents who have to get used to working a night shift. You have to accept that Baby is in charge and adapt to her schedule. There's really nothing you can do to change sleep patterns this early on. The luckier new parents will have a reasonable boss who does sleep a total of 8 hours a night; even so, this sleep will be broken into unsatisfactorily short chunks of anything from 20 minutes to three hours. Which is why, time and time again, we repeat the saying, "Sleep when your baby sleeps"—it's the only way to survive. Take advantage this time around, as it's unlikely that you'll be able to do so with subsequent babies. Daytime sleep is also fairly sporadic at this point, before true nap times are established.

In your child's second month until around six months, she will thankfully do more of her sleeping at night, needing about 10 to 11 hours of nighttime sleep and three to four hours in the daytime. Her sleep patterns are maturing, allowing her to sleep longer between feedings. The daytime sleep will gradually move to take the form of two naps: one around mid-morning and one mid-afternoon.

Between six and 12 months, Baby's sleep needs will reduce slightly to 11 hours of nighttime sleep and two to three hours of daytime sleep. Around the one-year mark, your child will start moving to one longer nap, usually in the early afternoon, instead of two short naps. This is great for you as it will provide you with a long enough breather to either get a project done around the house or, my preference, join in the napping.

Where?

While it is good to have some plans for where your newborn will sleep, don't be surprised if these are thrown away within the first few nights at home. Quite often a baby will have his own idea of what is a comfy sleeping spot, and it won't include the lovingly prepped bassinet. Of course, we are all well aware that Baby should be sleeping flat on his back, but since he has spent the last nine months curled up and rarely horizontal, sometimes it takes a while to adjust to the newly instated sleeping position. Babies who don't yet want to stretch out can sleep more peacefully in a reclined car seat. Our baby spent the first few weeks sleeping curled diagonally in a swinging baby chair. During the first month, within reason, go with the flow and let Junior sleep wherever works best for all of you, but always bear in mind that sleeping flat on the back is the least risky sleeping position where SIDS is concerned, so that's what we're aiming for. You will get so little sleep during this month (sorry, but it's the truth) that it doesn't really make much difference. Baby can't be spoiled yet and has nothing resembling a sleep pattern, so wherever is safe and comfy will suffice.

Moving forward a few weeks, a popular choice is to have Baby sleep in a bassinet or Moses basket beside your bed. This keeps him close so you don't have far to go at feeding times, but not so close that you could roll on top of him. A bassinet or basket won't last long, though, as Baby will have outgrown it by around five months, but it can be comforting to him to have a more confined space to sleep in initially.

I started out with the bassinet next to our bed, but soon found that I couldn't sleep through the noise. The night was an endless cacophony of snuffling, shuffling, snoring and farting . . . and Baby made quite a lot of noise too. A baby beats a husband hands down when it comes to making ridiculous noises in slumber. My son was very talented, giving me a nightly chorus of animal impressions, starting with the clucking and cooing of a brooding chicken, moving through honking geese and a family of pigs (the wee and snuffle of a piglet; the grunts and groans of a hog) to the finale of a strangled cat when hunger struck. He also made another bestial sound that I couldn't place until I saw a rerun of *Star Wars* on TV and it hit me—it was a perfect Chewbacca impression. I swiftly moved the bassinet to the other side of the bedroom, then outside the (open) bedroom door, then into the kitchen. Had it been summer, he may have made it outside onto the patio. He made the transition into his own room much earlier than we anticipated.

You may be considering co-sleeping in your bed, rather than having your baby sleep in a crib or bassinet. Even if you aren't, you probably have strong opinions one way or the other about co-sleeping. Some moms find it comforting to have Baby close, and they say it helps them bond. Mom feels relaxed knowing Baby is right beside her, and they often fall into synchronized sleep cycles. One friend would manage to breastfeed while still half asleep. Conversely, just as many moms find the idea of sleeping with Baby too stressful. They are unable to sleep soundly for fear of rolling and squishing the baby or from being agitated by a fidgety baby's movements; and believe me, some babies are very restless in their sleep. The few times we tried co-sleeping we ended up with Baby splayed horizontally between us while we clung to the edges of the bed by our fingertips. Needless to say, there was really only one of us sleeping at all on those nights. Unless you find it comforting to sleep with a small toe inserted in your nostril, co-sleeping probably isn't for you.

Your bed as is probably isn't as safe a sleeping environment for Baby as a bassinet or crib would be. It may have a gap between the headboard and mattress that Baby could roll into, and of course it has edges to fall off. If you choose to put your baby in your bed with you, there are precautions you should take to ensure Baby is safe.

- Forgo your quilt and pillows, as they increase the risk of SIDS if Baby is smothered or breathing stale air.
- Make sure Baby isn't too hot. It can get hot and sweaty with the combined family body heat.
- If Dad is a heavy sleeper, put Baby on your side rather than between you. Dad will generally be less sensitive to Baby's presence than Mom will.
- Do not co-sleep if your awareness is diminished from drinking alcohol or taking medication.
- For peace of mind, it's best to purchase one of the baby beds made especially for "joint sleeping" arrangements. These beds attach to the side of your bed or form a little penned-off area, providing enough of a buffer that you (or, more likely, your spouse) will not roll onto the baby while you are sleeping, and that Baby is not at risk of rolling out of bed.

When I told a good friend of mine I was expecting, her one and only blunt piece of advice was, "Whatever you do, don't let the little bugger sleep with you." While this sounds harsh, she was speaking from experience, as she was still trying to get her nine-year-old to sleep in his own bed. Of course, we all assume that one day our child will decide for himself that he wants to graduate to his own bed, but there's no guarantee that this comes before he graduates from high school. My friend's case may be extreme, but it is true that you need to carefully think about your methods before setting yourself up for battles ahead. You should have a time and a plan set for moving Baby to his own bed and his own room, and expect some resistance when you implement this plan, especially if it happens after he is six months old.

After the first month or three are over and Baby has a more regular sleep pattern—we hope (whether it's six hour-long stretches or one six-hour stretch, the stretches should be regular)—you will most likely think about moving him into his crib in his own room, paving the way to "sleep sanity" for you and your spouse. You'll meet less resistance if you allow your baby to become accustomed to sleeping on his own earlier in life. This will also give the grown-ups a chance to spend evenings engaged in adult pursuits. No, of course I'm not talking about sex (as if!)—I mean eating a meal together at the dining table or watching a movie instead of turning in with Baby at 7 p.m.

When Baby first makes the transition to the crib, you'll be shocked and amazed to see how tiny and lost he looks stranded on the vast flat plain. I always felt a little cruel observing my little one asleep in the spartan crib, face mashed and drooling on to the firm mattress, shielded only by a thin cotton sheet, not a fluffy pillow or cozy duvet in sight. He'd wake with red welts on his forehead indented by the crib bars. But that's really the way it has to be. Once a baby can roll over and starts crawling, he will probably complete numerous circuits of the crib during the night, and under no circumstances stay neatly positioned with his head on a pillow and a blanket covering him. To reduce the risk of SIDS, a baby should not have any thick blankets or pillows that he could burrow under or that could become bunched up in front of his face. Cot bumpers are also not recommended as they can restrict Baby's breathing if he maneuvers into the corner during the night. Another cautionary note regarding cot bumpers is that older babies have been known to use them as a step to climb on and launch themselves out of the crib. Luckily, babies don't seem to mind the basics; as long as he is kept warm enough with fleecy pajamas, he'll sleep fine.

Getting Baby to Sleep

With a newborn, all bets are off. You will likely spend countless hours rocking, pacing and cajoling Baby to sleep.

> ## "I wish I had known . . .
>
> a baby needed such a bizarre ritual to go to sleep. I don't remember how we hit upon the winning formula, but it involved swaddling and quite firm bottom-patting while swinging vigorously side to side—quite a workout."

New parents often assume that babies will just fall asleep on their own, but they soon learn that their assumptions are way off. Your baby is miserable and tired, so surely there's nothing easier than letting her succumb to the soothing rocking of the swinging chair and drift off for a battery-charging nap, right? In your dreams! Isn't it infuriating when Baby fights sleep so much? Why does she scream and bawl and only give in when Mom sings "Somewhere Over the Rainbow" from inside the wardrobe, with one hand through the crack in the door patting her bottom? Babies like to be held and swayed and are not easily fooled. It seems that comfort for some babies is inversely proportionate to the comfort of their parents. After spending 20 minutes pacing the room rocking a baby who appears to have finally fallen asleep, you carefully lower your aching butt onto the comfy sofa, diligently maintaining the rocking motion of your arms, and yet *ping*—she is instantly awake and miserable. Likewise, you can stand bent over the crib gently jiggling a seemingly contented, slumbering baby until your back can take no more. With the precision of a bomb disposal expert, you carefully extricate your hands, aborting the mission several times as Baby stirs . . . then *crack* goes your broken back as you try to straighten, and your mission is blown. As your quest continues, look forward to perfecting commando crawls and stealth rolls.

Even though I can count the number of diaper changes my husband has done on one hand, he will forever remain "Super Dad" in my eyes for discovering that my son liked being swaddled—finally putting an end to the back-breaking, sleep-inducing dance routines. Swaddling had the same effect as a mallet over the head (and believe me, that option was sometimes tempting): instant submission and sleep. I guess he was a sensitive baby that needed all stimuli switched off as a signal to sleep. Swaddling helps prevent random arm movements that rouse a baby from slumber, and can help babies develop a settled sleep pattern. There are a few things easier than swaddling a protesting baby—wrestling an alligator, for one. This is a parenting job where two hands are definitely not sufficient. Your elbows and knees (gently placed, of course) may need to come in to play. For some tips on holds, watch a few rounds of WWE before you start. And it wasn't long before my son got the hang of escaping his swaddle. I'd wake to the sound of him chewing his hands and moaning, and lie there contemplating more secure bindings: Could I fashion a suit with Velcro down the sides? Would luggage straps be considered too cruel? I was saved when I discovered purpose-made swaddling wraps, from which Baby would need to be a budding Houdini to escape.

Baby's biological clock will start maturing at around six to nine weeks of age. Her ability to fall asleep and stay asleep for longer periods or get herself back to sleep after waking should start to improve. Unless your baby is particularly cooperative, getting her to sleep may still involve an elaborate routine, but with any luck it will be a little less physically taxing.

Survival Secrets

- If a baby misses her window of opportunity for falling asleep, you can have difficultly getting her to settle. Watch your baby for signs of drowsiness (such as rubbing eyes or nose, fussing, yawning or the bug-eyed look) and try to respond promptly to get her to bed before she gets overtired.
- Good sleeping practices are best introduced and learned early, before Baby's opinions about which cuddly toys need to be in the crib, precisely how dark or light it has to be in the room, and how many lullabies should be sung complicate the situation. Even a young baby will soon learn that she prefers being rocked to sleep or falling asleep on Mommy's chest to being in a crib if

you continue to offer it. Try to have Baby fall asleep in her bed. Start putting her to bed alone before six months.

- Establish a bedtime routine that signals to Baby this is the end of the day and time for "the big sleep." Dress her in pajamas, give her some milk, read books, talk about the day in a soothing voice, sing lullabies, brush teeth (once they've appeared). Most suggestions of bedtime routines include a bath, but since we are told Baby doesn't need a nightly bath and that in fact it might dry out her skin, this isn't a good activity to include in a consistent routine.

- Keep the routine realistic; no longer than 15 minutes, for instance. Reading six books, singing 48 lullabies and lying on your child's bedroom floor until she falls asleep is not something you are going to want to maintain.

- Start the routine in plenty of time. I always fall into the trap of thinking everything will somehow get done in 15 minutes when it realistically takes 30 minutes. The extra time can be enough for Baby to get overtired.

- Put Baby to bed when she is sleepy, rather than asleep. If she learns to fall asleep on her own, it will be easier for her to get herself back to sleep if she wakes in the night.

- Make sure that your baby can distinguish nighttime from daytime. Some tricks to help your baby make the connection to bedtime is to dim the lights in your house beginning in the early evening, and to even lower the noise from the TV and radio. Make Baby's room dark at bedtime—darkness triggers the release of sleep hormones. Alternatively, let her nap in a brighter, livelier house during the day so there is a big contrast between nighttime and daytime.

- Soothing noise can help a baby get to sleep. Lullabies or nature sounds on CD or white noise can all be effective to calm Baby while helping to drown out disturbing noise in the rest of the house. Shushing (as in "shhh, shhhh, shhhhhh") is a sound that is known to calm fussy babies, probably because it is similar to the sound of rushing blood that they heard in the womb. You need to shush fairly loudly to drown out the crying, or do it close to her ear. That may not sound too challenging, but if you are all shushed out, you can even buy a CD of rhythmic shushing sounds.

- Try swaddling. Use a light muslin or cotton blanket to avoid overheating. In summer, leave Baby in just a diaper under the swaddle. You need to swaddle firmly or in two wriggles Baby will be out. Try one of the purpose-made wraps, such as Miracle Blanket and Swaddle Me.

- A late bedtime doesn't mean Baby will sleep in tomorrow. Babies are programmed for an early bedtime around 7 p.m. It will be so tempting to keep Baby up later on Friday night hoping for the weekend lie-in you enjoyed as non-parents, but in practice this doesn't work. Baby will more likely sleep better if you maintain consistent bedtimes and wake-up times.
- If Baby seems to thrive on routine (most do), extend the routine to the rest of day. Try to have regular meal times and nap times. Establishing a regular wake-up time can help Baby to learn a sleep pattern. She won't respond well to an alarm clock, but you can try drawing back the drapes or putting the radio on at a regular time each morning.
- Once you have established nap and bedtimes, try to stick to them. We were tricked time and again into letting Baby stay up beyond a regular bedtime if she was happily playing. Enjoying watching her at play, we were reluctant to spoil the fun. However, it had a habit of going pear-shaped all too soon when suddenly she would be overtired. From that point, getting her to sleep would be an arduous task.
- Resist the temptation to kiss that chubby cheek once Baby is asleep. As tempting as it is, it's not worth the risk—really! Make do with drinking in that serene face from a safe distance.

Sleeping Through the Night

Of course, as sleep-deprived new parents, your endeavor is to get Baby sleeping through the night. In the **Getting Baby Back to Sleep** section that follows, there are some tips on reaching this ultimate goal.

Some bright spark defined sleeping through the night for a baby to be five hours, say from 11 p.m. to 4 a.m. While this may be a marked improvement on newborn sleep, my definition of sleeping through means I don't get disturbed for a full eight hours. Our firstborn decided at seven weeks to sleep through (don't hate me), which I have since learned is really too young, but at the time I was more than happy to trust her judgment. I have to guiltily admit to feeling a little smug listening to moms of 6-, 10- and

15-month-olds tell tales of being up feeding Baby multiple times a night. "What are they doing?" I thought. Then along came my son . . . At five months there was no sign of him giving up two feeds a night, and if left to weak-willed me it would still have been four—it was only my husband's weekend interventions that cut the feeding down from every two hours throughout the night. It proves that I was just lucky first time around, and that some babies do it for themselves while others need training and a mom with a backbone.

Young babies shouldn't sleep through the night, even if they are able, so don't expect anything resembling a night's sleep for the first six to eight weeks. A newborn needs nourishment at regular intervals to thrive, and if you are breastfeeding, allowing Baby to sleep through can interfere with your milk supply, which is still being established. Some babies will give you three to four hours of uninterrupted sleep the first week home from the hospital, whereas some take three to four months to reach that point. Both age and size determine how long a baby can sleep. A young baby is usually unable to sleep for long periods due to an immature nervous system and immature sleeping patterns. A bigger tummy equals more sleeping-juice capacity, so a baby of 11 pounds should be physically able to sleep through the night without feeding. As a general rule, a breastfed baby should be able to give up night feeds by four months, while formula-fed babies can be ready earlier, between two and three months. Babies over six months shouldn't need a nighttime feed, but in reality many continue to request a midnight snack through year one and beyond. A girlfriend listened patiently and commiserated as I told her my tales of woe about my six-month-old's continued need for nighttime feedings. When I'd finished my rant and she finally had a chance to interject, she calmly said, "Yes, George didn't sleep through the night until he was four." Four months? No, four years! Apparently George was always hungry. In the end, feeding him two Weetabix before bed helped him last the night.

As with all forms of development, a premature baby will likely be a little behind in developing sleep patterns, so set your expectations based on your original expected delivery date rather than the actual birth date.

As feeding Baby in the wee small hours is unavoidable, you might as well make it as comfortable a process as possible, with little disruption for both Mom and Baby, in the hope that they can both get back to sleep as soon as the meal is over.

Comrades' Recommendations

- Keep night feedings as tranquil as possible to avoid unnecessarily rousing Baby. Keep lights low, and don't talk to him or play with him.
- Have everything you might need at hand: your nursing pillow, a burp cloth (or six), a glass of water for Mom and changing gear should you need it. This is more difficult to achieve if you are bottle-feeding, as most formulas can't be made up too far in advance, but get as far in the process as you can before going to bed.
- Diapering at night should be avoided if possible as a cold, wet wipie to the nether regions is sure to fully awaken Baby. Of course, if Baby poops it is unavoidable, but modern disposables are pretty good at keeping wetness away from Baby's bum to last the night.
- How long you continue feeding your baby during the night is a decision for you and Baby to make. Most babies are done with the night feeds by four months. If yours doesn't fall into the "most" category and you are happy to continue, by all means do what feels right. If not, you might want to try some tactics for weaning them off the night feeds that have worked for me and my friends.
  - Make sure Baby has a good feed before bed. Often a baby will doze off mid-feed at the end of the day and end up with a snack rather than a meal, which won't tide him over. This means he'll wake for a top-up a few hours later.
  - Ensure Baby gets plenty to eat during the day so he is not reliant on night feeds for nourishment.

- o Once your child is six months old and has started solids, feed him some cereal for supper, which is heavier than milk and may keep him full throughout the night. While experts say this doesn't work, some moms swear by it.
- o Prolong the intervals between Baby requesting food and you responding. Try putting the feed off for 30 minutes tonight, another 30 in a couple of nights.
- o Be aware that growth spurts often happen at three and six months, so be prepared for some setbacks at these times when Baby may need more regular nourishment for a few nights.
- o Try the "sleep feed" method. This is where you preempt Baby's requests for food by going to him at a specific time each night and feeding him while he is still half asleep. Since Baby doesn't wake up feeling hungry, he goes back to sleep very quickly and stays asleep. However, there is a risk that your child will become dependent on these nighttime feedings and won't be able to sleep through the night without one.

A very important "I wish I had known" tip to remember is that every night is different. Don't despair if your baby is up every hour on the hour tonight, as there could be a breakthrough tomorrow. And don't get too cocky if Baby sleeps through the night on week eight—it might be a one-off.

But eventually, Baby will sleep all night. Hallelujah! Something other than a crying baby will wake you, like your hubby's alarm clock. You've waited for this for what seems like forever, but I guarantee you won't lie there and enjoy it—you'll spring out of bed to the crib side to make sure everything is all right.

Once you're there, unfortunately, it's not all over and done with. Teething, colds and other illnesses, and developmental and growth spurts can all disrupt a baby's sleep routine (see **Sleep Regressions** later in this chapter).

Getting Baby Back to Sleep

When your baby wakes up in the middle of the night, your first instinct will be to wade straight in and rock her back to sleep, giving her the rest she needs to grow and thrive (and allowing you to get the sleep you need to function tomorrow). By rocking Baby back to sleep tonight, you may get instant gratification, but in the long run she will come to rely on rocking arms to get back to sleep. Similarly, a baby who always gets offered the boob when she wakes will assume this is the only passage to dreamland. One of the hardest things you will do as a new parent is to teach your baby how to fall back to sleep entirely on her own. One mom confessed to having bought a daybed for the nursery because she got fed up with falling asleep on the floor next to the crib. The general idea is to be involved as little as possible in the getting-to-sleep routine so that Baby can do it by herself. The middle of the night is not a good time for patience and understanding, especially when you are already sleep-deprived. However, a few nights of interrupted sleep now could save months or years of the same nighttime shenanigans if your presence is always required to help your baby, then your toddler, then your child fall back to sleep.

"I wish I had known . . .

how quickly and easily I could teach my baby to sleep through the night with a little Ferberizing. I look back and think I could have saved weeks, even months of sleep misery for the whole family."

You can Ferberize, you can take child sleep expert Elizabeth Pantley's sage advice, you can suffer or you can pander to Baby's every whim—how or whether you tackle sleep issues is ultimately your choice. Most of us have heard of "Ferberizing." Some swear by it, others say it's cruel and heartless. In a nutshell, it's the sleep training system, developed by expert Richard Ferber, in which you start a routine of putting Baby to bed awake and leaving her if she wakes in the night and cries. Comforting at arm's length is allowed, but picking Baby up and feeding are not, and you gradually extend the time before you go to comfort her. The optimum time to start is between four and six months of age. The theory is that Baby will realize in a few short nights that crying isn't gaining her anything, and she will learn to fall asleep on her own. Of course, it isn't that simple and it doesn't always work—which is why Ferber has a whole book dedicated to the method—and it takes steely determination from the novice parents not to give in to Baby's heartbreaking pleas. I can certainly vouch for the fact that picking my son up when he cried at night and rocking, cuddling and soothing him got us nowhere. Half an hour later, with an aching back, I would lower him into the crib and he'd start bawling again; but if I left him crying initially, he'd be asleep 10 minutes later.

Tips from the Trenches

- Don't assume Baby needs feeding every time she wakes.
- Actually, don't assume Baby needs anything every time she wakes or stirs. Babies come to the surface at the end of their short sleep cycles more often than adults. They also sleep lighter and make lots of noise during their sleep.
- Being in a room of her own might increase Baby's chances of being able to put herself back to sleep without Mom's interference. An overzealous mommy who jumps to Baby's aid whenever she moans might be inadvertently rousing her out of a light sleep. If you pick her up, she'll be wide awake and expecting action or milk.
- If Baby is in her own room and you have a baby monitor, turn it down so you can't hear every whimper. Then you won't be tempted to go in and further wake Baby when she may just be stirring and about to go back to sleep on her own.
- Seeing you in the middle of the night might not be as comforting to Baby as you might think. (No, I'm not talking about the terrifying sight of you with bed head.) A baby will likely get more frenzied when she sees Mom because she thinks a meal is imminent. If you then shush a few times and leave, it only exacerbates the crying, and now she's too worked up to fall asleep. Try to stay out of sight or away altogether at least for a trial period.
- If at all possible, let Baby fall asleep in her normal place of rest. If things have changed since Baby went to sleep—for example, she was being rocked by Mom with the TV blaring and now she's alone in a dark, silent room—it's a bit of a shock, and a brief awakening will likely escalate to distress.
- Try not to feed immediately before bed. Falling asleep at the breast with a full tummy leads Baby to think this is the only way to get to sleep. In practice, it can be difficult to avoid this as babies often fall asleep easily at the breast, and most moms are reluctant to mess with a method that works. Try moving the last feed to earlier in the nighttime routine, then change diapers, put on PJs and put Baby into her bed while she's still awake, leaving lullabies as the last move, for example.
- If Baby wakes, don't flick on the lights or carry her into a bright room since light is a natural wake-up call. Keep the lights as low as possible, even if you are feeding or diapering.

- Letting Baby "cry it out" is considered a bit harsh by most parents. The theory is that Baby will give up crying when she learns no one is responding to her. It will probably work in as little as three nights, but can you stomach it? The gentler approach of letting Baby cry a little and gradually extending the period before you respond will be easier on you.
  - When Baby does wake, try to wait five to ten minutes (which will feel like an absolute eternity) before you go to comfort her. You could be pleasantly surprised to find your baby can fall back to sleep within minutes of waking up.
  - If after 10 minutes the crying continues, go ahead and soothe Baby, but try not to pick her up. Instead, stand beside the crib, speak to her gently and give her a pat or rub, but try to avoid making eye contact. If you engage Baby, she will be roused out of the sleep zone and expect further interaction.
  - Over the next few nights, gradually increase your response time or your proximity to Baby. Don't touch her at all; just talk to her or shush her from a distance, then from outside the door. Eventually it may be enough to do some shushing from the comfort of your own bed.
  - Use your judgment, and (providing you have learned the meaning of each cry) if your baby means business, go ahead and satisfy yourself that everything is okay.
  - If your Baby falls sick or there is some other change to the norm, such as sleeping away from home, you may have to abandon the process and start again once things are back to normal.
  - It usually takes at least a week to notice results. Be consistent and stick to your plan if at all possible, as changing methods will only confuse Baby.

NAPPING

Why do babies need to nap? Because it's necessary for survival—or rather, their parents' survival. Without nap time I swear we wouldn't last out the year. I don't care how much you love him; time off from taking care of Baby during the day is *required*. Games of "ballie" or "knock down the tower" can run only so long. An older baby can run you ragged getting into mischief, and you'll soon find yourself checking your watch in the hope that nap time is approaching.

Okay, we should consider the baby too: babies need to sleep because sleep renews energy. A little baby body is using up so much energy growing, developing and learning that he can't last a full day without taking a battery-charging nap. Ninety minutes of learning to roll, sit or crawl is hard work for a baby. If Baby is cranky and it's over an hour since he got up, he might well benefit from a nap. After getting used to my firstborn's fairly regular and mature nap routine, I was constantly amazed that my son was "tired already?!" having barely lasted an hour since getting up. A good nap is an hour or more. Twenty minutes is considered only a catnap: while it may tide Baby over, it is not replenishing sleep.

While nighttime sleep is top of your agenda for knocking into shape, napping is extremely important because it affects nighttime sleep. You may have heard that a baby who doesn't nap doesn't necessarily sleep better or longer at night. I found this to be true—an overtired baby tends to have a broken night's sleep. Once overtired, Baby will likely miss the window of opportunity to fall asleep at night and will pep up again, resulting in fitful sleep and an early wake-up.

Early on, when sleep patterns are erratic, let Baby nap whenever he wants for however long he wants—catnapping around the clock is common. At six weeks to two months, start to expect some regularity to form. At three months, Baby might be having four to six naps a day as he can't last long without getting tired. By four months you can expect to have fallen into a nap routine.

As a rough guide, you can expect your baby to need naps as follows:

Four months: Three naps totaling four to six hours.
Six months: Two to three naps totaling three to four hours. If there is a third nap, it may be short.
Nine months: Two naps totaling two and a half to four hours.
Twelve months: One to two naps totaling two to three hours. Some babies hang on to the two naps until 18 months; others ditch the second nap around the one-year mark.

Comrades' Recommendations

- Don't let Baby nap too late in the day. Naps should be logically spaced between waking and going to bed; for instance, a nine-month-old baby on two naps a day will likely need one mid-morning and one mid-afternoon. A surprising number of babies fall into a 2-3-4 pattern of napping two hours after waking in the morning, napping again three hours after waking from the morning nap, and going to bed for the night four hours after waking from the afternoon nap. Once Baby is down to one nap, it usually falls just after lunch.

- Don't skip naps assuming that Baby will need more sleep at night.
- Keep the nap environment distinct from the bedtime environment. If Baby naps in the same bed as he sleeps, keep the room light and maintain noise and activity in the house.
- If you don't want to be trapped at home for all naps, it helps to vary the nap location early on: nap in the stroller one day, in bed the next and in the car for another.
- It seems that most babies are only admitted to dreamland once per nap. There's no hand stamp for reentry if they wake after only 10 minutes. Interrupt that sleep cycle, and Baby will be up and at 'em rather than snuggling back down for the rest of his 90 minutes. You will get to know your baby's sleep patterns and the points at which he'll wake if disturbed. For example, you might be able to move Baby from the car seat to the crib 30 minutes into a nap, but you may also learn that it is vital not to stop the stroller motion at minute 45.
- Try to extend catnaps by leaving Baby to get back to sleep if he wakes after a short time; in other words, less than his regular sleep cycle. Much as you would like to at night, don't rush in as soon as you hear awakening noises; wait and see if he goes back to sleep for a longer nap.
- Limit the duration of daytime naps to stop Baby from using up all his sleep tickets and confusing night and day. You've heard the one about never waking a sleeping baby? The exception is when he is napping too long in the day. Limit naps to three hours.
- When Baby is ready to transition to fewer naps, you'll find he protests more about going to bed and plays at naptime rather than sleeps. It will take a little extra patience and effort on your part to keep him occupied in the morning while you gradually move the nap later, until he slips into the new after-lunch nap schedule. He'll likely have a few episodes of falling asleep in the high chair over lunch or dinner during the transition period. You may need to move bedtime earlier to make up for the loss of sleep while establishing the new nap times.

SLEEP REGRESSIONS

Oh crap yes, that does say "sleep regressions." Just when you thought you'd cracked it too. Or maybe you haven't cracked it, but you assumed it can't get any worse. Think again. Studies show babies tend to regress in sleep patterns at certain ages, particularly around the four- and eight-month marks. For a night, several nights or maybe longer, they will sleep less, be restless and cry out.

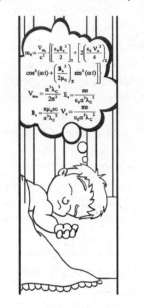

There are theories that these are ages at which a baby's little brain is so busy working on a new skill that sleep suffers as a result. The developmental spurt could be something obvious, like working up to crawling or walking. Or it could be something much more subtle—you'll never know exactly what—but just as demanding for Baby's little brain, such as a mental challenge like pattern recognition. After Baby's clocked up a few overtime hours and the skill is mastered, she'll fall into bed burned-out by the period of intense brain work and will sleep peacefully. Well, maybe not "peacefully" exactly, but back to her old sleep pattern or possibly, if you are lucky, a better one.

Allowing for developmental spurts, growth spurts, teething, illnesses, separation anxiety and bad dreams, you might calculate that you'll get a good night's sleep around Junior's second birthday. Actually, it's best not to think about it too much—sleep regression is a very interesting but highly depressing topic. However, it helps to be warned; now you won't worry that this is the new norm when Baby begins waking more frequently.

TV WATCHING

We are told kids under two shouldn't watch TV, period. Experts say TV takes away from the precious time babies have to interact with people and explore their environment, and have linked early TV viewing to attention deficit disorder in school-age children. Apparently the amount of TV I let my little one watch at 18 months old (about 90 minutes a day) means she is 30 percent more likely to suffer from ADHD later—oops! In the real world most of us find that using occasional TV or DVD watching as a short-term distraction for Baby is a sanity saver. In fact, right now I'm tearing my hair out because my curious 10-month-old is in that limbo stage between becoming mobile and having a vague understanding of his boundaries (or rather my boundaries) and the words "no" and "don't." He waits until I'm in the middle of filleting a piece of chicken to sneak off and lick the stroller wheels. Consequently, I can't wait until he's at an age where he'll become absorbed in a TV show long enough to allow me to cook dinner without having to drop everything every two minutes to rescue him from his latest predicament. Sometimes you just need 20 minutes to yourself to do something mundane like prepare a meal without the menace of a baby under your feet in the line of hot spills.

Only you can decide whether you want your baby exposed to TV in the first year. If you do decide to switch on the goggle box, here are some guidelines to maximizing the positive and minimizing the negative effects of television for your little one.

Tips from the Trenches

- Make sure Baby is interested and interacting rather than just staring. A young baby will let you know by fussing if he is not interested in watching.
- Whenever possible, watch with Baby and point things out. Later, encourage him to point things out to you and practice some first words. Treat it almost like a dynamic board book.
- I scoffed at *Baby Einstein* DVDs when I was a rookie mom, but I have to admit in our house they were a hit from about nine months to at least two and a half years old. Babies love looking at other babies, and the *Baby Einstein* series is packed with

babies doing their thing, plus eye-catching toys, puppets and images from the enticing big wide world. I have also heard the *Sesame Beginnings* and *Eebee's Adventures* DVD series are good bets for babies.

- There are a few quality, age-appropriate educational TV programs out there, like good old *Sesame Street*, but there are oceans of bad stuff too, so pick your programs wisely.
- Moderation is the best policy. Try not to be tempted to use the TV as a babysitter, but allow it to fit into a wide range of activities that your child participates in during the day.
- Try to avoid having kids' TV on in the background when Baby is otherwise occupied playing, as it is very distracting. Even adult TV can be distracting for little ones, particularly the commercials. If your baby seems fixated and keeps getting distracted, it's probably best to turn off the visuals and put on some music.

CHAPTER 3

Baby Map—Nose

CLEANING

It's inevitable that your baby will have copious amounts of disgusting matter emanating from his nose. Until a couple of years down the line when he learns the important childhood skill of nose picking, making sure the obstructions are removed falls to lucky old Mom—this job is so glamorous! However, you will notice that your finger is at least twice as big as your child's nostril, so picking the crusties out isn't going to be the best plan of action.

Tips from the Trenches

- As with the ears, we shouldn't go delving into the nose with a cotton swab. In general, stick to cleaning what you can see (or rather, what you don't want to see) with cotton balls dipped in water.
- If Baby is congested and uncomfortable, you're going to have to step in and help him breathe more easily. Your best bet is a device that resembles a very small turkey baster, called an aspirator, which you can buy at most drug stores. Basically, you squeeze the bulb, stick it into the baby's nostril and let it suck out all the goop. Admittedly, it may remind you of a scene from a horror movie in which you are the evil scientist attempting to suck out the poor kid's brains.

- If you want to go a step further, you can tip Baby's head back and use the aspirator to squirt saline solution into his nostril. This softens the crusties in a few minutes so that they'll stream out with the water, or you can suction them out.
- Okay, we are already into the realm of "way too much information," but we can go one step further. Come on, you're a mom, you can take it! I have heard it suggested by a very businesslike nurse that you can actually solve the problem by sucking the mucus out with your own mouth.

COLDS

While we're not attempting to write a medical book, we simply have to cover the common cold—a malady that will plague your life now that you are a mom. You can expect Baby to get between six to ten colds in her first year. If she starts day care in this time, you can add a couple more for good measure. In fact, my doctor once told me to expect as many colds during one year as there are children at the day care. Obviously this isn't a precise measure, but basically the more kids at day care, the greater the chance of catching a cold virus. Either way, the onslaught noticeably starts once Baby is old enough to start interacting with other children, sharing toys and thus inevitably also sharing germs.

Six to nine months of age is a particularly vulnerable period for an infant. Baby's natural immunity is wearing off but her immune system is still immature and therefore less able to fight off infection. While colds can hit at any time of year, there is an upsurge during the colder months when we typically spend more time cooped up indoors with the heating on. These conditions dry out nasal passages and provide an ideal nesting site for the virus. Every cold virus out there will likely latch on to your baby, and just as she's getting over one, she'll come into contact with a new virus the very next week. It will seem as if the winter months are one long succession of snotty noses.

A cold typically starts with a clear runny nose, which thickens up to yellow or green mucus over a week to 10 days. Colds are contagious from one day before to seven days after symptoms show. Sometimes Baby will sail through the cold, relatively undisturbed by her new role as a snot factory. Other times the congestion can cause discomfort and make sleeping and eating difficult, leading to a grouchy baby. My mom used to say she wished she could take over the suffering of my childhood illnesses herself. I'd certainly take on a baby's cold—after all, I can blow my own nose. Until your baby is stuffed up, you don't appreciate what torture it must be to have a cold and not be able to blow your own nose. Even a two-year-old will have trouble understanding the concept of nose blowing and can rarely do it effectively.

The snotty nose can also be accompanied by a cough, watery eyes and a low-grade fever. Often a cold will travel to the ear canal and result in an ear infection. Many babies suffer chronic ear infections, which cause far more misery than the original cold.

Survival Secrets

- A surefire way to combat a cold is to pump your baby full of fluids. This can ease congestion and stop her from getting dehydrated. Breastfeed or formula-feed your young baby regularly. You can also give an older baby water, and fruit juice if it has already been introduced to her diet.
- A stuffy nose affects Baby's ability to nurse, but she needs fluids for a speedier recovery, so try rinsing out Baby's nose (as suggested in the **Cleaning** section earlier) just before a feed.
- Be armed with a tissue at all times. You will be amazed at the horribly explosive sneezes a baby can produce. Because they can't blow their noses, there is a lot stored up to be ejected, and it will inevitably happen at the supermarket checkout.
- Sleep is a great healer, so help Baby get as much rest as possible. Let her sleep in a reclined car seat or stroller if lying down in a crib aggravates her congestion or coughing.
- A handy device for helping your baby get through her colds is a humidifier. It can be left running all night (most shut off when the water runs out) to moisten the air that Baby breathes. You can put eucalyptus, menthol or pine oil in most of them to help clear your baby's nasal passages so she can breathe easier. An alternative is to create a steam room in the bathroom, but spending the night on a cold tile floor beside a steaming hot shower isn't conducive to a comfortable sleep for Mommy.
- Don't medicate your baby's cold unless advised by a doctor. You'll just have to ride it out. If Baby has a fever, infant Tylenol may help. Cough suppressants are not recommended because coughing is the only way Baby can clear her airways.

- The doctor isn't going to be too enthusiastic about seeing Baby for every common cold, but don't hesitate to get advice if you feel she is suffering unduly or seems otherwise unwell, the cold lasts more than two weeks, you suspect an ear infection, Baby has a fever over 102° Fahrenheit (39° Celsius), coughing is severe or she is wheezing or fighting for breath. If Baby is younger than three months old, colds can easily develop into pneumonia, so consult your doctor.

Living in a plastic bubble is the only assurance against catching colds. Look around at any winter playgroup or activity and most of the kids will have snotty noses. Those who haven't will probably be busy incubating colds and will therefore be contagious anyway. Since babies get so many colds in their first year, keeping Baby away from others whenever she has a cold means you have to live the life of a hermit from November to March, which would drive you stir-crazy. We wouldn't recommend this lifestyle choice, but there are some measures you can take to avoid illness—maybe Baby will only get five colds this year instead of six.

- Use your discretion and try not to take Baby to a playgroup if she is sneezing or coughing and is likely to sneeze a shower of cold germs into the face of a buddy. It will take years before your child can begin to understand the concept of hygiene, and even then it is a tall order for a three-year-old to catch every sneeze in a tissue or consistently cough into her sleeve.
- Breastfeed as long as you can. Breast milk contains powerful antibodies that boost your baby's immunity against colds and other illnesses.
- Once Baby is on solids, keep the fruit and veggies coming, particularly immune-system-boosting varieties like blueberries, tomatoes, broccoli, sweet potatoes, citrus fruit and watermelon.
- It's obviously not practical for parents to wash their hands every time they go to pick up Baby, but there are times when it's important, such as when Dad gets home from work.
- Wash Baby's hands before and after playgroup to try to limit the amount of germs she shares.
- A small baby typically puts everything in her mouth, and since she won't check first to see if it's already covered in drool or a film

of snot from the last player, it's wise to avoid visiting the known sick. Or, take along your own toys if Baby is going to be mouthing them.

Usually colds are merely an unpleasant annoyance, but flu is not something you want Baby to suffer with, and it can be avoided. Flu typically does the rounds between October and May, and symptoms include a fever, chills, a cough and aches and pains. Babies can get a flu shot once they're six months old, and since postpartum moms have enough to contend with without battling a bout of the flu, it's probably a good time to consider getting one yourself.

CHAPTER 4
Baby Map—Mouth

BREASTFEEDING AND BREAST MILK

It's pretty amazing that a baby can thrive for a full six months, doubling his birth weight, on breast milk alone. What's more, it's free, easy on the little one's tender tummy, super healthy and on tap. The make up of the milk even alters to meet Baby's changing nutritional requirements as he grows.

If you have no breastfeeding concerns—Baby is feeding contentedly and gaining weight satisfactorily—you're probably not at all worried about understanding the mechanics behind it. Good for you; accept the magic and skip this section. However, a lot of rookie moms struggle with the concept of not knowing how much Baby has eaten. As soon as there is a hitch and we hear advice like, "Make sure you drain the breast," it all starts to get a little mind-boggling. I know my head was swimming with questions: What is foremilk? What is hindmilk? Both breasts or one? How long at each breast? All coming to the crux: is Baby getting enough?

We are told the trick with breastfeeding is to allow Baby to feed long enough from one breast to get the hindmilk, effectively "emptying" one breast before moving on to the other. So when is a breast drained? When that little gauge at the top of the boob reads empty, of course. Oh, you don't have one of those? When is hindmilk delivered? When the milk level drops below the green line on your boob. You don't have one of those either? With breastfeeding, you really have no idea how much Baby has eaten. While we can all tell when our boobs are full and firm, it's virtually impossible to tell the difference between half-full and almost empty. In truth, a breast is never completely empty, as there are always supplies being cooked up in the back kitchen.

Foremilk and Hindmilk

Foremilk is watery, low-fat-content milk delivered at the start of a feed. Think of it as the thirst-quenching part of the meal. There is no sudden switch to hindmilk; as you feed and your breast empties, the milk gradually gets fattier. The longer Baby feeds on one breast, the more fat is picked up from deeper in the milk ducts. This fatty hindmilk has more nutrients and is the key to weight gain. If there is only a short interval before Baby goes back to the same breast for another feed, the milk will already be fatty at the start of the feed— there will be no foremilk in that feed.

If you look at foremilk in a bottle, it is thin, watery and almost bluish in color, while hindmilk is thicker and creamy yellow. If left to stand in a bottle, breast milk will separate, with the fatty hindmilk floating on top.

How Often Do We Feed?

Breast milk is quickly digested, so we are initially told to feed the baby on demand; in other words, let her tell you when it's chow time. Baby may give subtle signs indicating hunger, such as sucking, lip smacking, rooting or the less subtle method of bawling her head off. In the early days, this will be a crazy schedule of 10 to 12 times in 24 hours. It's easy to panic and imagine that the baby will become a permanent fixture at your breast. After the first three weeks or so, once the milk supply is established, things usually slow down a little, with feeding every three hours. But let your baby set the pace.

"I wish I had known . . .
that nursing would be so time-consuming."

How Long/Much Do We Feed?

At first it may take ages to feed your baby. Feeding intervals are timed from the start of one feed to the start of the next, so if you're feeding every two hours and Baby is at the breast for 45 minutes or more, that doesn't give you much time off. Take heart; it gets easier. Once your milk supply is established and you and Baby become a more efficient breastfeeding team, it may take only 10 minutes to feed and you'll start to wonder how he can get enough in such a short time. All babies have their own pace at meal times; some take both breasts at a feed, others only one. Aim for 10 to 15 minutes at a breast to ensure that Baby is getting to the nutritious hindmilk, rather than spending five minutes at each breast and getting two low-cal foremilk feedings. An indication that you've emptied a breast is that it is soft and only a trickle of milk, rather than a squirt, will come out if you squeeze it.

Baby should also tell you that he has had enough by stopping feeding, pulling away, falling asleep or fussing. However, some babies will just enjoy the comfort of nursing and sit there forever if you let them, suckling rather than actively nursing. For the sake of your poor nipples, don't let Baby hang on for more than 45 minutes.

Is Baby Getting Enough?

The concrete evidence of watching milk drain from a bottle is comforting. At the breast, there is no such reassurance that Baby is getting enough, but here are some telltale signs of successful breastfeeding.

- Baby is gaining satisfactory weight. As a rough guide, she should gain 4 to 8 ounces (110 to 220 grams) per week for the first three months.
- Baby seems contented after a meal and does not cry or continue to show signs of hunger.
- Baby is wetting plenty of diapers. Four to six a day is normal.

It's possible your latch may not allow for effective feeding. In rare cases, your body may not produce enough milk. If you are afraid Baby is not getting enough nutrition, talk to your doctor or community health nurse to get a referral to a lactation consultant.

From six months, Baby can no longer get all the nutrients she needs from breast milk alone, so it's time to start supplementing with solids. But it's not an immediate switch. Milk continues to be her main source of nourishment through the first year, and you can continue to breastfeed for as long as you wish; the longer the better in terms of health benefits for Baby.

Don't forget that a breastfed baby doesn't get enough Vitamin D. Until she is drinking either 6.5 ounces (200 milliliters) of formula or 16 ounces (500 milliliters) of cow's milk a day, you should supplement with 400 IU infant Vitamin D drops per day.

In this chapter we are talking about breast milk from the perspective of a baby's nourishment. For the lowdown on letdown and breastfeeding from the equipment angle, check out the **Boobs** chapter of the **Mommy Map**.

Fussy Feeding

There are a few reasons why a baby might fuss during a feed. I never did work out why my son insisted on pulling, squirming and dragging my nipple two feet across the room while we fed, but here are a few possible causes of a little one's bad table manners.

- Milk tends to gush at the beginning of a feed and then decrease in flow, so if your baby fusses at the start of a feed it could be that your flow is too fast. This is particularly true when your boobs are fullest, typically first thing in the morning. It can cause Baby to choke, gag, get gassy or spit up. Try pumping or expressing some milk before he starts feeding.
- On the other hand, if Baby gets fussy after, say, 10 minutes, he may be bored of the slow flow from breast number one and impatient to move on to a new, faster-flowing boob.
- Fussing and pulling away part way through a feed could mean Baby needs a burp break. Or it could mean he's done. So try a burp, then offer more, and if the fussing resumes, assume he's full.
- Teething can make for miserable meal times, since Baby is hungry but the milk and sucking irritates his sensitive gums.
- It's difficult to nurse through a stuffed-up nose when Baby has a cold. See **Cleaning** in the **Nose** chapter for tips on clearing the airways.
- Some newborns like the environment to be calm and relaxing before they will settle down to eat. So if your infant seems to be a fussy eater, try going into a room where you can dim the lights and provide a quiet space for him to focus on eating.
- Once Baby is old enough to know what's going on around him, unless he's a real foodie, he may be easily distracted and prefer to play. A lot of head-whipping while he follows any activity in his proximity can be painful for Mom. Try keeping distractions to a minimum.
- During growth spurts, you may find Baby is disturbed when feeding, but this will pass once the growth spurt is over, probably within a few days.

- Fussy feeding could be the sign of intolerance to something in your diet, or it could be a sign of reflux. Baby is hungry, but if he starts to get gassy or uncomfortable when he feeds, he may pull away, arch his back or shake his head. If you suspect Baby may be reacting to something in your diet, take a look at the **Breastfeeding Diet** section in the **Boobs** chapter of the **Mommy Map** for more information, and seek advice from your doctor.

BOTTLE- AND FORMULA-FEEDING

At five months I came to the painful conclusion that, for the sake of my sanity, it was time to throw in the burp cloth and wean my son from the breast early. I frantically scoured parenting books trying to find out how much and how often I should be feeding him. What should I start with? What should I build up to? How many times per day? I was exasperated; I couldn't find the answers to my questions—every book and fact sheet I turned to was adamant that breast, breast, breast is best. I know that! Already feeling guilty about my decision, this lack of ready information on formula and the focus on breast milk did nothing to ease my remorse. So I was determined that stressed moms would have formula-feeding information at their fingertips in this book. It might seem like you're the only one, but the truth is lots of breastfeeding moms supplement with formula, and there are various reasons why others quit or cut down by six months. If formula-feeding suits you and your lifestyle, and helps you be at ease with motherhood, so be it.

Preparation

Formula is nutritionally adapted, iron-fortified cow's milk. It comes in ready-to-serve, concentrated liquid, and powder forms. Liquid formula is recommended for premature or sick babies and those younger than a month old. You must always follow directions on the formula packaging carefully to ensure your baby is getting the right hydration balance. Any diluting according to the instructions should be with previously boiled tap or bottled water for babies under six months. After six months, you can make the call on whether you continue to boil the water. Formula can be prepped in advance and stored in the fridge for up to 24 hours, but at room temperature it can only be kept for an hour before it should be discarded. Any half-finished bottles should be discarded. Opened cans of ready-to-serve and concentrated liquid formula should be covered and stored in the fridge for up to 48 hours.

The temperature at which Baby likes her formula is a matter of personal taste. One mom suggested it's best not to spoil Baby by providing warmed milk so that if you are feeding out and about, she won't turn her nose up at a slightly chilled bottle. Aim for body temperature initially, as she will be more likely to accept it, and experiment with cooler milk later. To warm a bottle, use a bottle warmer or stand the bottle in a bowl of hot water for a couple of minutes. Take extra care if you use the microwave as it's easy to create a hot pocket of milk that will burn Baby's mouth. Whatever method of warming you use, always shake the bottle well and check the temperature every time before serving by shaking a few drops onto your wrist—you may have performed the same ritual a hundred times, but "mommy brain" can strike and cause you to make a mistake at any time.

How Much and How Often?

The guidelines below will give you an idea of what to expect, but your baby will make the final decision about how much he wants and when he wants it. He'll tell you when he's hungry by crying, getting irritable, sucking or rooting. He'll let you know he's full by pushing the bottle away, turning away, fussing, stopping sucking, or in my son's case, doing a sudden 180 degree flip and attempting to rip his bib off—never one for subtlety. It's important that you allow Baby to self-regulate his food intake. Nearly all babies take exactly what they need if parents trust them and watch their signals. By forcing Baby to finish the bottle he may learn to continue eating even though he is full, which is not a good habit going forward in life. Under **Breastfeeding and Breast Milk** we mentioned the difficulty of not knowing how much a breastfed baby has consumed. On the flip side, consternation does arise from seeing as plain as day that Baby has not finished his bottle—in fact, he's barely drunk half of it . . . for the second time today. Panic sets in at this point for a lot of new moms. It's one of the hardest parenting rules to follow: pay attention to your baby's fullness cues and don't force it. Some days he will play it by the book and drink his recommended amounts; others he will not be so interested. Whenever I broke this golden rule and pushed Baby to drink more, I was rewarded with an almost instant return of the goods as a reminder.

Formula is not as quickly and easily digested as breast milk, so babies tend to feed less often—every three to four hours. When you first offer formula, start with a small amount, such as 2 ounces (60 milliliters). If Baby accepts the formula and there seems to be no adverse reaction, you can build up to larger servings. The amounts below are a rough guide to what a baby will probably drink over 24 hours. Not every feed needs to be the same size. You may find through trial and error that your baby is ravenous first thing and will gulp down 8 ounces, will barely manage 6 ounces at the rest of the day's feeds, then will fill his tanks with 8 ounces again at bedtime. The amounts here are also broken down into feeds. I don't mean to insult your intelligence; I'm sure you can do the math, but I know my fatigued mommy brain was so addled that the numbers swam before my eyes, so it can help to have it spelled out for you.

Newborn: 12–30 oz (360–900 ml) per day. That's six to ten feeds of 2–3 oz (60–90 ml). A newborn may even drink as little as 1 oz (30 ml) at a feed.

Three weeks to two months: 20–35 oz (600–1050 ml) per day. That's five to seven feeds of 4–5 oz (120–150 ml).

Two to three months: 20–36 oz (600–1080 ml) per day. That's five or six feeds of 4–6 oz (120–180 ml).

Three to six months: 25–36 oz (750–1080 ml) per day. That's five or six feeds of 5–6 oz (150–180 ml).

Six to nine months: 24–35 oz (720–1050 ml) per day. That's four or five feeds of 6–7 oz (180–210 ml). Offer milk before solids.

Nine to twelve months: 21–32 oz (630–960 ml) per day. That's three or four feeds of 7–8 oz (210–240 ml) per day. By now Baby is taking in more nutrients from his solid food, so you can feed solids first and milk as a dessert course or snack.

Equipment

It can take some time, patience and a surprising amount of money to find the bottle and nipple combo that Baby tolerates. I used to open my kitchen cupboard and be buried alive under an avalanche of rejected bottles and nipples. Some leaked, some poured milk down Baby's chin and others didn't allow enough milk out. You may be lucky and the first bottle you offer is accepted, but more likely there will be shenanigans. Baby may not be open to new ideas when it comes to mealtime. She may be reluctant, even adamant, that she's not going to settle for artificial when the real thing is right there in front of her.

There is no one bottle type that suits every baby, which is precisely why there are so many designs and brands on the market. They all claim to be the best—making it more difficult for us moms trying to choose. Modern artificial nipples are designed to have the shape and feel of the real thing. They are available in rubber or silicone, and Baby may even have a preference for one material over the other. Make sure you start with the right flow for your baby's age. In general, for older babies the hole in the nipple will be bigger, or there will be several holes, allowing a faster flow. Be sure to replace nipples every three months or sooner if they show signs of wear such as cracks, tears or stickiness. Bottles have various easy-flow features—collapsible drop-in liners, aerated bottoms, a hockey-stick shape—all designed to reduce the air gulped as Baby drinks.

All feeding equipment should be washed thoroughly in hot, soapy water and well rinsed, or it should be washed in the dishwasher. You can buy a special rack to keep the nipples, bottle rings and caps in place in the dishwasher. For at least the first four months, you should also sterilize the feeding equipment after washing it. To sterilize, you can use a microwave sterilizer or you can boil the equipment in a large pot of water for five minutes. Disposable drop-in liners cut down on the cleaning job, but you still have to deal with the nipples, rings and caps.

In this chapter, we're assuming that you have switched from breast milk. If your baby is formula-fed from day one, there are usually fewer issues since she knows nothing else. You were likely given a bottle and formula in the hospital, she drank it and the stage was set. If you're having trouble coming to grips with bottle-feeding, you may find the following tips helpful.

Comrades' Recommendations

- Start with breast milk in a bottle. This way, if Baby rejects it you can be pretty sure it's the method of delivery rather than the milk. By introducing two new things at once (the bottle and the formula), you won't know which is disagreeable if Baby balks.
- If Baby has never sampled formula, the taste may come as a bit of a shock. It may help to initially mix it 25/75 with some expressed breast milk. If Baby accepts this cocktail, gradually reduce the amount of breast milk in the mix until you are serving the formula neat.
- Sometimes Baby won't accept a bottle from you, but she will accept it from someone else or she'll accept it when you are not there. Don't assume this will always be the case and leave the

babysitter stranded. If you're not sure if she'll accept a bottle from a babysitter, stay in range for a speedy return from your night out.

- Try offering a bottle when Baby is not especially hungry and she will probably have more patience for trying something new. If that doesn't work, try when she's starving and doesn't have time to think about being fussy.

- Try a different position when offering Baby a bottle, such as seating her facing towards you, so that she doesn't expect to be breastfed. It's hard to accept artificial when she has the real thing as a cushion for her head. If that doesn't work, try a sneaky move: position Baby as if you are going to breastfeed, then slip the artificial nipple in instead. It won't fool most babies, but it's worth a try.

- Try a different formula. They all smell and (if you are brave enough to try it) taste foul. Baby may be a connoisseur and only like one variety.

- Keep at it. The first time he was offered a bottle, my boy screamed blue murder; the second time, he screamed blue murder; the third time, my husband fed him and he screamed blue murder; the fourth time, he drank it without a whimper.

- Try giving the formula at body temperature first. If Baby doesn't like it, try it warm, and if Baby doesn't like that, try it cooler (never hot or too cold).

- I made a huge rookie blunder in buying 20 bottles from a friend who swore they worked fabulously for her baby. I'm not doubting my friend (I know she wasn't trying to scam me), but all babies have their own idea of what is best, and mine hated that particular design. Start cautiously with one bottle and buy more once you have a winner.

- See if a friend can part with one of their bottles just so you can try it out.

- Start tentatively with the brand of formula too. Buy a small can to try—this stuff is too expensive to waste. Take care: once opened, a can of powder only lasts a month, and a can of ready-to-serve or liquid concentrate only lasts 48 hours. Once you have a preferred brand and are using it at a fair pace, buying in bulk is cheaper.

- Try your baby on a bottle sooner rather than later—babies quickly get familiar and reluctant to change. The optimum time is around two to three months. Even if you are breastfeeding and have no intention of switching to formula, it pays to not be the only feeding equipment in the house; you could get sick, want to return to work or just need a night off once in a while.

- Rub breast milk around the outside of the artificial nipple to make it smell and taste like you.
- Have formula prepped as much as possible for the night feed. Popping out a boob half asleep is easy; propping a bottle without bright lights and concentration is not wise and Baby won't like the wait. Ready-to-use formula is handy for the night feed.

NIPPLE CONFUSION

The definition of "nipple confusion" is when you introduce your baby to bottle-feeding and the lazy tyke realizes, "Hey, getting milk out of that bottle thing is way easier. I'll have that from now on, thanks." Then he starts fussing and refusing to breastfeed until Mom panics, gives in and produces the bottle. Round one of wrapping Mommy around his tiny finger goes to Baby. He's right: breastfeeding is hard work. He's got to open wide to get a good latch and use more muscles for less reward, since bottles have an instant, faster and continuous flow.

It's a confusing issue for moms as well as babies. Moms worry because they don't want to risk putting Baby off breastfeeding by introducing a bottle too early, yet they want Baby to accept a bottle so that they have a chance at a sort of life at some point in the coming year. If Baby will feed from a bottle, it means that occasionally Mom can sleep through while Dad takes over the night feed. It's also good to have an alternative to turn to if you fall ill, and it's especially important if you plan to return to work. The trick is to find the optimum time to introduce the bottle: after Baby has breastfeeding down pat and before he gets too opinionated and resistant to change. Several moms told us they were overly anxious about causing nipple confusion, yet it turned out not to be a problem. This is a case where well-meaning breastfeeding advocates may go a step too far in their quest to keep everyone breastfeeding as long as possible, frightening moms into making wrong decisions as a result.

If Baby is going to have a problem confusing the two feeding methods, it is most likely to happen in the first month when he is still learning breastfeeding techniques. So if possible, leave the introduction of a bottle until later, when you are sure you have your method perfected. Most of us can manage to breastfeed exclusively for a month—we're not likely to want to stray too far from home in the first few postpartum weeks anyway. It is also true that Baby is more likely to refuse to try bottle-feeding if you wait until four months or beyond. It seems the optimum time to introduce a bottle is two to three months; however, there is no guarantee that this solves the issue. Where one baby will take flipping from breast to bottle in stride, another will have problems, and there is no way to tell which yours will be. I know some babies who went from breast straight to a sippy cup, completely rejecting anything that came via an artificial nipple. I also know babies who rejected breastfeeding at a few months old in favor of the faster flowing bottle. One baby refused her first bottle at eight weeks and continued doing so until eight months. I even know a baby who at two months decided she would only feed from Mom's right boob. She would cry and arch her back when presented with the left boob. My friend's solution was to lay the baby as if to feed her from the right and then sneakily slide her pillow over to feed from the left. I don't think having a preference between right and left is exactly nipple confusion, but it demonstrates how finicky and wacky babies can be.

If you can't breastfeed Baby in the first month for health reasons, there's still no need to panic, as there is an alternative to bottle-feeding that is less likely to cause Baby to have problems breastfeeding later. You can express milk and use a nursing system that feeds Baby via a tube taped to a finger, which requires Baby to exert effort similar to when he is breastfeeding.

Tips from the Trenches

- If Baby fusses and refuses the breast, do not allow him to bottle-feed instead—hunger should eventually win him over.
- Express some milk before feeding to ensure it is flowing fast when Baby latches on, creating a sensation akin to the flow from a bottle.
- Feed regularly and don't wait for Baby to tell you he is hungry. A hungry baby is keener to get at the goods and has less patience to get the right latch.
- Use a newborn nipple on the bottle to ensure Baby has to work harder to get his milk and doesn't learn to equate bottle-feeding with fast food.
- If you want Baby to accept a bottle and arc meeting with resistance, see the **Comrades' Recommendations** under **Bottle- and Formula-Feeding** earlier in this chapter.

DRINKS FOR BABY

So, should you give Baby anything else to drink in this first year besides breast milk or formula? The simple answer is that you don't have to. It is, however, useful to introduce the idea of a drink coming from a source other than the breast or bottle around six months.

- **Water:** From six months, you can offer Baby little sips of cooled, previously boiled water from a cup. The aim is to let her learn to drink from a cup and introduce the idea of an alternative liquid from an alternative source. Don't let her fill up on a bottle full of water in place of breast milk or formula. Water is the best alternative drink to give Baby—it's refreshing and hydrating in hot weather or if Baby is feverish, and it helps to prevent constipation. It's also good as a mouth wash to rinse away milk residue before bed, helping to prevent tooth decay.
- **Juice:** Sure it tastes good, but what Baby doesn't know, she won't miss. It's really not recommended to give Baby juice this first year. If you do want to, it should be diluted at least 50/50 with water, preferably weaker, and limited to 2 ounces (60 milliliters) per day between six and nine months, and 4 ounces (120 milliliters) per day from nine to twelve months. Filling up on juice could decrease Baby's appetite for food and put her at risk of being malnourished.

Only serve 100 percent fruit juice: no cordials, diet or light juice, or cocktails, especially Harvey Wallbangers.

Never put juice in a bottle, as you're just asking for tooth decay. Allowing a baby to take nips of juice from a sippy cup throughout the day is just as harmful to teeth, so limiting juice to sips from a cup with meals is the best option as far as her teeth are concerned.

- **Cow's milk:** When we started writing this book, the recommendation was to wait out the first year before giving cow's milk to a baby. A couple of years later, we are now advised it can be introduced between nine and twelve months. Cow's milk is generally left until the latter part of the year because early introduction could promote allergies in your baby. The protein, minerals and fat in cow's milk are hard on a young baby's kidneys. Cow's milk does not contain iron, so unless you are confident Baby is getting plenty of iron from her solid food, it's best to continue with breast milk or formula through the first year and introduce cow's milk as an additional drink between nine and twelve months.

  When you decide to wean your baby off of breast milk or formula and onto cow's milk, a tentative, gradual approach is advisable for several reasons: cow's milk is harder to digest, Baby may not like a sudden flavor switch and you'll need to watch for allergic reactions. Start by mixing a little cow's milk with breast milk or formula; say, one-quarter of her bottle. Baby is likely to accept this slight change in flavor and, providing there are no adverse reactions, after a couple of days you can switch to a 50/50 mix, then 75/25, until you are at 100 percent cow's milk. The protein in cow's milk can cause Baby to get a bit bunged up. Don't worry; the constipation shouldn't last for long (you may even welcome the break in poopie diapers). Your baby should soon get used to the new input and return to her normal pooping schedule within a week or so. If she continues to be constipated past one week of introducing cow's milk, discuss it with your doctor.

  Baby needs the fat in homogenized milk for energy, growth and brain development, and should not have skim or semi-skim milk until she is at least two.

- **Beer:** Oh yes, at the summer barbeque or Christmas party, Dad is bound to give your little one his first swig of beer. Not that we are recommending it, of course.

SIPPY CUPS AND GROWN-UP CUPS

Babies as young as five months old can drink from a cup—not a sippy cup, but a big grown-up cup. Then again, who is patient enough to let a six-month-old loose with a spillable cup? Not me, for one. He may master a brief sip and an even briefer hold, but how many beverages will cascade onto the floor when his next move is a frantic hammering of the highchair tray or a random arm fling? You will also find that Baby has an overwhelming desire to investigate the bottom of any cup in his grasp. As a result, most of us turn to the spill-proof sippy cup as a transition from bottle to cup or for supplementary drinks. They are useful for drinks on the go, save us from yet another reason to have to change Baby's outfit, and save the rug from yet another soaking. "I swear this carpet will float out of the door one day," my mom would exclaim on the frequent occasion of us upending a drink. Your floors have years of spillages ahead to cope with.

When you shop for sippy cups, you will be overwhelmed by the selection. There are just as many design choices as there are for bottles, and just as many will end up relegated to the back of the cupboard when they prove to be dribbly, leaky, difficult to hold or just not quite to Baby's liking.

Comrades' Recommendations

- For a baby who is just starting to use a sippy cup, try one with easy-grip handles for easy holding.
- A spill-proof lid or one with a cap is useful for drinks on the go.
- As you'll need more than one sippy cup, we recommend the multi-packs of interchangeable cups and lids such as those made by The First Years. They are fairly durable and inexpensive, and they seem to work well for most babies, judging by the number of them you see in use in baby circles. Once they are worn out they can also be recycled. However, if your baby is a chewer, a cup with a harder plastic spout may be in order.
- If Baby is allowed to nip juice or milk from a sippy cup throughout the day, his teeth are at risk of decay. It's best to limit sippy cup use to meals and snacks. If Baby has one at hand throughout the day, make sure it is filled only with water.
- It's best to keep a sippy cup on hand but out of reach. If Baby is allowed to tote one around while he plays, it will soon become

a comforter akin to a soother. Plus, it's easy for Baby to lose the sippy cup amongst his toys. It may lie forgotten for days before Baby rediscovers it, and he'll not think twice about finishing the contents.

- Help your baby learn to use a grown-up cup at meal times in the highchair, when the spillage is limited to the chin, bib and tray.
- Babies don't tend to drink enough volume from a cup—the cup may be emptied, but three-quarters of the drink will be soaked up by the bib. To be sure your baby is properly hydrated and nourished, continue to breastfeed, or serve formula in a bottle or sippy cup throughout the first year.

SOOTHERS

I wonder what the stats are for soothers purchased by bleary-eyed dads at the all-night pharmacy. Both my pacifier purchases were panic buys, and although it didn't solve my immediate problem of a screaming infant, I was actually relieved that both babies rejected them as it saved me from the longer-term issue of when to "lose" the soother once they were hooked. Some babies don't like soothers, and some can't live without them because they just love to suck. I know babies who spat soothers out after a two-second suck, babies who ditched their own soothers sometime in the first year, babies who had their soothers ditched for them around 18 months and one who doggedly kept sucking on hers until age seven.

You may guess from my tone that I personally lean towards the anti-pacifier camp, although the jury is still out on whether soothers are actually bad or good for your baby. While I applaud anything that gives rookie moms an easier life, it saddens me to see a toddler at play with her face obscured by a plug, when she'd obviously be perfectly happy without it. It's advisable to limit a soother to doing just that: "soothing," rather than becoming a permanent piece of face furniture that will interfere with interacting, smiling and talking.

On the pro side, a baby who has a pacifier is less likely to suck her thumb. When it comes time to break the sucking habit, you can take away a pacifier, but you can't take away a kid's thumb (well, strictly speaking you can, but I wouldn't go there). On the con side, a thumb is always there to be found by Baby in the middle of the night (unless you've taken it away, but I thought we weren't going there), whereas she is likely to need your help to locate and retrieve the soother that's dropped out of her mouth. While a pacifier can save you time at bedtime by soothing Baby to sleep, it's likely to give her more cause to interrupt your sleep in the middle of the night once she's reliant on it to get back to sleep.

Tips from the Trenches

- Buy multiple soothers that are the same. That way if you really do lose a soother, you can replace it before there is a meltdown.
- It's not advisable to give a breastfeeding baby a soother before two months of age. If Baby is doing all her sucking on a pacifier instead of ordering milk supplies, it may interfere with your milk production. There is also a possibility it could cause nipple confusion (see earlier in this chapter).
- Some parents put a couple of spare soothers in the crib in the hope that Baby will be able to locate one if she wakes in the night.
- Think about how far you want the attachment to go and specifically what Baby needs the soother for. Don't assume that a fussy baby who is calmed by sucking during the day also needs the soother to go to sleep. Soothers that go on your finger are great for babies who like to suck but aren't hungry—you can control how long they suck on it.
- Try to ditch it before it becomes a crutch or a "lovie." You will get less argument from Baby if you take it away between three and six months.
- No matter how many nocturnal fumblings you've had to endure to locate the dropped soother, don't pin it to Baby or the crib with a ribbon or cord as this could cause strangulation. Leave a spare soother on the dresser next to the crib so you can find it easily.

ORAL EXPLORATIONS

Babies do not discriminate when it comes to putting things in their mouths. They would just as soon mouth their own toys, the dog's toys, or even less sanitary items: grass, dirt, magazines, dust bunnies, cat food, stroller wheels, Dad's toe or that dead ladybug you've been meaning to vacuum up for weeks. All it takes is a swift one–two action—grab and chew—or if he can't bring the object to his mouth, he will take his mouth to the object so he can lick and slobber on it. I understand that in this exploratory phase Baby is using the supersensitive mouth to investigate the taste and texture of objects, but it doesn't strike me as a particularly good survival instinct when the reaction to finding a week-old dried-up piece of ham under the dining table is to stuff it in your mouth. (This may not be possible in your house, but sadly it is in mine. Aw, come on; remember the advice about letting the housework slide when you are busy with a new baby? I took that to heart.)

While a lot of moms, including myself, shudder at the thought of Baby mouthing some of the grosser items listed above, we are assured it's not something to worry about; it's good for Baby to be exposed to dirt and germs to develop a strong immune system. What we do have to watch for are "chokables." Anything that can fit through the middle of a toilet roll tube can be swallowed. Tiny things will usually pass straight through causing no harm, but if something, say, the size of a coin "goes down the wrong way," it can get lodged in the trachea and block the airway. Enter ever-vigilant mom. Once Baby is mobile, it's time to do a clean sweep of your entire house. You may fancy yourself a pretty tidy person (obviously I don't), but if you scrutinize on all fours looking for potentially hazardous Scooby Snacks, the first thought that will spring to mind is, "Do I ever need a maid service!"

Baby starts mouthing objects as soon as he can coordinate the movement of hand to mouth at around two to three months old. This is because the mouth is his primary sense organ until about eight months. Around five months this tendency may lessen, when he learns there is more to playing than mouthing stuff and adds banging, passing and turning toys to his repertoire. Whenever there is a tooth breaking through, you may notice a renewed vigor in chewing on things as Baby tries to ease the discomfort of his gums. Towards the end of the first year, most babies start to use eyes and fingers instead of their mouths to learn about their world.

My son put virtually everything in his mouth. When we played ball, it involved an extra step, with him mouthing the ball before rolling it back. It was a lot like having a puppy in the house: he trotted around with a chew toy protruding from his mouth; everything was covered in drool; the dining chair had a ragged edge where he'd been gnawing on it. He'd have happily chewed our shoes if I'd let him. Then came the day I gave him his first finger foods. The Cheerios were flicked, rattled, crushed, thrown and dropped, and the bowl used as a drum, but not one did he attempt to put in his mouth—go figure.

Survival Secrets

- Provide safe, soft, durable teethers for Baby when he's in a munching mood to save him hurting delicate teeth and gums on pointed objects, wooden toys that may splinter or long-handled rattles that could be shoved down his throat.
- Keep a toy on hand when you're going to the supermarket to dissuade Baby from sucking on the cart handle or chewing on your car keys.
- We made good use of toy links to attach a teether or toy to the high-chair, preventing Baby from mouthing toys retrieved from restaurant floors. The same technique is useful in the stroller and car seat.
- Paper doesn't stand up well to chewing. Even board books are soon destroyed by enthusiastic munching. Save the story books for reading by keeping them out of reach, and give Baby rag books to chew on.
- A lot of plants are toxic (English ivy is an example), so keep house-plants out of reach and watch for fallen leaves. Watch for holly and mistletoe berries if you use them in Christmas decorations.
- If you don't want something to go into Baby's mouth, keep it out of reach and remember that Baby's reach is rapidly expanding. Remember, anything that fits into a toilet roll tube could be swal-lowed and cause choking.
- Check larger toys for little pieces that can detach.
- Watch out for small see-through plastic items. Bits of plastic bag, sticky tape and tags from new clothing can't easily be seen if they have been dropped, yet Baby will undoubtedly find them.
- Take an infant first-aid course, specifically to learn what to do if Baby is choking. I learned this vital survival secret firsthand when I had to try out my technique on my nine-month-old, who was choking on a cardboard tag I'd just removed from new clothing. A choking baby will not necessarily be coughing; he may have dif-ficulty breathing, he may not be making any noise but be flailing his arms and legs, or he may be turning blue around the mouth. If you think Baby is choking, summon emergency help immediately.

DROOLING

Drool, spit, foam, bubble, razz. Babies are drool machines from around three months old until they master the whole swallowing business towards the end of their first year. Until then, they just don't know what to do with their saliva and that it's polite behavior to swallow (something that seems to recur in teen years—mostly in boys, judging by the amount of spitting on sidewalks that goes on).

If the drooling gets out of control for a period of time, Baby could be teething. Of course, she'll save the full-force drool for the "turn and burrow" move into your best jacket just as you head out the door for a rare night out, confirming that you really should have resisted the temptation for one last hug.

Tips from the Trenches

- A chin that's permanently bathed in drool will likely get a rash. Help prevent this by periodically mopping up Junior's slobber.
- Slap on a bib. Sure it ruins the outfit, but it saves you having to change Baby's clothes three times a day. Leaving her in drool-drenched clothes will likely cause a rash on her neck and chest.
- If Baby does develop a rash, use barrier cream like Vaseline and it should clear up relatively quickly.
- For a more severe or sore rash, your doctor may suggest a cortisone ointment.

TEETHING

Thankfully, there are only 20 toothy peg eruptions to survive in this first set of baby teeth. Usually bottom teeth will appear first, followed a month or so later by their top counterparts (although the top outer incisors usually break this pattern). As with everything in Baby World, there are no set rules for teeth growth, but as a rough guide, the two front incisors will appear first around six to seven months, followed by the outer incisors by nine months. Then it jumps to the first molars breaking through between 10 and 14 months, and Baby won't likely get his fangs or second molars until he's out of this first year. Some babies start teething at three months; it's even possible for a baby to be born with a tooth. On the other end of the scale, some don't pop a pearly white until a year old, but by age three he will have all 20.

Don't despair and start calculating the sleepless nights ahead just yet; in actual fact, a lot of babies are only mildly affected by teething. He could pop a tooth overnight without any prior warning so that the first you know about it is when you feel a grating against a spoon, or spot the little white line when Baby gives you a cheesy grin. He may suffer more with the first teeth because it's a new experience, but soon become familiar with the sensation and take it in stride. Any discomfort from teething happens days, weeks or sometimes months before the actual appearance of the tooth, and as soon as it's broken through the gum, the fuss is over. You may notice a lump on the gum or a split before the tooth appears. Molars tend to be more troublesome due to their larger surface area.

If Baby is uncomfortable, you may notice ear pulling and increased crankiness or fussiness, particularly when he's feeding because the sucking causes irritation to his sensitive gums. Teething babies are likely to drool more than usual and frantically chew on their toys and hands. Their gums may be swollen and sore, and it could lead to a runny nose. And yes, unfortunately, sometimes it affects their sleep.

Comrades' Recommendations

- Give Baby traditional teething rings as a safe and comforting chew toy. Their modern counterparts—the water-filled teethers that you can chill in the fridge or freezer—work great as well.
- Freeze a wet facecloth for Baby to suck on.
- Rub the gums with your finger. Watch out once there are a couple of teeth—a little nip bloody well hurts!
- Sips of cold water or cold food such as fruit sauce may be soothing.
- Teething symptoms are normally mild, so if your baby seems overly distressed, consult your doctor.
- To ease more serious discomfort, it's okay to give Baby a mild pain reliever such as acetaminophen (for example, infant Tylenol).
- There are ointments for soothing gums, such as Orajel, but the jury is still out on whether these products help. Ask your doctor for advice.

TEETH CARE

Oh crap, I just put my son to bed forgetting to clean his teeth once again. Well, it takes time to remember that it should be part of the bedtime routine. Somehow his four little pegs don't register as the real thing—it's like they're toy teeth just there to look cute in photos. But they do count. It's easy to overlook the care of Baby's teeth because it's set in our minds that these are temporary, yet you wouldn't let your four-year-old slack off in her teeth brushing, and they're the same teeth. From the moment you spot a tooth broken through, you should consider it worth taking care of. This first set is going to be needed for a number of important tasks until school age: keeping space for the second teeth, speech, chewing and eating and biting other kids at playgroup. These teeth are the placeholders for the second set. If she loses them to decay, there is more chance of orthodontic problems later. Goodness knows the dentist bills are going to be high enough without creating more problems.

Tips from the Trenches

- Get into the habit of wiping Baby's gums with a clean, wet washcloth before the teeth even appear.
- Once teeth make an appearance, you can continue to wipe them with a cloth or get a very soft-bristled, age-appropriate toothbrush and brush them at least once a day, particularly at bedtime.
- Brush very gently to avoid damage to delicate teeth and gums.
- Toothpaste isn't really necessary, but if you use any, make sure it is age-appropriate and fluoride-free as Baby mustn't swallow too much fluoride—it's actually harmful to the formation of permanent teeth.
- Think of sweet, tooth-rotting drinks and juice springs to mind, but there are also natural sugars in milk that can be just as harmful to teeth. You should try to avoid giving your baby milk in a bottle right before bedtime. There is little saliva production to battle the sugar while Baby sleeps, allowing bacteria to attack the teeth.
- Never put Baby to bed with the bottle. This can result in brown spots on the teeth known as "baby bottle mouth." Make sure feeding is finished and teeth are cleaned before Baby goes to sleep.
- If Baby will only fall asleep with a bottle in her clutches, make sure it contains plain water only.
- Bottles should be drunk in one sitting, not carried around and sipped on. Prolonging a meal gives more time for sugar to coat teeth. Constant grazing on snacks is harmful too.
- Sippy cups containing juice or milk are just as harmful if Baby is allowed to nip from them all day long. Limit drinks to supervised sessions.

- Ideally, only serve juice from a cup, watered down and with a meal or snack.
- Aim to ditch bottles by the end of the year for reduced risk of tooth decay. Sucking from a bottle increases the time sugars are in contact with the teeth.

BITING (OR "FANGS FOR THE MAMMARY")

Hot on the heels of the proud breastfeeding mom's joyous recording of the "first tooth" milestone in the baby book comes the spine-chilling realization: that razor-sharp little gnasher is going to be in proximity to her nipple at feeding time.

While your baby isn't going to gnaw on you, they have been known to occasionally bite the boob that feeds them, and you obviously won't want it to become a habit. They aren't being vicious, just chomping down because it feels good to those irritated teething gums. This is no consolation to Mom, though.

The pain is unbearable, and the anticipation of the bite is worse than the bite itself. While your six-month-old may seem too young for discipline, it's time to start teaching table manners for the sake of your nipples. Treat it like anything you implicitly don't want your child to do. Of that lengthy list, biting your boob has to be right up there in the top three with eating the cat's food and investigating the contents of her own poopie diaper.

Pit bull owners should be well versed in the technique of prying apart jaws clenched around miniature poodles. Assuming you still want your nipple attached to your boob, you'll similarly need to know how to rescue it from the jaws of death. Rather than yanking

Baby away with still-clenched teeth, get a finger in the corner of her mouth to break the suction and part the jaws.

It is going to be hard for most moms to carry out a "punishment" that involves ending the feed, since it goes against instinct, so maybe try this as a last resort. There are a few other deterrents you can try first.

- **Shout:** You probably don't need to be told to do this as it will likely be your initial reaction to the pain. It might be enough to startle Baby and make her cry, and therefore let go.
- **Put Baby down:** Dump Baby safely but firmly on the bed or sofa.
- **Pull Baby in:** Pull her into your chest so that her nose is smothered just for a split second; that's all it will take. Her natural reaction will be to stop biting to breathe.

Wait for a reaction, calm Baby if necessary, then resume feeding. With any luck she will soon learn that biting leads to an unsatisfactory meal time.

TALKING

Like walking, talking is something that just makes it under the wire to be considered in this first year. Most babies are using one or more words with meaning (however bad the pronunciation) by the end of the year. However, you've probably heard the saying "early walker, late talker," suggesting that if babies are ahead in physical development, they are less so in their language development. Babies won't always follow this rule—some will have a few words and be toddling around at the end of this year; others will still be working on both skills, and that's fine.

While your baby may not be talking by his birthday, his language development and communication should be well under way. In fact, he's been communicating with you in some form since birth, albeit only squawking for the first three months. Even those squawks had meaning—the hungry cry was different from the sleepy cry—and if you listen to baby language expert Priscilla Dunstan, newborns actually use their own lingo to give you a hint of what they want before they cry. For example, a "neh" sound means she's hungry, while a "heh" sound means "I'm uncomfortable," and apparently they even have two different sounds for "I have gas" and "I have lower gas." My aural sensitivity must be appalling; as hard as I tried, I couldn't hear pre-cries or detect any difference in cries—it all sounds like bawling to me.

Around six months, Baby practices sounds like razzing, "agoo," laughing, squeaking, squealing and singing. He may even utter a "mama" or "dada," but don't get too excited—it has no meaning at this stage and could just as easily be "vava," "yaya" or "baba," depending on which consonant is currently his favorite. He also learns to communicate non-verbally by smiling, waving, pointing and showing he's hungry or full, and possibly by 10 months knows some sign language—very puzzling if you haven't been teaching him any.

In fact, beginning to talk around age one is the end point of the language development that Baby has been working on for the last six months, and he understands a whole lot more than his few words suggest. At six months, Baby probably knew his own name and turned to look at you when you spoke. By eight months, he probably cried if you sternly said "no" (or in my son's case, laughed—I think my angry tone needs work). Towards the end of the year, he should be pointing to the picture in a book when you ask, "Where's the cat?" (providing there is a cat in the picture—don't get too tricky, Mom); following simple requests like "Go and get your ball" or "Can I have that?"; and when you ask, "Where's your nose?" he should demonstrate his understanding by answering, "In the middle of my face where it always is, Mother." Well, given the stupidity of some of the things we say to a baby, it wouldn't surprise me if this was his response.

Encourage language development by reading, singing and talking to Baby. The more words he hears, the better. Tell him the names of objects, people and body parts, and point out things when you are out. Tell him what culinary delight is on the spoon making its way towards his mouth. Give him a running commentary while you perform mundane tasks like the diaper change (his first word may be "stinky," said with a gag). It helps to keep things simple by using words of one syllable. Why then, with baby talk words like "ball-y," "bird-y" and "dogg-y," do we complicate matters by adding a syllable?

Baby may start by using his own words for familiar things, but they're often quite far removed from the actual word. "Ba-ba" might mean bottle, sheep, ball or all three. (At last count, "na" meant no less than six different things to my daughter.) You'll soon get to recognize what he means—you can probably tell if he wants his bottle rather than a sheep. Don't be tempted to adopt his word. Instead, use the proper word in your response. For example, "Okay, Mommy will get your bottle." If you lapse into his language, he will never learn, and one day he'll be totally embarrassed in the bar when he asks for a ba-ba of beer.

CHAPTER 5

Baby Map—Ears

HEARING

Babies can hear well at birth; in fact, hearing is a baby's primary sense for the first three months. She even relies on it to recognize Mommy and Daddy initially, before she can see them clearly. A young baby is attracted by rhythmic sounds and high-pitched voices, which means babbling away in baby talk to your infant is not such a silly thing to do. Much of the first year of your baby's life is spent learning about the world she's now in from the soundtrack. Here are a few hearing milestones to look out for.

Birth to Three Months

- Baby should startle at loud noises (providing she's not in a deep slumber).
- She should turn her head or eyes to listen to your voice and should react to your voice even when she can't see you.
- She should be soothed by your voice as a general rule—obviously Mommy's voice isn't magical enough to solve all ills.

By Five Months

- She should turn towards new, interesting sounds.
- She should be able to recognize her name and turn to you when called.
- She should start to repeat simple sounds like "ba-ba."

Seven to Ten Months
- She should react to sounds she can't see but can recognize, like the door opening when Dad arrives home, a dog barking or the phone ringing.
- She should be babbling away in baby talk.

End of the First Year
- She should begin to point at the sources of familiar sounds.
- She should start using a few simple words like "hi," "bye," "mama" and "dada."
- She should be able to identify a picture in a book when asked, for example, "Where's the ball?"

If you feel that your child might not be hearing well or progressing as indicated above, you should consult your doctor. The screening process to test a baby's hearing is very simple. It is important to detect and deal with hearing issues as early as possible because speech and language development hinges on it.

CLEANING

The key word in the old adage "Never stick anything smaller than your elbow in a baby's ear" is "in." While it is sometimes tempting to delve in with a cotton swab and help the wax out, you should resist. The wax will work its own way out, cleaning the ear of dust and debris as it goes. The ear canal is short and easily damaged. It's easy to push the wax back in rather than hooking it out as intended, leading to blockages and possible infections; you could even puncture an eardrum. "Clean what you can see" is another good guideline. Stick to cleaning only the outside of the ear. The folds can easily accumulate grease and flaky skin.

Baby's ears are very sensitive. You should use a cloth or cotton ball and plain water—no soap. Make sure your cloth has been wrung out first before putting it up to your baby's ear to minimize the amount of water going in the ear, which can be uncomfortable or disturbing for Baby. If you feel that Baby has excessive wax or a blockage, consult your doctor or community health nurse.

EAR INFECTIONS

Ear infections are a very common occurrence in young babies because the shortness and angle of the ear canal make it easy for bacteria from the nose and throat to travel to the middle ear. Fluid and bacteria can build up inside the ear when the ear is blocked, resulting in painful swelling around the eardrum.

An ear infection will often follow hot on the heels of a cold. Some babies are highly susceptible to ear infections and succumb after every cold. Other babies may only suffer one or two bouts before outgrowing the condition, and some never noticeably experience ear infections. Allergies, changes in elevation, reflux, drinking a bottle while lying on the back or irritants such as cigarette smoke can also be behind ear infections.

Ear infections are very hard to detect, especially since babies aren't particularly good at telling us what hurts. Most babies will cry or scream if they have an ear infection, but then that's just one reason out of 20 they might be doing so. Fever, fussiness, difficulty sleeping or escalated complaints when Baby is laid down can be signs. A baby with an ear infection can have diarrhea or be less interested in eating, as the same virus can cause stomach upsets. Also, sucking with blocked ears can be painful and make Baby fuss at meal times. Surprisingly, a baby who is pulling on his ear rarely turns out to have an ear infection, as he isn't yet able to understand where the pain is coming from. He is more likely just exploring interesting body parts or teething. However, if he's doing this in addition to some of the previously mentioned symptoms, you can take his word for it.

Survival Secrets

- If you suspect that your baby has an ear infection, consult your doctor right away. Most ear infections can be treated with antibiotics, and Baby will feel better in a couple of days. An ear infection may go away untreated, but it will take up to a week of misery and suffering.
- Infant acetaminophen or ibuprofen are effective pain relievers to get Baby (and you) through the night.
- A warm cloth over the ear can help reduce the swelling.
- If Baby appears to be in more pain when lying down in his crib, try letting him sleep reclined in a car seat. (Best to bring it in from the car first.)
- If your child is prone to ear infections, you can reduce his chances of developing one by following the guidelines for avoiding colds in the **Nose** chapter.

- If you suction Baby's nose whenever he has a cold, you reduce the chance of bacteria entering the ear (see **Cleaning** in the **Nose** chapter).
- Don't feed Baby lying down—make sure his head is elevated to about 45 degrees.
- Breastfed babies are less likely to suffer from ear infections, at least in the first six months, so if you are breastfeeding, keep the magic milk coming.

MUSIC

In the early days when Baby might be a little discombobulated by her unfamiliar surroundings, soothing sounds and music can make her feel more at home. She's lost in a big new world and relying on her sense of hearing to understand where she is and who's there with her, so recognizable sounds can be reassuring. It's been proven that spa or aqua sounds remind Baby of being in utero. A rhythmic and consistent sound like the ticking of a clock reminds the baby of her mommy's heartbeat. There's no need to put "The Wheels on the Bus" on a constant play loop from day one because, unless you have very strange musical tastes, Baby is not yet familiar with this particular music genre. At this point she's more likely to enjoy the rhythmic beat of some adult music you were listening to during pregnancy, since from 20 weeks she was listening along with you. Try playing music to help calm and comfort Baby if you are having trouble getting her to sleep or if she is fussy.

Of course, eventually you will succumb to the kiddy music. It's not compulsory, but since music is a proven tool for aiding brain development, you'll probably find yourself selecting a couple of nursery compilations some time soon. Besides, you're going to have to learn a few old favorites if you don't want to be left behind at the playgroup singing circle. Some kids' CDs are more palatable than others, depending on whether you can stomach the squeaky kids' choir renditions; maybe the slightly more tuneful singing of a kids' entertainer is more your line. Either way, you will be sick of the sound of them in a year or two. Repetition is important to little ones. Language and memory skills are developed by learning easy rhymes and songs. Action songs help develop motor skills and coordination. They can also encourage exercise in an older baby—and Mom too, if you care to join in. All together now: "Head, shoulders, knees and toes, knees and toes."

READING TO BABY

You can start to read to your baby as soon as you like. Reading too early is not going to be a problem. Research shows reading to babies is a very important step in helping them develop verbal and listening skills as well as vocabulary, memory and imagination, and it builds the foundations for reading and writing. Language skills are related to how many words Baby hears each day. For the first few months, Baby is most interested by the rhythm of language; he doesn't understand objects, let alone stories, yet it's good to start including stories as part of a bedtime routine. If your baby library isn't stocked yet, improvise by telling him the story of his day. Even if it's been the dullest of days, Baby will enjoy the soothing sound of your voice, and you'll be stimulating his senses, aiding brain development. An infant's attention span is only a few minutes long, so little and often is the key to reading to Baby early on.

To a young baby, a book is just another toy to chew on, so books to play with should be cloth books. Even a fairly tough-looking board book can be destroyed in a few earnest gnawing sessions. Real books that you don't want drooled on and dog-eared are best saved for supervised reading. Books with simple images and lots of vibrant color and contrast are attractive to infants. "Touchy-feely" books interest babies as they love to explore the different textures.

Around four to six months, when Baby will be interested in looking at books for himself, hardy board books withstand more abuse. Pictures of baby faces are usually a hit, as are toys and objects familiar in a baby's world. A vocabulary-building book of photos of everyday things like eating, sleeping and bathing will be a hit since

Baby can relate to the subject matter. When reading to Baby, watch his eyes for signs of interest, and when they start to wander, move on. You will notice a change in Baby's enjoyment of the books and stories around this time. He still won't understand why the Hungry Caterpillar is munching his way through an entire picnic, but he will enjoy the visuals and repetitive text regardless.

Baby will start to develop an understanding of the book content between six months and a year. As soon as he is able, at around nine months, give him the responsible task of turning the pages. Start to ask him to point to things in the book. Baby will soon be able to master flap books, which are usually popular. While reading as part of the bedtime routine is a must, it's important to also read to Baby at other times of the day when he's not so drowsy. Check your local library to see if they hold a weekly baby story time session, where you will be introduced to age-appropriate books, and where reading is often enhanced with entertainment involving puppets and props.

By the end of the first year, Baby will be developing preferences and will choose the same old book every night. The repetition will drive you mad; however, research shows that babies become more confident when they can anticipate what is coming up next and guess it correctly. By the tenth time you've read the same book you'll probably want to hide the darn thing and never read it again. Console yourself by remembering that you are building the foundations of a confident and academically smart child. Stimulate Baby (and amuse yourself) by hamming up the performance, providing character voices and varying the pitch of your voice. This helps language development, because he's learning tone as well as vocabulary and pronunciation, which are important when he starts to talk.

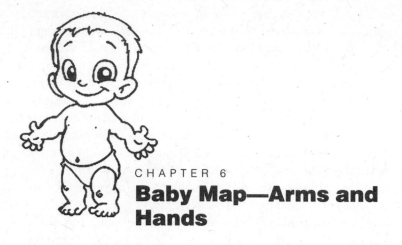

CHAPTER 6

Baby Map—Arms and Hands

CUTTING FINGERNAILS

"Your mission, should you choose to accept it, is to cut Baby's fingernails." The nails are miniscule; the skin so soft; the fingers wriggly. Your palms are clammy, and sweat drips from your brow as you endeavor to navigate giant clippers around that speck of nail without drawing blood. I failed and nicked my baby's pinkie on the very first attempt, and boy did I feel bad. Trimming Baby's fingernails is a nerve-wracking, but important, new parent's job, as Baby's flailing limbs and spastic movements coupled with sharp nails will inevitably result in some nasty self-inflicted scratches on the delicate skin of his face.

Comrades' Recommendations

- Invest in a decent pair of baby nail clippers. This will help eliminate any accidental clippings of the skin around the nails. It can be hard to find an effective pair. Some are good safety clippers, but don't actually cut nails, just chew futilely on them.
- Clip one side of the nail (it's hard to navigate the clippers under the entire nail at once), then you can just pull the rest of the nail off. It sounds painful, but the soft nails pull off easily.
- If you are worried about cutting a wriggling finger and less worried about waking a sleeping baby, try cutting nails while Baby is asleep.

- If you are just too nervous to put a sharp instrument anywhere near those tiny fingers, you can try biting them off instead. Babies' nails are fairly soft and pliable and easily bitten off, especially if softened by a bath.
- Baby can sleep in mittens if scratches around his eyes are worrying you.

You've barely had time to breathe a sigh of relief that the job is done when the inquisitive little fingers raking your face just two days later are once again razor sharp. That's when you realize that Mission Impossible II already needs to be undertaken.

FLAILING ARMS

Due to an immature nervous system, Baby will initially have flailing arms that she has no control over. While it is somewhat amusing to the cruel parents amongst us to have a little giggle at Baby's expense when these spasmodic actions cause her to smack herself on the head, it is no laughing matter when that smack on the head wakes her from a sleep. Some babies (and sleep-deprived parents) benefit from being tied up—sorry, I mean swaddled—to keep the jerky arm movements from rousing them from slumber. (For more information on swaddling, see **Getting Baby to Sleep** in the **Eyes** chapter.)

The flailing arms will start to come under control around three months when gross motor development starts to take over the reflex actions, but there will still be plenty of uncoordinated movement. The swipes may be clumsy and random, yet it is uncanny how often Baby will connect with the object she's going for, like your glasses or earrings. If her favorite grab is your hair and it's getting painful, encourage her to move on to Dad's chest or leg hair.

PLAY

Toys aren't really that important in the first year. We're not suggesting you leave Baby with a toilet roll tube (he'll only eat it, although he could use it to measure potential choking hazards), but stacks of fancy toys are not really necessary. At this point, everything in his world is interesting.

Before three months, while he has very little control over his movements and no grip, Baby is really only ready for visual toys such as mobiles. Look for bright, bold colors and high-contrast patterns that are visually stimulating, like polka dots and checks. Reaching for dangling toys in an activity gym will encourage the development of his gross motor skills and coordination. By the third month he'll start grabbing at things (although he'll rarely get what he's after and may start to get a bit annoyed by this) and is ready for something to hold. This is a good time to introduce rattles because the sound will also be stimulating. Lightweight or fabric models are best to avoid the stunned expression and tears when the rattle inevitably connects with his head.

Once he's reached three to four months and can usually coordinate his arm movements, his first achievement will be to reach for a toy and bring it to his mouth to chew on. That is pretty much his range of play for the time being. In fact, with a young baby it's hard to know whether the subject of toys belongs in the **Arms and Hands** chapter or the **Mouth** chapter, since it is implicit that every toy gets slobbered on. A baby has a highly developed sense of touch on the lips and tongue, making investigation with the mouth a satisfying experience. Later there will be more frantic chewing on objects such as teething soothers. Until Baby is mobile, the activity gym is still a good bet for kicking and batting at objects and discovering shapes, colors and patterns. Textured toys are also interesting for Baby's developing senses, as are sound-making toys like squeakers and rattles. The primary-colored squashy animals with mirrors, a squeaky tummy and crinkly, textured limbs are a sensory delight. One that can be attached to the car seat, stroller or high chair for entertainment on the go is even better. You can encourage Baby's developing mobility by placing toys just out of reach.

Play is how babies learn. At play he is working on his motor skills, coordination and sensory development. Gradually his aim will improve and his fingers will become more dexterous. By eight months, Baby will likely have mastered sitting, and then his hands will be free to play. Blocks are no longer just mouthed, but turned around, dropped, passed from hand to hand and sometimes thrown, which is why soft blocks instead of their wooden counterparts are a good early buy. Don't underestimate the versatility of a basic toy like stacking cups. Apart from the obvious stacking (which will be your never-ending job while Junior enjoys the demolition), they can be shouted into, banged together or rattled. They can also be used as hiding places, pretend drinks, drums, hats and anything else Baby's little brain thinks up.

By the end of the year you'll notice that Baby is playing with toys more appropriately. He is now becoming more interested in investigating objects visually and with fingertips in preference to his mouth. Finally, he'll be pushing the car instead of sucking on it, and more interested in turning the pages of a book than eating them.

Comrades' Recommendations

- Early on, place bright hanging objects that make noise within hitting range. A distance of 8 to 14 inches (20 to 35 centimeters) is the optimum range for Baby's eyesight.
- Since he will gnaw on everything, it's best that Baby has his own items to chew on rather than your car keys or other grubby or sharp objects that might damage delicate teeth and gums. Provide clean, safe, chewable textured toys that he can't swallow.
- Pick toys that will be most appealing to Baby's eyesight rather than your own. While the adorable pastel-pink bunny immediately grabs your attention, it's more likely Baby will prefer the hideous primary-colored monstrosity with the googly black and white eyes.
- Around six months, Baby may form an attachment to a certain toy. Try gently persuading Baby to latch on to a washable toy. If he gets attached to a "surface wipe only" soft toy, it will soon be disgusting.
- If Baby falls in love with a particular toy, it's a good idea to go grab an identical backup. Then if, heaven forbid, one gets lost or, more likely, needs a visit to the laundry for barf removal, the reserve can be conjured up and Baby will be none the wiser.
- Fuzzy animals need to be age-appropriate with no potentially dangerous attachments: some shed; some have cords or ribbons; some have loose buttons.
- Any toy less than 1.5 inches (4 centimeters) in diameter (or that fits in a toilet roll tube) is a potential choke hazard.
- Don't be swayed by the battery-driven, all-singing, all-dancing "educational" toys that guarantee to turn your six-month-old into a brainiac. Quite often these are too complex and don't entertain Baby as much as you would expect. There are years of battery use ahead, so for now save the batteries for the swinging chair and leave the complex toys until next year.
- Here are a few staples moms recommend:
  - stacking cups
  - stacking rings

- ○ spinning toys
- ○ mirrors
- ○ soft blocks
- ○ soft rag books with squeakers, crispy-crackly pages, etc.
- ○ links
- ○ rattles
- ○ activity gyms
- ○ shape sorters
- ○ balls
- Get Baby to play with that "other kid" in the mirror.
- Babies quickly become immune to familiar toys. Rotating the toys is a good ploy to keep him interested. Every couple of weeks, put one set away and break out a new batch—the new batch being the set you put away two weeks ago. Keep a few toys in each room of the house rather than having one overwhelming heap of toys. "Hide" some toys in a wardrobe or behind a chair to be discovered during Baby's daily investigations. Somehow toys are far more interesting this way.
- Always be suspicious of a baby who is too quiet. A double-check will almost certainly find him with something unsuitable in his clutches: he'll be gnawing the buttons off the remote control or diligently attempting to reinsert the lamp cord he's just unplugged.

It's easy to overlook the biggest, best and most versatile toy Baby has. No, I'm not talking about the life-size teddy bear with the winking eye and the musical tummy that Granddad insisted on buying. It's you. You are a climbing frame, a horsey for bouncing games and a cuddly toy all in one. You have eyes for probing and hair for pulling, you make funny faces and silly sounds, and you are musical (maybe off-key, but babies aren't fussy). But be warned: the injuries inflicted on parents reads like a list of torture techniques employed by the villain in a James Bond movie. He'll almost scalp you when he uses clumps of your hair to pull himself up. He'll poke you in the eye, claw at your face, pinch and twist your skin, grind his clammy feet into your flabby thigh skin (okay, maybe that's a personal one), head-butt the bridge of your nose, bite the thin skin on your shoulder with razor-sharp teeth, bounce on Dad's groin and pull at chest and leg hair (that's Dad's, not yours). I have yelped in genuine pain many times, and so will you.

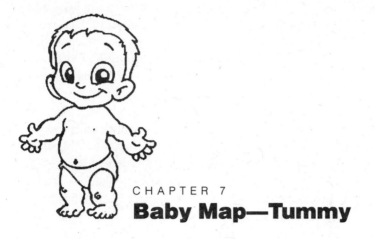

CHAPTER 7

Baby Map—Tummy

GAINING WEIGHT

Rookie moms are naturally obsessed with weight gain—after all, it's the primary indication that Baby is thriving. For the first three months you'll probably find yourself religiously heading to the clinic or parent–infant drop-in at least weekly for a weigh-in, and meticulously charting her weight, counting every half ounce. "How much does she weigh now?" is a standard opening line in mommy circle conversations and interrogations by grandparents. You answer in pounds/ounces/half-ounces; however, pretty soon the ounces become insignificant and you'll be talking only in round pounds. Then one day someone will ask how much Baby weighs and you'll say, "Not sure; about 25 pounds, I guess," realizing you haven't weighed her or worried about it for weeks.

Formula-fed babies typically gain weight a little faster than breastfed babies over the four-months-to-one-year period. Weight gain will also depend on factors that similarly affect adults, such as metabolism, body shape and activity level. As a rough guide, in the first month you can expect a weight gain of 4 to 7 ounces (110 to 200 grams) a week, then 1 to 2 pounds (450 to 910 grams) a month for the next few months. By four months your baby should have approximately doubled her birth weight. From six months on, the growth rate slows to around a pound a month.

GROWTH SPURT ALERT

Just as you've settled into a feeding pattern and are coming to grips with understanding Baby's hunger cues, he is suddenly fussy and seems to want milk, milk and more milk, demanding a feed every hour. Don't worry; this is not the new norm. It's most likely Baby's first growth spurt, which commonly happens around three weeks of age, and then again at six weeks, three months and six months. A temporary increase in milk intake for a couple of days provides Baby with the energy he needs to develop, whether it's physical growth or working on a skill such as rolling or crawling. If you are breastfeeding, additional nursing sessions will prompt a boost in your milk supply, and after a day or two demand will settle back down to a regular, less frequent pattern. A formula-fed baby can be given an ounce or two extra per feed or an extra bottle if he seems hungry. The common times for growth spurts were given above, but as babies don't work to a schedule, you could find growth spurts happening more frequently or at times other than those listed. Or you may not notice any.

INTRODUCING SOLID FOOD

Two extremely important things to remember before you introduce your baby to solid food are:

1. Cover your entire room in plastic sheeting—the fallout zone is way bigger than you anticipate.
2. Have a camera handy to capture priceless grimaces at the first sampling of veggies.

Starting solids: the fun, the mess! Once my little girl was ready to graduate to a booster seat for meals, we pried the high chair from the spot it had been occupying for almost two years and found that not only had the carpet in the vicinity permanently changed color, but the wall behind had been redecorated with a Jackson Pollock relief; the primary medium being spaghetti sauce. I estimate that she would actually consume 10 percent of a box of Cheerios, while the remainder was distributed around the house, car, grandparents' houses and various local restaurants and coffee shops. I even found whole Cheerios in her diaper at changing time and can only assume they hadn't passed through. I expect I'll still be uncovering them from the recesses of the sofa when she's started school.

Babies like to investigate, play with and wear their food. They'll grab at the spoon and stick their fingers in the bowl to study the texture before smearing the rest around their face and reaching over to share some with your sleeve. They'll squish pasta, crush crackers and spread cereal. And hammering on a tray of bouncing Cheerios makes a great game.

When?

With allergies on the rise, the current recommendation is to wait until Baby is six months old before introducing solids. A baby's digestive system needs time to mature to be able to handle the solids, and early introduction can cause bad reactions such as gas, constipation and upset stomach. Your baby should show signs of being ready to eat: making open beak baby bird moves towards food, seeming hungry after milk and being able to sit (not necessarily unsupported, but not slumped) and hold his head steady. When you do offer the food, he should make some effort to chew and swallow rather than pushing it straight back out with his tongue. Research says that feeding solids before six months doesn't help a baby to sleep through the night, so don't be tempted to start early thinking it will get you some extra rest. But if your baby does seem hungry and ready for food early, discuss it with your doctor. It's also a good idea to hold off until you've checked with your doctor if there are serious food allergies in your family.

Over the next six months, Baby will gradually take more and more nutrients from solids, but breast milk or infant formula continues to be the most important source of nutrition throughout the first year. The main reasons to offer solids are to get Baby used to different tastes and textures, find out his likes and dislikes, test for allergies and ensure he is getting enough iron. Initially you should feed Baby his usual breast milk or formula first and follow it up with solids. Around eight months, Baby will likely be more interested in his grown-up meals, and from nine months you can start to give solids first and leave the milk to the dessert course.

What?

We start with mush, officially known as iron-fortified infant cereal. Iron is essential for Baby's health and development, and by six months she is using up her inbuilt iron supply. (A baby's daily iron requirement is actually more than her dad's, so continue serving the iron-fortified cereal throughout this first year.) It's best to try rice cereal first because it's the least likely of the cereals to provoke an allergic reaction. If she accepts it, move on to other single grain cereals like oats and barley, leaving wheat until around eight months, as this grain is the most likely to cause an allergic reaction.

After a couple of weeks, once Baby is used to cereal, you can start to experiment with various pureed veggies and then fruit. That order is advisable since the sweet taste of fruit may reduce the chances of her accepting the stronger flavor of vegetables. Good bets to start are squash, sweet potato, carrots and green beans. Yellow and orange vegetables tend to be sweeter. Follow up a couple of weeks later with fruits such as applesauce, peaches, pears, apricots and bananas. Once Baby is eating a few vegetables and fruits, protein and iron sources such as pureed meat, poultry, fish, tofu, lentils and beans can be introduced. Leave dairy products such as plain or baby yogurt, grated cheese and cottage cheese to nine to twelve months of age.

In this first year, you should not give Baby high-allergen foods such as peanuts, shellfish and eggs (egg whites, to be precise; if you can be bothered to extract the yolk, it's a good source of iron and Baby can have that at nine months). Also, strawberries and chocolate should be avoided. Honey could make Baby sick because it contains botulism spores. No matter how sorry you feel for her having to eat wallpaper-paste infant cereal, a young baby shouldn't have additives like sugar, salt and spices.

The recommendation is to leave three to seven days between each new food. At this rate, your child will be starting school before her first taste of brussels sprouts, although from her point of view this is probably a good thing. This cautious, organized approach makes it much easier to determine the cause of an upset stomach, rash or more serious allergic reaction. If you suspect a particular food to be at the root of a minor reaction, wait a few weeks before trying it again. Start cautiously, and if Baby has no adverse reactions, it's probably safe to leave the minimum time between each new food. However, if you have a family history of allergies, continue with caution. It may be a good idea to talk to your doctor about the best approach before starting solids. Keep written logs noting the date each food is introduced. One jar of green mush looks a lot like another, and it will be a strain on your Mommy Brain to remember whether it was broccoli or peas you tried last week. Mixed fruit and veggie combinations and more exciting recipes such as beef casserole should only be offered after all the individual ingredients are tried and tested.

Baby shouldn't be forced to eat anything. There are plenty of years ahead of "encouraging" her to eat her greens. If she doesn't seem to like a particular flavor, forget it for now and try it again in a week or so—babies can be very fickle with their tastes. We've provided some **Comrades' Recommendations** below for sneaky methods of getting Baby to eat the things she is not so keen on.

At seven to eight months you can let Baby loose with the real fun stuff: finger foods. It's something to behold watching Baby try to coordinate a Cheerio from tray to mouth and actually eat it without a spill. She can fall at the first hurdle, dropping it into her lap, or it can get lost in the folds of her pudgy hand and become impossible to extricate. Even as close to the finish line as in her mouth, the game still isn't over—chewing is also a skill she hasn't yet mastered, and a mouth opened too wide can lose its prize. It must be an exercise in frustration, but she'll persevere and be very proud of herself when she succeeds, as feeding herself is an important step towards independence. It can take ages for Baby to eat a handful of finger foods, so it's also a useful ploy to keep her busy and entertained feeding herself while you eat your own meal.

For finger foods, stick to the soft fruits such as banana, peach, pear, mango or well-cooked vegetables peeled and cut into small pieces. Also try grated cheese (always pasteurized), rice cakes, plain crackers, small pasta shapes and, of course, cereals such as good old Cheerios. Avoid round fruits like whole grapes that will easily slip down the throat, and hard fruits and vegetables like apple and raw carrot.

Consistencies

The first foods you give Baby should be almost liquid. Early servings of cereal should be runny, then as time goes on you can mix the dried cereal with less water or milk to a thicker consistency. Fruits, vegetables and meats should initially be pureed. However, it's best not to wait too long before introducing lumpier foods, otherwise Baby may be resistant to learning to chew on the chunks. Seven to nine months is a good time to switch to chunkier baby foods. As a rough guide, move from pureed to mashed around seven to eight months, to minced around nine months and to diced around ten months. Lumps should always be soft and small enough to avoid choking when Baby inevitably forgets to chew and swallows them whole. Be prepared for plenty of gagging during the learning process.

Oh, blah blah blah—every now and again I catch myself regurgitating advice and overlooking what happens in the real world. Before we start to sound just like every other baby book out there, let's step back and be honest: babies don't like lumps. It's a good idea to try to get Baby to eat chunkier foods before he gets too set in his ways, but don't be surprised if you meet with resistance. Sure, he'll eat lumps in the guise of a Cheerio or cracker, but try to slip him a lump or two of veggie and he'll not hesitate to spit it back out. When we're desperately trying and failing to potty train, the advice goes, "Don't sweat it, they'll learn eventually—do you ever see a kid at school in diapers?" Well, the same follows here: no kid goes to school with a pureed packed lunch.

Also, remember that in the same way Junior has to learn how to crawl, walk and talk, he also has to learn how to eat. It surprised me that eating didn't come naturally; it also surprised me how long it took for my son to learn that he had to chew his food rather than inhale it. He may have been an early walker, but he was a complete nincompoop when it came to eating. The cough-and-vomit became a regular occurrence at meal times when he would forget to chew and then would gag, cough and bring up whatever he'd eaten so far—not a pleasant diner to share the table with.

How Much and How Often?

From six to nine months, you can feed Baby two or three times a day whenever it is convenient for you. Initially, the feedings are learning and experimentation sessions more than meals, so pick a quiet time when you can make her first meal a pleasant experience rather than trying to shovel food in five minutes while you multitask trying to prepare your own evening meal. Baby doesn't care if her first taste of beef stew is served for breakfast or if lunch isn't on the table until three o'clock, if that is the time that suits you. Eating together isn't always practical if Baby turns in really early, but gradually you can move to serving food at more conventional meal times, allowing you to eat with Baby as much as possible. Including Baby in family meals ensures she learns by example and feels included. Aim for increasing to three or four consistently timed meals a day by nine months. By the end of the first year, Baby should be enjoying three meals and two snacks a day.

Start with a tiny amount—just a tablespoon of infant cereal is ample. When introducing a new type of food, start with just 1 to 3 teaspoons (5 to 15 milliliters). If the food is a winner, you can increase serving sizes based on your baby's appetite and the guidelines given later in this section.

A baby may show she is hungry or pleased to see her food by waving her hands, opening her mouth, reaching forward or smiling or squeaking excitedly. If she's still hungry at the end of the meal, she may get upset when the dishes are taken away. Signals that she is full may include shutting her mouth, turning her head away, pushing away the spoon or getting agitated, especially if you keep trying to force more on her. Babies know a lot (you will be surprised how much). With a few exceptions, they all know how much food is right for them at a given time. You'll soon become familiar with your baby's appetite and how she signals an empty and full tummy—be sure to let her instincts guide you. For most moms, this is an extremely hard rule to follow. I had ongoing inner battles to stop myself from trying to stuff my baby with food when, in my opinion, she had not eaten enough. Inevitably, a swift barf would remind me to heed her full signals next time.

Some babies will have big appetites; others small. Some have stable appetites; others change like the weather. One day your baby might not be particularly interested in food, maybe because she's teething or feeling a little under the weather, and you'll immediately start to panic. Then the very next day she'll be back to normal, or she'll be having a growth spurt and will be ravenous and screaming blue murder because dinner isn't served 30 seconds after her first whimper. Teaching bad habits with regards to overeating is also a common trap for new moms intent on a well-fed infant. Try not to resort to food every time Baby cries (try to work out if there is something wrong first), as a reward, to combat boredom or as a comfort.

With varying appetites in mind, the following is a rough guide as to how much per day your baby will eat in this first year, in addition to regular breast milk or formula feedings (see the **Mouth** chapter for more information). To make the amounts easier to picture, a small jar of commercial baby food is roughly 8 tablespoons (120 milliliters).

Six to Nine Months
- 4–8 tbsp (60–120 ml) infant cereal
- 4–8 tbsp (60–120 ml) fruit and vegetables
- 6 tbsp (90 ml) meat or alternatives

Nine to Twelve Months
- 8 tbsp (120 ml) or more infant cereal
- 8 tbsp (120 ml) or more fruit and vegetables
- 6–8 tbsp (90–120 ml) meat or alternatives

Comrades' Recommendations

- Don't sweat it too much on a daily basis. Look at the bigger picture and consider how much Baby has eaten over a week rather than a day—you'll probably find it evens out to the recommended amounts.
- Bibs: the bigger the better. The fallout zone extends way beyond a small square beneath a baby's chin.
- Always watch your baby carefully when she's eating because she will often not chew properly. She'll usually manage to cough up the offending article, but you need to be on hand just in case she does start choking.
- Unless Baby will eat the whole jar, do not serve food straight from the jar. Once saliva gets mixed with the food, enzymes start to break it down, and it becomes watery and will start to spoil. Use a clean spoon to serve up as much food as you expect Baby to eat into a bowl.
- Throw away anything left in Baby's bowl, as it will quickly start to go bad.
- Always feed Baby solid food with a spoon—never put cereal in a bottle.
- If you feed Baby canned fruit, avoid fruit in syrup. Buy it in juice instead.
- Over the next few years you will be forever telling your little one to "share," so start by setting a good example and share with your mommy friends. Serving sizes for babies are very small, and opened packets or jars will often go out of date before you've had a chance to use them, so it's a good idea to split large packets with your friends.
- Pass on your rejects. Instead of tossing things that your baby rejects, give them to someone else. If you open a packet of banana raspberry cereal and Baby thinks it's disgusting, pass the rest of the box on to a friend. Another baby might find it yummy.
- Share your success stories with friends. If you find or make a tasty baby treat, give friends a sample so they can try it without buying a whole big bag, or if it's a recipe, before they go to the trouble of making it.
- Babies are not usually fussy about the temperature of their meals—they don't realize chicken casserole should be warm.

They will likely eat anything at room temperature. Food can be warmed by standing the bowl in a pan of warm water. Microwaving is not recommended as it can lead to hot pockets of food that can burn Baby's mouth. Take care to stir and test warmed food before serving it to Baby.

- In some little ones, an empty fuel tank will trigger what moms generally term a "meltdown." If you notice Baby is getting cranky, tearful or impatient, or there is an escalation in naughtiness, it might be time for a meal or snack. A new and improved baby will emerge after the nutrition blast.

- Get a Dustbuster! Handheld cordless vacuums are absolute lifesavers when it comes to the quick and easy cleanup of the twentieth spill of the day. Remember how few Cheerios actually get eaten? The rest are ideal Dustbuster fodder, as are the toast crumbs and spaghetti strands in the high chair. If you don't suck up the leftovers, Baby will find them on her next exploration and not hesitate to eat them as a little Scooby Snack.

- Relax, Mom! Sure, feeding is stressful: Is Baby getting enough? Eating her greens? Getting her iron? We can easily over think the whole topic. Only the safety rules should be followed to the word; otherwise, interpret as you see fit, and enjoy feeding your baby.

BABY FOOD

For lazy, culinarily challenged moms like me, the pop on the seal of a jar of commercial baby food is music to the ears. However, according to my less kitchen-phobic friends, it's apparently quite simple and less expensive to make your own baby food. Just boil or steam the fruit or veggies until they are really soft, then blend or mash, depending on what consistency Baby is currently working on, and add a little previously boiled water if needed. This will keep in the fridge for up to three days, but as Baby generally eats such little portions, and assuming you don't want to bore him with 12 consecutive meals of carrot, freezing some is a good idea. An ice cube tray is useful to divide up the pureed or mashed food into baby-sized portions. Your frozen food cubes can be transferred to a freezer bag and are good for up to four weeks. You can do the same with meats and fish, but they take a little more prep—several blendings might be needed to get a smooth consistency. All meat and fish must be lean, skinned, deboned and of course carefully cooked until tender. Always thaw the frozen foodcicles in the fridge overnight, never at room temperature.

If you find cooking enjoyable, have fun with some baby recipes. Be sure to share portions with your culinarily challenged friends when you find a winner (hint, hint). If you're in my pro-jar camp, don't beat yourself up—Baby's tastes aren't that discerning. He will probably be just as happy with chicken lasagna from a jar. The few baby recipes I experimented with got the short shrift at one sitting and the rest was discarded, although this could well be a reflection on my cooking.

Give your kids a chance to eat healthily by starting them on the right path. Even if you don't eat the right things or know you could do better, try and do right by your baby. When you introduce bread, pasta and rice, serve the whole grain variety, not white; offer plain cereals rather than sugar-coated ones; try cereal bars rather than sugary cookies. If you introduce processed, sweet and chocolate-coated foods early, Baby will get used to the taste, and it will be hard to switch to a healthier option later. Also, excess sugar in a baby's diet may spoil his appetite and harm his teeth, so save the first taste of cake for his first birthday party to make the event extra special.

Provide a variety of fruit and vegetables and try not to force your own food preferences on Baby by only serving what you like. Keep in mind that a baby's diet in the first two years strongly affects what you can expect him to be eating at age seven. I found that my own eating habits actually improved as a result of ensuring my baby had healthy food choices. While I was prepping fruit for Baby I would have some with my lunch, and as I was cooking whole wheat pasta for her I served it to myself and hubby too.

NOT EATING AND FUSSY EATING

One of the most common and significant worries of a new mom is whether Baby is eating well. If Baby has a "healthy appetite," you feel at ease; if she's off food for a day or two, or point-blank refusing to eat vegetables for weeks on end, you see it as a personal failure. Unfortunately, a lot of babies are fussy eaters, piling on the stress for their poor moms. I've seen rookie moms reduced to tears by their little ones' finicky eating. After tolerating one or two veggie purees from a jar early on, my baby girl decided to restrict her diet to infant cereal, banana and avocado until 18 months. I bumped into a fellow new mom purchasing a blender to make smoothies in a last-ditch attempt to get her little one to eat any veggies whatsoever.

The problem may not be what you're serving, but rather the method of delivery. While some lazy tykes are prepared to sit back and let Mom feed them ad infinitum, other more independent souls will want free rein to wield the spoon themselves, and may go as far as to resist anything delivered to them and insist upon feeding themselves. Unfortunately, when left to their own devices, quite often little of the nutritious meal actually reaches its intended target of Junior's tum. Mom's frustration grows as she watches the food spread around Baby's person and drop into the recesses of the high chair. She despairs as Baby is distracted by investigating what happens when she crushes a cracker and mixes the crumbs with a drop of spilled milk. But to an 11-month-old budding scientist, conducting experiments is way more interesting than eating.

As mentioned earlier in the **How Much and How Often?** section, it's important for us to encourage babies to eat and try new foods, but not to force food on them. Our well-intentioned badgering is likely to turn every meal time into a battle and put Baby off food. That said, we've learned some devious tricks a mom can employ to encourage her baby to eat a variety of healthy foods, and we've shared some here.

If you get to nine months and are struggling to feed your baby foods from the various food groups discussed in this chapter, it may put your mind at rest to get some advice from a doctor, community health nurse or dietician. But as long as Baby is gaining weight as expected and seems alert, energetic and generally happy, she is likely getting enough nourishment.

Comrades' Recommendations

- If Baby balks at the strong taste of veggies or meat, try mixing them with infant cereal to water down the flavor.
- On the flip side, once Baby is used to flavor and texture, the sloppy, wallpaper-paste blandness of infant cereal may not be exciting enough, so jazz it up with fruit to make it more enticing.
- If your older baby won't eat that iron-fortified cereal because it's just too dull, try using it to make muffins.
- Don't be tempted to switch to adult cereals with added sugar or salt and less iron, as these are not as good for Baby.
- Try foods in different shapes. It is possible Baby may not like carrot coins but will eat carrot sticks. She may not be keen on square toast but will eat triangles. Or, she'll prefer to gnaw on a big lump of bagel rather than be given bite-sized pieces.
- If Baby goes off a food that she previously enjoyed, try reintroducing it after a week in a different shape—she may be fooled into thinking it's something new.
- Baby will often find food off your plate more desirable than what you have served her, even if it is the exact same meal.
- Practice the art of mixing two types of food together. If Baby doesn't like peas but loves carrots, mix a spoonful of peas with a few spoons of carrots to dilute the flavor, and she may enjoy the flavor mix.
- A good rule of thumb is you decide "what" (working around your baby's known dislikes), while Baby decides "whether" and "how much" she will eat. This way you are not pandering to fussiness too much, but allowing Baby to eat according to her appetite.
- If your baby does not eat meat, aim for at least 8 tablespoons (120 milliliters) of infant cereal daily, on average, by nine months of age to ensure she is getting enough iron.

FOOD ALLERGIES

It is not until about six months that a baby begins to produce enough antibodies to prevent allergic reactions. A younger baby is more prone to an allergic reaction to any input other than breast milk. Of course, infant formula is carefully manufactured to resemble breast milk as closely as possible, but even so, some babies can react to the cow's milk protein in the formula. Some babies can even have a bad reaction to cow's milk protein in Mom's breast milk. The longer we avoid high-allergen foods like egg, cow's milk and peanuts, the more time Baby has had to prepare for these inputs and the less chance there will be of an allergic reaction.

An allergic reaction occurs when the body's immune system fights a particular food it has mistaken as harmful. Once an allergy is developed, a reaction occurs every time the food is eaten. Children can outgrow food allergies; for example, a cow's milk allergy is often outgrown by age three. About six percent of babies have food allergies, and since allergies tend to run in families, your baby is more at risk if you or Baby's dad have food allergies or other allergic conditions such as eczema, asthma or hay fever.

Signs of a food allergy can occur within minutes or up to two hours after eating, and may present as a mild intolerance or more severe symptoms. Some symptoms, such as eczema, may take longer to appear. Obviously, if there is a severe reaction such as difficulty breathing, you should seek immediate medical attention. The following is a list of possible signs of a food allergy.

- excessive gassiness; explosive poops
- diarrhea, or poop that contains mucus or blood
- excessive spitting up or vomiting
- sore, red bottom
- rash or eczema
- runny nose, wheezing, watery eyes
- swelling of the mouth, tongue and throat
- difficulty breathing or swallowing
- blue face or lips

If you suspect a food is causing an allergic reaction, stop serving it and talk to your baby's doctor or a community health nurse or dietician for advice on the best course of action.

SPIT UP

What advice can we give on spit up? Not much, because there isn't a great deal you can do about it. With babies, "spit happens." With some babies, spit happens a lot.

Here are the top five reasons a baby may spit up.

1. She ate too much.
2. She gulped air with milk.
3. Her immature digestive system causes regurgitation.

4. You've just changed her into her best cute outfit.
5. She is sitting on Great-Aunt Muriel's lap.

Four out of ten babies spit up regularly, and the puking peak is around four months. If you have a puker on your hands (shoulder, chest, sofa, carpet), you'll need to stock up on bibs and burp cloths and get the washing machine serviced because it is going to be working overtime. Then it's a waiting game as the valve that's supposed to keep stomach contents from being regurgitated matures enough to do its job. This will likely happen at around six or seven months, after which physics lends a helping hand. Gravity holds down the stomach contents once Baby is sitting up and the consistency of solid food is harder to regurgitate. Some babies do persist in creating excess laundry until a year old, and it starts to get a bit gross (and colorful) when they are spewing solids.

Spit up caused by eating too much or trapped air bubbles normally happens immediately or soon after the feed. What comes up looks much like the milk that went in. Reflux due to the underdeveloped stomach valve can happen a while after a feed, often triggered by being jiggled around. By then, the milk has been in the stomach and mixed with stomach juices, so it will be sour smelling and curdled like cottage cheese on its return. Spit up can even occur one to two hours after a feed. Spitting up may increase once Baby is putting pressure on her stomach when rolling or learning to crawl, or when she is teething due to swallowing lots of saliva.

A little spew goes a long way. It often looks like a worrying amount, but it is in fact only a couple of tablespoons. Test it out by putting three tablespoons of water in a cup and spilling it on the kitchen counter—it looks like a flood, doesn't it? A rookie mom will often worry that Baby must be hungry again and need more nourishment judging by what she's brought back up, but there is no need to feed her again. One friend of mine would end up with what looked like a jumbo carton of yogurt down her back after burping her baby, yet he was growing like a weed.

Breast milk spit up is quite innocuous and easy to clean, whereas formula puke tends to stain more. Rarely does Baby hit the spot designated for spit up; i.e., the 5-inch-square bib. We spend most of our efforts defending baby clothes against the spit up, when in fact most of the ejections get us. Perhaps we should be the ones wearing the bibs. Most of my "mommy" wardrobe is one big burp cloth—to be ritually burned along with the nursing cushion and nursing bras shortly after Baby's first birthday. You'll soon become accustomed to *eau de vomit* as your new perfume.

Spit up does not distress a baby: stealth puke can be delivered without a whimper. Alerted by a splatter, you'll look down to find a trail down her arm, her leg, your leg, and the final splat on the floor or your shoe. The best ones are those you don't find until you step in them. Vomiting is different—it's often projectile or forceful, it distresses Baby and it is probably due to a bug or something in her diet. Excessive spit up could also be the sign of an allergy; the most likely offender is cow's milk products (in Baby's or Mom's diet). If Baby spits up a lot and seems to be choking or gagging, and if she's fussy when feeding, she could be bothered by acid reflux (GERD)—like bad heartburn. If your baby seems distressed or uncomfortable, if she is not gaining weight or if the spit up is projectile or doesn't look like something resembling curdled milk, it's best to discuss it with your doctor.

Tips from the Trenches

- Don't overfeed. Feed Baby little and often if her tiny tummy is prone to overflow.
- Babies often spit up when they get too much milk too fast. This can happen particularly if your breasts are really full, such as first thing in the morning or if you switch sides too soon or too often. If your supply is too forceful, try expressing a little milk first.
- Heed your baby's signs that she's had enough. If she pulls away from the breast, gets fussy or pushes the bottle away, she's probably done. Whenever I persisted in "coaxing" Baby to take more in, it came straight back out again.
- Burp Baby mid-feed. Air bubbles coming back up can bring up any milk in their path, so burping part way through reduces the amount of spit up.
- Try to keep Baby from getting too distressed before a feed since she'll gulp lots of air when she's crying. Attempt to calm her down before feeding (yeah, try telling that to your ravenous baby).
- Ensure you tilt the bottle correctly so your bottle-fed baby isn't gulping too much air. Try bottles that reduce air intake, such as ones with liners that deflate, and make sure you have the right sized nipple.

- Feed Baby in an upright or sitting position.
- Keep Baby upright for 20 to 30 minutes after a feed by putting her in a baby carrier or ExerSaucer. An infant seat or swingy chair is not such a good bet as it puts pressure on the tummy from bending in the middle.
- Don't tilt, fold, jiggle, jostle or squeeze Baby after a feed. Save hugs for later and specifically remind Dad not to play airplane rides just after lunch.
- Number four on our list of top five reasons why Baby spits up was a joke, but looking at it logically, a lot of jiggling around getting her into that cute outfit probably caused the regurgitation. Leave diaper and clothes changes for a while after feeding.
- Watch out for tight waistbands and diapers squeezing her middle.
- If you're going out or to work and really don't want spit up on your shoulder, put an old shirt over your decent clothes and shed it once you are completely clear of Baby. It's Murphy's Law that she'll barf on you during that last goodbye hug.

TUMMY TIME

"Tummy time" is a baby's first exercise class. It is important for a couple of reasons. Since so much time is spent sleeping on the back, time on the tummy will help to prevent Baby's head from developing a flat spot. Also, lifting the head and pushing up on the arms is an important neck, back, chest and arm muscle workout, enabling Baby to develop head control, which is the key to sitting and all movement. Research shows that babies who spend less time on their tummies are slower to develop skills like crawling.

Not all babies like tummy time. It's hard work and not too much fun in the beginning, when all you get out of it is a face full of mat. It's a good idea to start early, before Baby gets too accustomed to lying on his back all day long. Lifting the head a couple of inches might not look like much of a workout, but it can quickly get very tiring, so be sure to keep the sessions short and stay nearby to keep him company. Provide lots of encouragement, and if Baby is upset, just string it out a little longer by playing, but don't force it. You can gradually increase the time Baby spends on his tummy—when he gets used to it and better at it, he will likely protest less. By three months old, he should be able to lift his head somewhere between 45 and 90 degrees from the horizontal. If your baby is not showing signs of developing head control by six months, discuss it with your doctor.

Tips from the Trenches

- Join Baby on the floor to keep him company. It's a good idea to kill two birds with one stone and do your postpartum exercises at the same time (see **Body Repairs** in the **Body** chapter of the **Mommy Map**).
- If Baby gets upset spending tummy time on the floor, try placing his tummy down across your lap or on your chest to work the same muscles.
- Provide toys that Baby can see and play with while he's on his tummy.
- Getting Baby to look up at objects while on his tummy will encourage him to lift his head and neck.

GAS

You won't believe the smells that can emanate from such a sweet and innocent little body. They can be way worse than a grown man after five pints of beer and a curry. My son's aroma would alternate between bad eggs and rotting garbage. He could clear a room—really unfortunate when I was trapped breastfeeding him and he let rip. Maybe the diaper provides an echo chamber, because the volume of the farts was something to experience too. I expect acoustics take a back seat to absorbency in diaper design.

Baby farts are a constant source of embarrassment. People approach to coo over the baby only to recoil with watering eyes, trying to find some polite way of pointing out that obviously Baby has a load on board and needs changing. I got tired of people assuming I was a slovenly mother (without a sense of smell, apparently). An "I haven't pooped—it's just gas" bumper sticker for the stroller would have saved me repeated explanations. The loudest farts are saved for quiet social gatherings such as church, and the smelliest for confined spaces like the elevator. Of course, on the flip side, if you happen to let one slip yourself (not unheard of postpartum), you can always blame the baby.

Gas is common in young babies due to kinks in their immature digestive systems. There is usually nothing that can or needs to be done except wait it out until the digestive system matures. Babies who go longer between poops are typically gassier. If Baby seems distressed by trapped gas, look for a tight waistband on her clothing or diaper that could be hampering digestion. A little leg cycling, slow circular tummy massage or putting pressure on the tummy by lying Baby face down across your lap (or along your arm in the football hold) can help her to pass trapped gas.

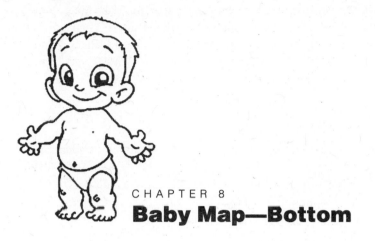

CHAPTER 8

Baby Map—Bottom

THE SCOOP ON POOP

Poop isn't something you tend to talk about—until you have a baby. Then it suddenly becomes a very important, much discussed topic, both at home and on the mommy scene. It's pretty much unavoidable given it's what Baby does best and most after sleeping and eating. To a mom, almost as worrying as how much goes into Baby is how much (or how little) comes out, and of course whether the color and consistency is "normal." Whenever my husband changed the diaper (I didn't have to worry about this too often), he found it most disturbing that I had to know "what was it like?" It's hard for others to understand a mom's fascination with her offspring's poop, but normal diaper contents are a load (hee hee) off her mind when she's worrying whether Baby is healthy. There's nothing guaranteed to get you flying to the Internet quicker than opening Baby's diaper to find it full of bright orange poo. (It's best to finish the diaper change before logging on—that could get really messy.)

Runny, pasty, rabbit droppings, a big log, a pancake, mustard-yellow, green, black—you can find all manner of color, quantity and consistency lurking in (and unfortunately, sometimes escaping from) Baby's diaper, but the big question when it comes to baby poo is: "What is normal?" Essentially, normal is whatever is normal for your baby, and you'll soon get used to Junior's personal bathroom habits. There may be several changes over the course of the year, inevitably causing you to worry, although most changes are simply a response to a new input. I know I was alarmed when my son's poop suddenly transformed from mustard paste into dark green pond sludge. A few minutes on Google confirmed this was fairly normal poop for a baby drinking iron-fortified formula, and sure enough I was midway through weaning him from the breast. Typical poop evolution occurs as follows:

- when transitioning to breastfeeding or formula-feeding after a newborn's meconium days
- at about eight weeks when there is a drop in poop frequency for breastfed babies
- if you start supplementing with or switch to formula
- at the introduction of solids
- at the introduction of a new food group, like dairy.

Breast milk is easy to digest, so for the first couple of months breastfed babies tend to be serial poopers, depositing a little liquidy offering after every feed, which is expensive on diapers and wipes. Breast milk composition changes as the baby grows, and the pooping schedule usually slows down somewhat around six to eight weeks and settles into a pattern. Until they start solids, most breastfed babies will poop at least once a day, but as with most baby-related subjects, some babies are naturally less regular.

"I wish I had known . . .

it was okay for a breastfed baby not to poo for a week. It got to the point where I was wondering how come he wasn't exploding."

Most baby books will tell you that "some babies will only go every two to three days," as if this is the outside figure. Yet both of my babies and those of a friend would often go more than a week without offloading. Old hands may insist this is constipation, but that is not likely the case—very few breastfed babies get constipated. Mother-in-law is probably thinking of what she was used to—a formula-fed baby would be considered constipated in similar circumstances. According to my lactation consultant, after eight weeks of age, breast milk is extremely efficient and there is very little solid waste, so 10 days without a poop is normal for some babies.

When it finally comes, beware: it's likely to be an über-poop. As you wipe, it will almost certainly trigger another pump, and another, until you're not sure where it can possibly be coming from and what you're going to do with it. Babies who skip several days between poops also tend to be gassier. As long as you know your baby is capable of pooping and he seems comfortable and happy (in relative terms, for a baby), everything is likely fine. To ease your mind and get your mother-in-law off your back, you can mention it to the doctor—she may suggest an infant suppository to get the muscles contracting. It's wise to keep a log (hee hee again) of poop action so you can report the facts correctly. When fatigue causes days to merge together in a fog, you won't recall whether it's been five or seven days since Baby's last evacuation.

Breastfed baby poo is a whole different kettle of fish when compared to adult poo; it's something to be reckoned with. It's pasty, seedy, curdy or even runny. It's also expelled with explosive force at times. The diaper is only the general area for baby poo to go—it's likely to escape, shooting up the back and dribbling out the leg holes. Quite often the diaper would need to be a spacesuit to cope with the containment. It will seep into every fold and wrinkle of skin around the diaper area. It's mustard yellow and it stains. It will come at the most inopportune time and will most certainly ruin your favorite designer baby outfit. It'll probably ruin your favorite outfit too, or rather the only clothes that fit you right now.

When my daughter was having six-week baby pictures taken by a professional photographer, we went for some cute naked shots. To my horror, she pooped mid-shoot. Not a little nugget on the carpet, but a projectile shower targeted at the photographer's lighting sheets. The photographer, being an old hand at baby shoots, claimed it happened all the time. I suspect she was just being polite, but at least she didn't run screaming from the room.

Our advice is to always pop a change of baby clothes in the diaper bag when you go out, even if it's just to the store to grab some milk, because you never know when the diaper will fail you and you will have a huge mess on your hands. Don't let the fact that Baby just pooped lull you into a false sense of security either. Take that change of clothes with you, because he can easily decide to poop again, even if he's typically a once-per-day man.

While we're on the subject, I have to include another "I wish I had known . . ." from my own list, albeit a mild gripe. Once we had Baby home and settled, and the meconium days were thankfully over, we were waiting for the telltale odor of poo to tip us off that she had filled her diaper. I did the famous baby's-bum-to-the-nose sniff test several times, but detected nothing. When it came time for a wet diaper change I was amazed to find the diaper full of poop. Poop that didn't smell! Okay, it did smell, but sweet and not unpleasant—not unlike cake mix. I've also heard the smell described as creamed corn, apricots or curried yogurt.

Formula-fed babies' poop will typically be firmer than breastfed babies', it will happen less frequently and it is generally stinkier. The poop can be various colors and textures depending on the type of formula, the iron content and how Baby digests it. Yellow, yellow-brown, green-brown and dark green are all common colors. Moms have described the consistency as peanut butter, Play-Doh or sludge. Typically a formula-fed baby will go once or twice a day, but again there are no set rules. Formula-fed babies are expected to go more frequently than breastfed babies since formula is not as easily digested as breast milk and produces more solid waste.

Breastfeeding moms can wave goodbye to any fragrant diapers and start keeping a clothes-peg handy for their nose at the change station once Baby starts solids. The new wide range of input will radically change a Baby's poop, and what goes in will often be reflected in the output. Remember that bright orange poop? Junior probably polished off the better part of a jar of carrots the night before. Similarly, peas can tint the poo green, and of course sweet corn will reappear unaltered (what is it with sweet corn)? The high iron input of iron-fortified cereal on top of iron-fortified formula will often result in dark green to greeny-black poop. Generally the consistency will firm up considerably to patties once Baby starts solids. Movements might become irregular as Baby's intestines learn to digest the new foods. Grunting and going red in the face is quite normal, but no less embarrassing when Junior starts doing the deed in the middle of the living room while you have guests.

Given that this huge variety of color and consistency is considered to be perfectly reasonable output for a healthy baby, what is actually cause for concern?

- **Diarrhea:** Normal baby poop can be frequent, watery and greenish, so how do we tell if a baby has diarrhea? Diarrhea in a baby will be more frequent, more watery and greener. Now isn't that helpful? A foul smell might tip you off—okay, a fouler smell than normal. A bout of diarrhea is probably not serious; it could be a virus, a food allergy or a reaction to extra saliva being swallowed when teething. Try to make sure Baby stays well hydrated, and speak to your doctor or community health nurse for advice.
- **Red in poop:** The one color that no mom wants to see in Baby's poop is blood-red, yet even this is not necessarily anything to worry about. Blood streaks can appear in Baby's poop for a few reasons: constipation, little cuts around the butt hole that can appear as a reaction to dairy products (in Mom's diet or Baby's own), or even blood ingested from Mom's cracked nipple. Occasionally it can be the sign of something more serious, so it is always best to check it out with the doctor.
- **Black poop:** After meconium you shouldn't see tar-black poop again. Since dried blood could be the cause, black poop should be checked with your doctor.

CONSTIPATION

If constipation didn't cause Baby discomfort, I'd welcome it with open arms. What mom wouldn't if it meant changing only one poopie diaper every three days instead of three times in one day? Just because a baby is pooping less often than usual, it doesn't mean she is constipated. Telltale signs of constipation are if the poops are harder and dryer, or if Baby has difficulty doing the deed. Because it is harder to expel, the poop stays longer in the intestine and consequently gets dryer and harder, creating a vicious cycle. A constipated baby can get stomach pain and some leakage of liquid poop that bypasses the blockage.

Constipation is rarely a problem in young babies; after all, their diet is pure liquid. There is a slight chance formula-fed babies will suffer from constipation as formula is harder on the stomach than breast milk. It is when solids are introduced that the lottery begins. Often babies get constipated at transition time because their digestive systems need to adjust to the new input. We typically start babies on rice cereal, which can be binding. Also, they are taking in more solid food that is dehydrating. The switch to cow's milk from breast milk or formula can also be a time when Baby might suffer from constipation.

Tips from the Trenches

- Try some abdominal baby massage. You may find a class in your neighborhood, or you can buy a book.
- Get Baby moving. Exercise is great for getting the digestive system functioning. If Baby is mobile, encourage more crawling or walking. Lying Baby on her back and cycling her legs can help.
- Give Baby a warm bath. (Be prepared with a fishing net if this does have the desired effect!)
- Increase Baby's liquid intake with previously boiled water that's cooled.
- If Baby is six months or older, add a cocktail of 1 ounce (30 milliliters) prune or apple juice and 1 ounce water to her diet. If she isn't keen on drinking it, try mixing it with cereal.
- Providing that Baby is on solids, increase the fruit and vegetable servings. Particularly effective are pears, apricots, peaches, plums, peas and, of course, prunes.
- Move from rice cereal to barley or oat.
- Give Baby whole wheat bread or crackers instead of their white counterparts.
- Bananas, rice cereal, applesauce and cooked carrots are binding and should be avoided.
- Try giving Baby some probiotic yogurt to aid her digestion and help regulate her poop schedule.
- Don't give a baby laxatives or suppositories unless given the okay by your doctor.
- See your doctor if your young baby appears constipated and is not gaining weight, is distressed or in pain, is vomiting or has blood in her poops (although a little blood can be from the difficulty in passing the poop), as there could be an underlying illness or problem.

- When should you mention your baby's infrequent bowel movements to the doctor? The general guideline is if a breastfed baby goes more than seven days without a poop and a formula-fed baby more than four.

DIAPER RASH

Diaper rashes are inevitable. Sensitive baby skin can be irritated by the ammonia in pee and poop and can get chafed by a damp, warm diaper. You may find your baby only experiences occasional flare-ups, or you could be fighting a constant battle. Babies are particularly susceptible to diaper rashes in their "sitting phase," around eight to ten months, when they spend more time with their tushie in contact with the damp diaper. The term "diaper rash" encompasses various unpleasant skin conditions in the diaper area. It typically involves red, sore spots or areas on the bottom, genitals or inner thighs. Once skin is damaged it is easily infected, leading to a worse rash. You may see broken skin or blisters.

The main causes of diaper rash are:

- a wet bum
- irritants in poop from foods like citrus fruit
- scents, chemicals or detergents in the diaper or wipes

A diaper rash will normally clear up in a few days if you follow a few simple home remedies. Think clean, cool and dry.

Comrades' Recommendations

- Keep Baby's bum as clean and dry as possible. The standard rule is to change the diaper every two to three hours max or as soon as it is poopie. Enzymes in poop can quickly irritate already wet skin.
- Make sure you clean the poop out of every nook and cranny. Any poopie residue will quickly irritate and an angry red patch of skin will no doubt greet you at the next diaper change.
- Completely dry the bottom before putting on a diaper by patting it with a towel.
- Allow the bottom to get air. This is an easy-to-follow tip while Baby is young. Lay him diaperless on a towel on the changing

mat and let him kick as nature intended; supervised, of course. Once Baby is mobile, it may be a little less practical. A baby on the loose without a diaper . . . hmmm.

- Use a barrier cream to soothe rashes or protect against them. I swear by the magical zinc oxide cream—one or two applications and the rash disappears. Or you can use petroleum ointment. Make sure you thoroughly clean and pat the bottom dry before applying; otherwise, you are trapping moisture against the skin, which will exacerbate the situation. If the regular barrier creams aren't working or the rash is severe, ask the pharmacist to mix up a stronger cocktail.
- Our behinds were typically smothered with good old baby talc when we were young, but it is now considered a no-no as it can get into Baby's lungs.
- Try a different wipe. Make sure you select the unscented ones. Sometimes just a particular brand can irritate your baby. Happily for my budget, a cheap store brand of wipe was fine, whereas one name brand caused a rash.
- While Baby has a rash, use just a clean, wet washcloth or cotton balls (with or without mild baby soap) for cleanups. Or save unscented wipes for poop cleanup and use a washcloth and water for the wet ones.
- If Baby is in disposables, try another brand that may be less scratchy or fit better, reducing the friction that adds to irritation.
- If Baby is in cloth diapers, try switching detergents. Rinse diapers twice to remove as much of the chemicals as possible.
- Plastic pants over cloth diapers create a warm, damp greenhouse environment where bacteria thrive. Try to find breathable pants.
- Some rashes, particularly a red ring around the butt hole, could be due to an irritant in the poop. This is more likely to occur when Baby starts solids or when new foods are introduced and the poop content changes. For instance, whenever my daughter ate strawberries she got a diaper rash without fail. Acidic foods like citrus fruit or tomatoes are typical offenders. Finding the culprit can be tricky, however.
- See your doctor if:
  - there is no improvement after more than three days of trying the home remedies
  - the rash worsens or appears infected or swollen

- ulcers or blisters form
- the rash spreads out of the diaper area
- the rash is yeasty. (A warm, moist diaper is the perfect environment for yeast infections like thrush to thrive. A yeast infection typically affects the genitals and thighs but not the buttocks. An antifungal cream will be needed for treatment.)

DIAPERS

One thing you are going to see a lot of in the next two to three years is diapers—unless you are brave enough to attempt "elimination communication." But I'm guessing there aren't many out there prepared to let Baby go diaperless from the get-go, watching for poop and pee body language and racing to a receptacle to catch the fallout. Hey, I'm not knocking it. I think it's admirable, but I suspect it's more than most of us are willing to take on. So it's on, and off, and on . . . with the diapers—probably nearly 5000 of the things before your little one is potty trained. You are left with the decision of using disposables or cloth diapers. Actually, the options are:

- disposables—Pampers, Huggies, Luvs, store brands, etc.
- eco-friendly/biodegradable disposables
- cloth diapers with a diaper service
- cloth diapers laundered at home
- new flushable diapers (gDiapers), which sound promising.

Disposable Diapers

In the words of Kermit the Frog, "It's not easy being green," and there is never a more difficult time to stop and consider our effects on the environment than when we are new parents. So many eco-unfriendly, ridiculously over-packaged disposable products are thrust at us, and we accept them gratefully because they're so darned convenient. Take the obvious example: the disposable diaper. It's scary to think that every disposable diaper that has ever graced a baby's bottom in the world is still out there somewhere, ever so slowly biodegrading. Even the first diaper from 1961 apparently still has a good 400 to 500 years of biodegrading to do. I'm not sure how they know this when none have actually managed to complete the task yet. Will some landfill worker in the year 2511 hold aloft a little cute character waistband and say, "They lied, it's still here"?

I am guiltily conscious of how much trash we've generated in our house over the last couple of years with our disposable diapers, but at the end of the day the darn things are so effective and convenient. The next generation may have to find a use for used diapers, like building houses out of them. For my part, I will try to persuade my child to go into a scientific field where she can develop the diaper that turns into a cloud of smoke two hours after being removed from the bum. Of course, another option for us guilty but lazy consumers is to let Baby wear the same diaper all day. This is eco-friendly (or does toting a small bundle of methane around contribute to global warming?), but not really baby-friendly, and not advisable considering the advice in the "Diaper Rash" section.

There is no doubt that modern disposables work well. It's true that leaks do happen with small babies, and I'm not just talking about pee. It's hard to get a good fit on a newborn, and as mentioned in **The Scoop on Poop** section, due to its liquid consistency, poop can be hard to contain early on. Soon the poop will solidify to a much more manageable consistency and tend to stay put, and you'll rarely have a leak problem with a well-fitting diaper.

You really won't know which diapers work best for your baby in terms of fit, comfort and reliability until you try them. The ads all tell you the same thing: theirs are the best fit, they never leak and the other brands suck. You will probably have a couple of unpleasant incidents before you find what works best for your child. My firstborn's butt was only ever graced by a big brand name because I just assumed the store brands wouldn't be good enough. By the time my son came along I was conscious of the big hole that disposables were leaving in our bank balance and decided it was worth giving store brands a test run—some are given high ratings by parenting websites. I was pleasantly surprised to find that for two-thirds of the price they worked just fine.

Eco-Friendly/Biodegradable Diapers

I would have happily put up with a few leaks if there were a brand of diaper that advertised being truly biodegradable. I'm sure most of us would. Unfortunately, it seems like there is little point in beating yourself up to find, and to pay more for, biodegradable diapers. While biodegradable brands are made of cornstarch, which decomposes quicker than regular disposables, air and water are needed for the process and a landfill is typically lacking in both. So unless you are going to lay your dirty diapers over the back lawn until they biodegrade, you shouldn't bother. The neighbors probably wouldn't be too happy with this approach either.

If, on the other hand, you are interested in reduced chemical waste, there are several brands that are chlorine-free, latex-free, fragrance-free and hypoallergenic—better for Baby's bottom and the environment. Look for Seventh Generation, Nature Boy and Girl, Tushies and Ecobaby. Looking for these brands is sadly what you'll have to do, as most supermarket chains don't carry them.

Cloth Diapers

Lucky for us, cloth diapers have come a long way in the last 30 years. For a start, most now come with Velcro fasteners, so you don't have to worry about wielding sharp objects around your baby's sensitive parts. Modern cloth diapers are also smaller and sensibly shaped to fit Baby's butt, with stretchy waistbands and the all-important leak guards. The covers are now cloth-like and breathable, rather than the plastic bag that used to insulate our bottoms. You have an initial outlay to buy your supplies and the cost of running your washing machine day and night to factor in; however, cloth diapers are much cheaper than disposables. Diaper services that take away the soiled ones and deliver you a clean batch once a week make the option much more convenient, if more pricey—but still marginally less than disposables. Of course, cloth diapers aren't off the hook when it comes to harming the environment, as you have to factor in the energy used in laundering and the water and air pollution byproducts. In fact, in some areas, landfill issues are less of a worry than pollution and energy and water consumption.

My friends who use cloth diapers are really happy with them. They advise frequent changes to avoid diaper rash, since cloth diapers do not wick away moisture as well as disposables. At night, it's best to double up the diapers to avoid leaks. The only real disadvantages are that group day cares often refuse washable diapers for hygiene reasons and convenience, and Baby's bum does look rather humungous.

Flushable Diapers

It's worth a mention, even though at the time of writing this advance in baby waste management still seems to have a long way to go. These gDiapers have a liner that you can flush down the toilet (or compost if it's only wet), a second snap-in liner that can be washed if soiled, and outer pants. At the time of writing, they are not yet widely available and toilet clogging remains a risk, but having watched (and been terrified by) *An Inconvenient Truth*, I feel this option does at least offer some promise for our future.

CHANGE STATIONS AND EQUIPMENT

Whichever diapering method you choose, you are going to spend a lot of time at the change station, so you might as well set up a convenient and comfortable base camp. It's true that you can do the job without any expensive equipment—a towel on the floor or the bed will suffice—but if you set up a change table at waist height you won't be straining your back every time you change a diaper. It's important to have everything you need (i.e., diapers, wipes, wash cloths, diaper rash cream, clothes-peg for your nose) close at hand in drawers or baskets. It's no good realizing you're missing something vital half way through a change. You shouldn't leave Baby unattended on a change table, so you'll have to take the whole messy cargo with you if you have to retrieve something you have forgotten.

To make change time as pleasant as it can be, you want Baby happy and wriggling as little as possible. A squirming baby does not help matters when you are trying to minimize poo transfer. A squishy, soft mat with cupped edges will keep Baby warm, snuggly and somewhat contained. Sometimes it helps to have a little mobile hanging above the change table or a couple of toys handy to keep Baby distracted while you work on the business end. A good tip is to have a designated area far away from Baby's flailing limbs to stash the dirty diaper while you finish off. If it is within reach, you can guarantee Baby will manage to get a hand into the mess or deftly kick it onto the floor.

Finally, the disposal. For disposables and cloth diapers you'll probably use some sort of diaper pail. The diaper pail should have a lid that is easily opened and closed and that keeps in the odors. Alternatively, for disposables there are specialized diaper disposal systems, such as the Diaper Genie. Sorry to nag, but I really am offended by the inefficiency of some of these machines. We are already stocking the landfills at an alarming rate, and on top of that some of these devices use a yard of plastic to wrap a single wet diaper, closing that tiny window of opportunity the diaper ever had to biodegrade before the year 2500. There are less wasteful versions that allow you to choose when to seal the bag and start a new one. Wet diapers aren't serious even into toddlerhood, so you might be happy bagging and tossing a day's worth, or even just popping them in with the household trash and saving the bags for the more offensive poopie diapers. Once the poops become solid enough, flush them down the toilet. At least this reduces smell in your garbage (which your garbage collector will be thankful for) and toxic human waste in the landfill.

HOME SPRINKLER SYSTEM

Having a demure little baby girl first, I was happily oblivious of the trouble in store when changing a baby boy's diaper. The feel of fresh air to the sprinkler system as the diaper is removed often encourages a timely pee-pee contribution. You don't always see it as you attend to business, cleaning the nooks and crannies, but you are alerted by the tinkling sound of pee landing on a surface across the room. Don't underestimate Baby's ability: distance, angle and timing are vital skills in this new sport. You may think the damage goes only as far as a wet onesie, but look again and you'll find further wet spots at the top of the change mat—and on his chin. Changing time can involve a lot more than just the diaper by the time he is finished. While sterile pee has to be the least offensive of the copious baby bodily excretions you will be adorned with daily, the extra laundry is best avoided. Even if it's already happened once during a change, don't let down your guard. They are sneaky like that—they'll have more stored up for a second spray.

We had reports of Baby peeing in his own eye or Dad's eye, or finding pools of pee in Baby's ear. But I'm pretty sure I can top them all with the time I looked up to see Baby's face completely drenched in pee and him smacking his lips.

Survival Secrets

- Have a washcloth or spare cloth diaper handy to drape over the mini garden hose as soon as the diaper is removed to avoid unwanted showers.
- "Pee-pee Teepees" are little cone-shaped, washable, cotton contraptions specifically designed for this purpose. You just pop one on top of your little one's penis while you change him. These are popular shower gifts (ha, ha) for parents of baby boys, so if you have them, give them a try, although word on the street is that they don't do as good a job as a simple

washcloth. Trying to place a very small teepee on your son's very small pee-pee can be quite a fiddly job, and just as you're leaning in close to secure the shield . . . bingo, you're right in the firing line.

- Never mind "Do you dress to the left or the right, Sir?" just as long as it is down. Ensure the penis is pointing down into the clean diaper before you fasten it up. If your little soldier's "little soldier" is pointing up to the waistband of the diaper, you're likely to get a wet onesie as soon as he pees.

While on the topic of little boys' mucky habits there's one more warning to heed. We don't wish to go too far into the topic of self-exploration: suffice it to say boys like to fiddle with their bits, and it starts early. While it's up to you whether you condone or discourage a bit of self-exploration, take care: Baby will not think twice about moving in for an investigative session when you are in the middle of a messy diaper change.

CHAPTER 9

Baby Map—Legs and Feet

SITTING

Learning to sit up may not seem too thrilling a milestone, but the skill requires neck strength and head control that are also needed for crawling, standing and walking, so it's an important developmental stage en route to more exciting mobility.

Babies start with virtually no control over their movement. You'll become familiar with the flapping and flailing reflex movements of a newborn. By three months the brain, nerves and muscles all come into play in the development of gross motor skills, the strengthening and control of the large body muscles needed to achieve all the major physical milestones: rolling, sitting, crawling, standing and walking. Development starts at the top of the body and works down, so head and neck control is first on Baby's learning list, and rapid progress is made in this skill beginning when she is four months old, allowing Baby to start to learn to sit up. There is a lot going on for Baby at this stage. Work on rolling is also in progress, and creeping or crawling is in her sights. There's no set order to which skill she will master first.

By five months, Baby may be able to sit for short periods unassisted, but it will probably take another couple of months until she's completely in control. She needs to learn how to position her legs for stability and work on fine-tuning the back and neck muscles to get the trunk wobble under control. For the more sadistic parents, a lot of fun can be had when Baby is learning to sit. Bet on which way

Baby will fall next, or play a form of chicken—who can get to Baby at the last minute to save her from the face plant? She will crunch forward until almost bent double until she learns to use her arms to support her forward weight. Due to the folding action, a face plant tends to be a gradual collapse. Be sure to pad behind and to the sides with pillows or use the U-shaped nursing cushion to guard against a backwards fall, as this can be quite a bump to the noggin.

You can't "teach" sitting, but you can provide opportunities to let Baby practice and get used to the idea. Tummy time (see the **Tummy** chapter) is important exercise for neck strengthening and head control. You can sit Baby up on the couch or leaning against you from the time that her neck is strong enough to support itself, usually around three months. You can buy molded foam seats like the Bumbo Baby Sitter to support Baby in a seated position. These are fun, but they only give Baby a taste of the new position rather than teaching her to sit. Sitting gives Baby a new perspective on her world. You'll see from her beaming smile how pleased she is with herself.

Once sitting, she's able to use her hands to play freely instead of using them to support herself on her tummy. Sitting is also one of the prerequisites for starting on solid foods. Baby doesn't need to be able to sit totally unsupported before you give the high chair a trial run, but she needs to keep from slumping, and she must be able to bear the weight of her own head. You can always pad the chair with cushions if Baby is still a tad wobbly.

MOBILITY

> ### "I wish I had known . . .
> that there isn't necessarily a period of learning and buildup to crawling. I found out the hard way with an afternoon spent in the Emergency Room that a baby can be suddenly mobile."

We can't tell you exactly when your baby will become mobile. It's usually anytime between five and eight months, but for certain it will be when you aren't looking. Babies are sneaky. Your baby will move inches while you watch, but as soon as your back is turned, he'll fire up the rocket boosters. You leave him innocently flopping around on the rug in the center of the room as you pop in the kitchen to grab a reviving coffee. You return to find he has materialized six feet from where you left him. Once I left my daughter on the play mat and dashed off for a much-needed bathroom break. During my 90-second absence she'd managed to coordinate her shuffling and rolling into effective mobility and was on the other side of the room with her fingers in the plant pot, yet the day before she was barely managing to roll over. Of course, when you want your performing seal to show his newfound skill to Dad later that day to illustrate how attentive you'll need to be from now on, Baby will lie there inert and innocent looking.

Some babies are content to play where they are supposed to; others who have a sense of adventure or mischief roam far and wide, by whatever means possible, looking for trouble. With this devious behavior in mind, it's wise to do your childproofing (see the next section, **Crawling**) in advance of Junior officially learning to crawl. Experience says he will be innately attracted to forbidden items and will get to them the minute your head is turned.

Be careful not to leave a baby anywhere elevated, such as a bed, couch or change station. A friend recalled the day she put her previously immobile and somewhat lazy son in the center of the bed and turned to the wardrobe to forage for spit up–free clothes. A sickening *thunk* announced that Baby had somehow maneuvered to the edge of the bed and launched himself off headfirst. Panicked phone calls to grand-parents and a trip to the ER to rule out concussion ensued.

CRAWLING

Once Baby is bored of pivoting in circles and curiosity spurs her into moving to get something out of reach, she'll start to work on a type of crawl. This usually happens between five and nine months of age. Mastering crawling often comes around the same time as sitting up when Baby learns to lunge forward or sideways from the sitting position. It's rare for babies to just suddenly crawl; there's more often weeks or months of bizarre yoga poses and tentative buildup to the event. Some babies initially get up on their hands and knees, and rock back and forth, but take a while to muster courage and coordination to actually move. Others start with bottom scooting, tummy slithering or commando crawling, which are valid alterna-tives that serve the same purpose of enabling them to get at stuff. From here she may move on to traditional all-four crawling, or she may be perfectly content to stick with her own preferred method of ambulation. Some figure out backwards crawling first—frustrating for Baby, but highly amusing for parents when she backs herself into tight spaces and corners and becomes stranded.

There are babies who skip crawling and go straight to walking. Encourage whatever mobility your baby favors by giving her lots of tummy time and placing toys just out of reach. The Christmas presents under the tree were the lure for our baby girl to start crawling forward. If your baby has shown no signs of mobility by the end of the year, consult your doctor.

As mentioned earlier in the **Mobility** section, Baby's first independent movement is a special time for new parents, but it's also a time for extreme caution. Suddenly she has the means to go anywhere and get into everything. Life as you know it has changed; it's time to babyproof your home if you haven't already. Only the most doggedly determined and style-conscious parents will manage to keep their living space looking like anything other than a McDonald's Play Place by the end of the first year. I used to look at friends' kid-friendly living rooms, where the coffee table had been replaced by a primary-colored floor mat, and sneer. I wasn't going that route. But by the time my baby was six months old, the Mexican chest suddenly started looking more like a lethal weapon than a coffee table. I capitulated, and our stylish furniture was swiftly replaced by said-same foam mat.

Tips from the Trenches

- Try some role-play and see the world through Baby's eyes. Get down on your hands and knees and pretend you are the inquisitive baby. Find all the enticing, dirty, dangerous things that are now at your level and that you could put into your mouth or tinker with.
- Cordon off danger zones like staircases with baby gates. You may think you will not be leaving Junior alone long enough to come to any harm, but once she has perfected the speed crawl, you'll have a hard time keeping up with her.
- I'm not sure of the damage that occurs when you stick your finger into an electrical socket (I didn't want to try it to find out), so I thought it best to have outlet covers. Outlets are handily at crawl height, and it doesn't take a mastermind to realize a baby might find it fascinating to poke fingers or toys into these interesting-looking holes in the wall.
- Wires are enticing, so hide them from view, tack them to walls or use wire tidies. Around six months Baby can be told "no," but her reaction, if there is one, will be slow and probably the wrong reaction for the situation. Yours may be fast, but not fast enough

to catch the lamp as it is yanked off the table by its cord. You might be lucky and the lamp won't break because its fall is cushioned by Baby's noggin.

- To be on the safe side, consider anything that will fit inside a toilet paper roll to be a choking hazard and make sure it is out of Baby's reach.

- Baby will soon be using every available object to pull herself up. But plants and floor lamps, for example, may not be stable enough to support Baby's weight. Move anything precarious, easily knocked over or delicate, and particularly anything that if knocked over or fallen on would do serious damage.

- Be especially careful to check for furniture that could fall on Baby if she pulls or climbs on it. (Don't underestimate the climbing ability of a baby who can't walk yet.) Freestanding chests of drawers, side tables, shelf units and bookcases are fine in an adult-only household, but in Baby World it's safer to have them fixed to a wall.

- Towards the end of the year, Junior will be getting tall enough to reach up onto tabletops, dressers and bookcases. Curious fingers will grab hold of anything available and drag it down, oblivious of a possible avalanche of items waiting to rain down on her. Take particular care of tablecloths and placemats with hot drinks on top. A hot drink can cause serious burns to delicate baby skin.

- When it comes to taking further safety precautions, like using door safety catches, there are the "for" and "against" camps. It makes sense to keep dangerous items such as cleaning supplies, medications and sharp kitchen utensils locked away. But some new parents put catches on everything, including the toilet lid, and others, like me, don't use them for fear our husbands will no longer be able to use the toilet or make a cup of tea. Regardless of your level of childproofing, back it up with discipline and set your child's boundaries early on. Don't rely on the safety catches to teach Baby where she can't go and what she shouldn't touch, since safety catches won't be in every home she visits.

- It's easy to be brainwashed by all the safety merchandise that's out there and assume that if they sell it, you must need it. Keep this in mind when childproofing your home, and set the level where you feel comfortable. A new parent can easily be overly cautious and go safety crazy, padding the walls, removing all furniture and buying every safety device on the market to save Junior from harm.

STANDING

I remember one day I heard my daughter through the monitor singing to announce she had awoken from her afternoon nap. As I walked into her room I was stopped in my tracks by the sight of her standing up for the first time, hanging onto the side of the crib, looking extremely pleased with herself.

Some babies love the standing position from early on and are most impatient to master the skill—around five months they'll be happiest bouncing on your lap, strengthening their leg muscles. At about eight months, your baby will probably start pulling himself up while holding onto furniture. It pays to remember he has no sense of what is suitable to pull up on. Make sure there are no unstable items around such as plants, toys with wheels and freestanding lamps. Dad might also want to avoid wearing shorts as Baby can bring tears to his eyes using the hair on his legs to pull up.

At about nine or ten months, Baby will begin to learn to bend at the knees to sit back down from standing. Yes, that's right; Bad Baby Design Point #4: babies learn to stand up, but don't know the best way to get back down again. There is a short transition period when the new skill is a bit of a pain, especially in the middle of the night when he pulls himself up in the crib, can't figure out how to lie down to go back to sleep, and gets upset. For the sake of sleep-deprived parents everywhere, perhaps the Great Baby Designer could take a look at improving this in future models. This is also a time of heightened consternation for parents until Baby learns that bumping down onto his handily padded bottom is less painful than falling like a bowling pin. It may help to show him how to bend his knees to get down without toppling over.

Eventually, around 11 months, once the leg muscles are strong enough, Baby will try the "Look Mom, no hands" move. Some may boldly let go of the furniture and wobble solo a month or two earlier; some won't gain enough confidence to try until a while later. Soon he'll be standing and squatting, bending and bobbing—it's tiring to watch.

There are several pieces of baby gear that can assist Baby in strengthening leg muscles and learning balance. No doubt on one of your many visits to the baby stores, while you were selecting your color-coordinated nursery decor, you stumbled across a vivid monstrosity known as an **ExerSaucer** and immediately vowed something this big and ugly would be entering your house over your dead body. I know babies like bright colors, but is there research saying they have a preference for a combination of lime green, purple and orange? Unfortunately, the manufacturers seem to think so and make the contraption as garish as possible. Despite their lack of visual appeal, these immense plastic beasts are lifesavers for keeping Baby safe and captive yet happy. Baby is loosely supported in a swivel sling seat in the middle of an exciting array of squeakers, rattles and chewables, so is encouraged to use his leg muscles to hold himself up and turn around. If you want to be able to cook, eat a meal, shower and spend more than 20 seconds on a bathroom visit during year one, you might want to bite the bullet and get one. An ExerSaucer can be used from approximately five months until Baby is walking. It is an expensive piece of kit, so it's worth looking at consignment sales or borrowing from a friend. Believe me, people are glad to get these things out of their houses as soon as possible, so there are plenty on offer.

The **Jolly Jumper** is the suspended seat you hang in a doorway that allows Baby a taste of the vertical with the added attraction of a good bounce to strengthen his leg muscles. After a couple of tentative sessions, most babies go wild in a jumper and find it especially entertaining if Mom does a bit of jumping for encouragement. (Make sure you're contracting those pelvic floor muscles!) Be sure to keep watch while Baby is in the jumper as he will soon get tired. If he is a puker, the bouncing is going to trigger some barf, so put a blankie on the floor to save the rug.

The **Learning Table** is a stable, entertaining mini table of delights that Baby can pull up on and maneuver around from upwards of six months. Be careful where you position the table—when Baby is first cruising and is still unstable, he may get carried away with the play and misjudge a step, fall into a sharp corner of a bookcase and dent his noggin. Be sure to position the table away from furniture, in the center of the room.

A walker that Baby sits in and scoots around with is fun, but it is not recommended. Walkers give babies speed beyond their level of judgment and control. Falls down stairs in walkers have resulted in serious injuries. Walkers are also known to make it too easy for a baby to get around, and therefore they don't help with upper leg muscle development.

WALKING

Walking could be the pièce de résistance of Baby's physical development this year. If she hasn't already mastered it by her birthday, it should be around the corner in the next few months. Three quarters of babies are walking by 13 months. Perhaps "mastered" is too strong a term for the drunken, staggering gait the likes of which you haven't seen since Uncle Albert hit the champagne too enthusiastically at your wedding. It'll take months before Baby is a proficient walker.

When she first learns to stand, Baby will hang on to the furniture for dear life, but soon she'll start "cruising." This buildup to unassisted walking is where she navigates her way around the room using all available props to steady herself: the furniture; the drapes; your legs; the dog's back. If she musters enough courage, she may take an unassisted step from the couch to the coffee table. You can encourage her to walk on her own by kneeling in front of her and holding out your hands. Suddenly one day she'll take the plunge and stagger off full of confidence, soon to be followed three or four steps later by a bump onto the handily padded backside. If babies didn't wear diapers for the intended purpose, we'd likely be protecting their bottoms with some other form of padding. Cautious babies will toddle along quite competently but hold on to your finger for dear life, extremely reluctant to try it completely on their own. Don't worry if Baby walks on tiptoe—this is quite common initially.

You'll be lucky to capture the actual first steps on camera as they'll catch you unawares, but keep the camera handy and Baby will likely repeat her new trick soon after, taking another three or four steps. The facial expressions—a mixture of pride and surprise at her newfound ability—are priceless. Soon she'll graduate to eight or nine steps before a tumble, and gradually over a period of weeks she'll improve to walking all the time unassisted. However, don't feel like you can let her loose just yet; there will be countless tumbles and fumbles as your baby transitions to a toddler. It takes all her concentration to move her legs and keep her balance, and she won't be able to navigate at all well for a while. You don't have to pad the entire house, but steer her clear of sharp corners, stone hearths and tiled floors, and try to keep her path somewhat clear. A nasty fall will likely be the result if her first tottering steps are across an obstacle course of toys with a glass coffee table at the finish line.

Toddle trucks and pushcarts aren't always a good idea when Baby is a novice walker. They can speed away leaving Baby spread-eagled, face down on the floor, or worse still, nursing a bruised chin from coming into contact with the handle on the way down. Careful and constant supervision, or sticking to anchored toys, until Baby is a more proficient walker is recommended.

SHOES

They look cute, but at the end of the day, baby shoes are an unneces-
sary annoyance since they rarely stay on. Mostly they serve as a chew
toy and get lost when kicked off in the stroller. Shoes really aren't
necessary until your baby is walking outside and needs some foot
protection. Indoors, barefoot is best for Baby's balance, coordination
and unrestricted foot growth.

There are some excellent soft-soled shoes on the market to keep
Baby's feet warm out on the town. Robeez makes soft leather shoes
in a variety of colors and fun designs that will match any outfit you
have in mind. They are durable, comfortable, designed to stay on
and even machine washable.

BANDY LEGS AND BENT FEET

New moms are quite often concerned about their baby's bandy legs.
The bowed shape of the legs is a result of the cramped living quarters
in the womb. It's an old wives' tale that letting a baby stand too early
will cause his legs to bow. A wad of diaper between the legs doesn't
make it easy to stand or walk with anything but a bowlegged gait.
The legs will gradually straighten once Baby starts walking. Feet,
too, can be slightly turned in, bowed or banana-shaped from being
curled up inside you. Walking will usually cause your baby's feet to
spread and straighten.

CHAPTER 10
Baby Map—Skin

BATHING

After a day at home with Baby, you'll have fed him several times, changed his diaper several more times and stared at him for a few hours. And then you'll probably wonder what to do next. Goodness, newborns don't really do much, do they? At this point you'll have the bright idea of giving him a bath to try out what you learned in the hospital. Then once you've got the slippery, squirmy little sucker in the tub, you'll immediately wish you hadn't started.

Baby gets little more than a dunking while you and Dad are drenched and the floor is flooded. Baby has a head full of suds that just won't rinse off, and no part of him has been washed, particularly that underside—the very part you wanted to get at. He is screaming blue murder (the baby, not Dad), and you're seized with panic that you will never manage this feat on your own. Even with the two of you on the job, you are so obsessed with supporting his head that there are no hands actually available for washing the baby. Yet it all looked so easy in the hospital. If you are anything like me, most things you were told in those few overwhelming days on the maternity ward went in one ear, fluttered around your vacant lot of a mommy brain, found nowhere to roost and floated out the other side. You should have taken notes; no, you should have taken a video. Never mind getting the first shots of proud Mom and Baby, get the good stuff on tape: competent nurse bathing Baby.

Don't worry, like everything it gets easier with time as you get more experienced and less nervous about handling the baby. Plus, in a few short months Baby will be markedly more robust. Until then, it's perfectly acceptable to keep baths to a minimum since bathing only dries out Baby's delicate skin. Before he is mobile, the only really grubby bit of Baby is his bum, and this gets regular cleansing at diaper changes. A proper bath once or twice a week is ample; the rest of the time, navigate the nooks and crannies with a washcloth or sponge bath.

On the subject of nooks and crannies, have you noticed that babies have no necks? They also tend to be a little on the chubby side and consequently have extra skin folds and creases that harbor dirt. Drool and spit up can find their way into these crevices, particularly under the chin. Although it's not an easy task—Baby doesn't willingly tilt his head back to allow access, and you'll likely get lots of protestation—you need to tackle it because, apart from becoming unpleasantly stinky, these deposits can fester and irritate, leaving red, angry, sore spots.

Comrades' Recommendations

- Have everything ready before you start. You simply cannot leave Baby unattended in the bath, and carrying a slippery, sudsy baby around as you gather forgotten equipment is almost as hazardous.
- One thing I did note when the maternity nurse bathed the baby: before she started she poured a little shampoo and soap onto the side of the bath to dip into. This saved her the virtually impossible task of trying to squeeze soap while holding the baby.

- Wash Baby's hair before you put him in the tub. Keep him diapered (for obvious reasons) and wrapped in a towel while you hold his head over the tub to shampoo and rinse. Dry off his head, then bathe the rest of him. This prevents Baby from getting chilly from sitting in the bath with wet hair, and it ensures we're cleaning the head and hair with clean water. The general rule is to wash the cleanest part of Baby first and work to the dirtiest.
- If Baby is not a fan of the hair wash, tackle it last to avoid tears through the rest of bath time, but be sure to use fresh water for rinsing rather than the bath water that's already serviced the dirtiest body parts.
- Use only the mildest unscented baby products. You may find even these dry out or irritate baby's skin (see **Dry Skin**, below).
- There are a number of infant baths on the market. They all do the job, and so does the kitchen sink if you don't wish to "splash" out on a bath. If you do get a baby bath, look for a no-slip bottom and lots of support for Baby to make life easier for you. A drain or plug at the bottom of the bath is a useful feature, saving your back from the strain of lifting a tub full of water.
- Early on, baths may be a disaster. Nervous handling of the baby can make him feel unsafe, so reassure him using a calm voice to talk through the process or sing a song. If you have any hands left, try distracting a fussy baby with a toy as you wash.
- Bathing just after a feed isn't wise—spit up might be induced by all the jostling and jiggling.
- Bathing an infant is awkward, so to make life easier and save your back stress, use the baby bath wherever it's convenient so you're not hunched over the tub. Try a high work surface or the floor (covered with a towel). In a few months when Baby is playing and splashing, you'll likely need to move to the tub, but by then he'll be sturdier and won't require constant support.
- Try baby bath products with extras: lavender to calm and help him sleep; eucalyptus to help him breathe better if he has the sniffles; moisture-enriched baby wash to ease dry skin.

DRY SKIN

You've probably heard the saying, "As soft as a baby's bum," referring to the silky smoothness of a newborn's skin. However, Baby's skin isn't always peachy soft; quite often it can be rough or flaky because it's dry. A baby's delicate skin is particularly susceptible to dryness and may benefit from moisturizing.

"I wish I had known . . .
even baby products can be too harsh for a baby's skin."

So lamented one mom, recalling the occasion she slathered her baby's flaky forehead with baby lotion. Within minutes his head was glowing like a ripe tomato. We assume a moisturizer made especially for babies would be fine to use, but their delicate skin is particularly vulnerable to irritants like perfumes, so some babies could have reactions to the mildest of products.

Tips from the Trenches
- Bathing can exacerbate dry skin because it removes skin's natural oils. Keep baths short and soapsuds to a minimum.
- Use only the mildest unscented skin products and laundry detergents.
- Nightly bedtime routines that include a bath are not a good idea if your baby has dry skin. If you like to bathe Baby more often because it soothes him for sleep, use plain water for most baths and bring in the suds for a thorough wash once a week.
- Moisturize skin immediately after bathing and towel-drying to seal moisture into the skin.
- Try a lotion or cream on a small patch of skin to test for a reaction before applying.
- My doctor warned me that popular baby shampoo is actually often the cause of dry skin. If you find Baby has very dry skin, ask your doctor to recommend good alternative mild, plain shampoo, soap and moisturizing products.

BABY ECZEMA
Infantile eczema is fairly common, appearing between two and six months for up to 20 percent of babies, and is not necessarily the sign of continued suffering in later life. Most cases of baby eczema clear up by 18 months to three years at the outside. However, if there is a history of eczema, asthma or allergies in your family, it is more likely that Baby has inherited the complaint and it will persist into adulthood.

Baby eczema is a red, scaly, itchy rash that you find on the cheeks, neck and behind the ears, as well as other areas, like the backs of knees and elbows. It is an allergic reaction, maybe to food or to other irritants such as detergent, soap, grass, dust or certain fabrics. Typical food allergens are cow's milk, wheat and eggs, which is why we are advised not to introduce these foods until late in the first year, once the risk of developing an allergy is lower.

Comrades' Recommendations

- Recommendations in the previous **Dry Skin** section are also applicable for eczema treatment.
- Consult the doctor, since eczema will need some treatment. The doctor will recommend a suitable moisturizer and likely prescribe steroid cream. Some moms may balk at using steroid cream, but the concentration is low, and it is important to combat the condition early.
- Stick to simple clothing in breathable fabrics to minimize sweating and overheating.
- Be vigilant for the cause of a flare-up. Think about where you've been (on grass? around pets?) and what chemicals Baby's skin has been in contact with (fabric softeners, lotions, sunscreen), and try avoiding or changing these possible irritants.
- Keep a food diary to help you determine whether a particular food is the culprit.
- Avoid swimming, since pools and salt water will both irritate.

SUN EXPOSURE

Doctors recommend keeping babies out of direct sunlight for the first year. Hmmm, sage advice, but not entirely practical. Although you may be up a good part of the night, you probably don't want to become completely nocturnal for the entire first year. However, sunburn is no joke. You know how itchy and painful it can be, and besides not wanting to inflict this misery on your little one, we need to ensure we reduce the risk of skin cancer in later life. Baby's delicate skin hasn't built up any sun resistance, so it's particularly susceptible to sunburn. It's not just on a day at the beach that Baby is exposed to the sun; even an early afternoon trip to the grocery store can do it. Therefore, aim to minimize sun exposure. Since sunscreen is not recommended for babies before six months, we have to find other ways to protect Baby's delicate skin.

Survival Secrets

- While tank tops and shorts might seem fitting for a hot, sunny day, lightweight cotton long-sleeved shirts and long pants will cover more of Baby's skin and provide more protection.
- Wide-brimmed hats protect the head, face and neck from sun and shield the eyes. Chin straps make it harder for an unwilling wearer to remove his hat. Don't take no for an answer to wearing hats—battle with Baby to keep them on. Introducing hats from an early age will help Baby get used to wearing them.
- Draping a blanket over the stroller for a makeshift sunshade seemed like a reasonable precautionary measure until I tried to walk and hold the blanket in place at the same time on a windy day. On a hot, still day it made an oven for my baby to ride around in. Changing the angle of a parasol every time you turn a corner is a pain too. By far the best piece of baby gear I found in the first year was the custom-made stroller UV shade. It enabled me to go for long walks on sunny afternoons with the peace of mind that Baby was well protected from the sun, and the light mesh allowed her to enjoy the scenery when she wasn't napping. It also serves as a bug shield, protects eyes from the sun's glare and provides a cooler shady spot for a nap. Plus it stays in place! If you're going to be spending any significant time outdoors and that nocturnal thing isn't going to work for you, it's worth investing in one.
- Avoid the sun's strongest rays between 10 a.m. and 3 p.m.
- Sit in the shade whenever possible.
- As a last resort, when adequate shade is unavailable and some sun exposure is unavoidable, you should use sunscreen on Baby. For example, on a day at the beach, Junior is going to protest at being cooped up in a stroller all day. Apply sunscreen 20 to 30 minutes before you go out. Be careful to avoid eyes when applying as it will sting.
- Stick sunscreen is excellent for applying where you want it on a squirming baby.
- Try a patch test of the sunscreen ahead of time in case it causes a rash.
- For holiday wear, check out sun suits made of UV-resistant material.

CLOTHES

Fancy fashion outfits and babies just don't mix. Unless you've the patience of a saint or a very clean baby (is there such a thing?), easy on and off is the key. Babies have excellent timing. They can judge to the second when to let rip a super barf: just as you fasten the last snap on their best clean outfit. This may not be as intentional as it seems, because you've probably just shaken her up a bit in the act of dressing her and initiated the upchuck. The bigger the battle you have getting clothes on, the more likely they are going to need to come off again quicker than you can say "spit up." Even if Baby is not a puker or drooler, remember the number of times you'll need easy access to the diaper area in a day. I feel guilty for wasting clothes, but have to admit some outfits were only worn once, then swiftly abandoned in favor of less attractive, more practical items. As an expectant mom, no doubt you couldn't resist collecting a cute outfit or six every time you went to the baby store for gear. Yes, they are adorable, but keep one for the baby shower or baptism and take the rest back. Save yourself headaches and swap them for onesies and sleepers. Reality check: the outfit will be covered by a receiving blanket or hidden under a bib most of the time.

Plus, they grow so fast in this first year. Typically Baby will triple her birth weight and grow about an inch a month. If she continued on this growth curve, you would have a 600-pound, 8-foot-tall four-year-old on your hands. Now there's a scary image! A cute outfit the price of a pack of sleepers will be lucky to have more than one outing before it's outgrown, providing it even makes it out of the house before being puked, pooped or peed on and thrown in the laundry after five minutes' wear.

"I wish I had known . . .

not to bother with newborn sizes. It was such a waste of money. She literally wore them once each before growing out of them."

Tips from the Trenches

- Sleepers with snaps from feet to neck are baby-wear essentials since babies are often distressed by things being pulled over their heads. Also consider that if it's covered in spit up or diaper leakage, getting the item over Baby's head without mess transfer is going to be challenging.

- Don't buy too much newborn clothing. Unless you have a preemie, this size will fit for such a short time that you'll be lucky if Baby wears it more than once. Go for "up to 3 months" and "3 to 6 months," and roll up sleeves and pant legs initially.
- Onesies and shirts with snaps under the butt are better than regular shirts, which ride up and become uncomfortable or leave Baby with a chilly midriff.
- Buy, beg, borrow (but don't steal) plenty of the basic onesies and sleepers. You can find yourself changing Baby four to five times per day due to spit up, drooling, sweating, diaper leakage, etc., and unless the washing machine is on constantly, you will need a ton of these staples to get you through.
- Dresses are often impractical. They ride up on infants, and can hamper an older baby's efforts to crawl and stand. Look for dresses with a onesie built in that are shorter than knee length. As cute as that little frilly satin dress is, don't be tempted—especially if you have a boy.
- Embellishments are usually a pain, something baby-wear designers sometimes forget in favor of following the latest trend. Watch out for uncomfortable clothes with zips at necks, scratchy collars and lumpy, bumpy trimmings.
- Avoid sleepers with hoods. They bunch up uncomfortably under a sleeping baby, and although they won't choke Baby, they can become uncomfortable around the neck as he wriggles about. Your offspring will have plenty of time to skulk around in a hood as a teenager.
- Breathable 100 percent cotton is most suitable for newborn skin. Watch for scratchy man-made fibers.
- Bibs are a must if you are formula-feeding. While breast milk is fairly innocuous and dribble is minimal with breastfeeding, there tends to be more leakage with formula-feeding, and formula stains. Clothes are quickly ruined by yellow discoloration at the neck.
- Once Baby starts experimenting with solids, the bigger the better as far as bibs are concerned if you don't want to change outfits after every meal. The fallout zone isn't restricted to the area directly beneath the chin. Baby will have his fingers in his mouth after every spoonful, then smear the mess on every inch of exposed clothing. Watch out for banana—a staple first-year food and a menace for staining clothes.

- It's wise to start with a mild detergent for washing Baby's clothes. Baby's sensitive skin is easily irritated. If your baby winds up with a rash, double rinse the clothes to remove as many chemicals as possible or re-wash all of his clothes in another type of detergent. If the rash persists, consult your doctor.
- Often you find that clothes like cotton onesies shrink quite a bit in the wash, even if you follow the washing directions to the letter. I was caught out several times waiting for Junior to grow into something, he'd wear it once, then after it had been laundered I'd find it had shrunk to barely fit. Wash the clothes when you first get them so you can see in advance what size they shrink down to.

BODY TEMPERATURE

The general rule for dressing Baby is to add one more layer of clothing than you are wearing. However, I tend to think this isn't applicable all year round. In summer, if you are sweating in a tank top and shorts, are you really going to dress Baby in a onesie with shirt and pants in addition? He's going to be a sweaty mess, and he'll overheat, get cranky and wind up with heat rash. Over-bundling Baby is a common rookie mom mistake. Baby does need to be kept warm, since with immature sweat glands he cannot regulate his own body temperature, but not hot. In the modern world, overheating is much more likely than hypothermia.

To test if Baby is hot or cold, feel the back of his neck or tummy. Extremities are often a bit chilly, so don't bundle him in a blanket just because he has cold tootsies. The top of the head is a heat regulator and will often feel warmer than the rest of the body. Baby's normal body temperature is 98.6° Fahrenheit (37° Celsius). An official fever is 100.4° Fahrenheit (38° Celsius) and above. There, I vowed to get that information in this book because I was forever taking my baby's temperature and then, clueless as to what it should be, spending the next 30 minutes frantically dashing around the house checking books and the Internet trying to find out what was normal. Too much clothing and exertion from crying can raise Baby's body temperature, but it's not usually a concern. However, if you've tried cooling Baby down by removing some clothing and calming him and he is still feverish, you may want to check with the doctor. In babies younger than six months, all fevers should be reported to the doctor, and a temperature above 102° Fahrenheit (39° Celsius) in babies over six months should also be checked. Furthermore, if Baby is at all feverish plus has other symptoms such as lethargy, a rash, coughing or wheezing, or if you just feel something is not right, trust your instinct and get him checked over.

The best ways to take Baby's temperature are under the arm or with a digital ear thermometer. Rectal and oral readings are not recommended for infants; however, these are recognized as the most accurate readings. The guideline is to add a degree to whatever temperature you get from an underarm reading—it will indicate whether a fever exists, rather than being an accurate measure of his actual temperature.

"I wish I had known . . .

about febrile seizures. When it happened to my baby I was terrified."

If a baby's temperature spikes suddenly, a fairly common occurrence is a febrile seizure. One quarter of children will have one at some point, usually between six months and three years of age. These convulsions involving rolling eyes, shaking limbs and a possible brief loss of consciousness are frightening for a parent to witness, but fortunately they usually aren't serious. They are merely a physical reaction to the sudden high fever. The seizure will probably be over in a matter of minutes, and the underlying reason for the fever is usually something like an ear infection, but it's best to get Baby checked over immediately afterwards to rule out any more serious causes. Some children are more prone to seizures, especially if it happened to Mom or Dad as a child, and you may find it occurs again until they outgrow the tendency by age five.

At night we are told to aim for a room temperature of 64.4° to 68° Fahrenheit (18° to 20° Celsius), but as I regurgitate such recommendations I wonder again what our grandparents did. I remember as a kid that my grandma's house was so cold you needed to don hat, coat and gloves to venture to the bathroom upstairs. You would do your business and race squealing back down to the only fire to thaw out your goose bumps. I swear it was several degrees colder inside than out. Yet she raised two babies in that icebox, and they certainly didn't sleep in a room heated to 68 degrees.

Survival Secrets

- For a newborn, use several lightweight cotton blankets rather than one thick one. This enables you to add or remove a layer if Baby appears too cold or too warm.
- Older babies rarely stay under blankets. Once he can roll and shuffle, you'll probably find Baby does at least 10 circuits of the crib per night. Any blanket you try to put him under will be little use for keeping warm and may pose a risk of entanglement. Baby could burrow down beneath it and breathe stale air, which increases the risk of SIDS. Fleecy sleep suits are great for keeping Baby warm on winter nights—it's as if he is wearing the blanket.
- A young baby may like swaddling, which is a good way to keep him warm on a cold night. However, on the flip side, if Baby will only sleep in a swaddle, overheating can be a problem in summer. On a hot night, go for just the diaper and a lightweight cotton swaddle blanket.
- In the heat, stick with lightweight cotton clothing. Synthetic fibers won't allow skin to breathe and will cause sweating and heat rash.
- A hat is an important accessory to keep Baby warm—we lose a lot of heat through the head.
- In the stroller, a rain cover helps to keep Baby warm. It can prevent your napping baby from being woken by a blast of cold air on a blustery day.

BIRTHMARKS

Examining the large strawberry birthmark in the center of my daughter's tummy, our pediatrician commented that "birthmark" is a misnomer since not all blemishes we label as such are actually present at birth. Some appear later, some go away and some are here to stay. Birthmarks are generally named after their appearance: café au lait; strawberry; port wine; stork bite.

Stork bites are the marks left on the back of the neck from the nip of the stork's beak when he delivered your baby. Nice idea, but you remember labor all too well to be fooled by that one; nip of the forceps, maybe. These red or salmon pink marks, usually on the base of the neck but also on the forehead and eyelids, are just blood vessels visible through the skin, and are very common, occurring in around half of all newborns. They are often more prominent when Baby has been exerting herself crying. They aren't permanent marks and will likely fade away by age two.

Café au lait birthmarks are flat, brownish (or black on dark skin) marks of various size. They can be there at birth or appear later. Existing marks can also grow. While one in five babies will have one to three of these permanent blemishes, it is uncommon to have more, and you should tell your doctor if your child has or develops more of these marks.

The **strawberry hemangioma** can be present at birth or not be noticeable until a few weeks later. These marks can be quite shocking to new parents as they are a lumpy, bright red clump of tiny raised blood cells and are often on the face. Further distressing is that over the first six months they often increase in size. However, gradually over the years, the strawberry will flatten and fade, and then sometime between ages five and ten completely disappear. At age four my daughter's strawberry is a flat red patch, and our friend's seven-year-old showed us that hers had diminished to a faint brown freckled area. Because it will resolve itself in time, the doctor will only talk to you about intervening to remove the hemangioma if its position interferes with sight, breathing, hearing or speech.

Port wine birthmarks are much less common, occurring in only three in a thousand babies. These are caused by abnormal blood vessels and will appear as flat, pinkish-red marks at birth, then deepen to darker reddish-purple. These are permanent marks and can be treated to some degree in later life if their appearance is upsetting to you or your child.

Mongolian spots look like bruises at the base of the spine and on the buttocks, as if Baby has bumped down on his bottom one too many times. They can also appear on the legs, sides and shoulders. These flat bluish spots or patches may be present at birth or appear later, and are most commonly found on Asian, Indian, African, Native American and Latino babies, while only 10 percent of Caucasian babies have them. They usually fade by age two and disappear by age five, although occasionally they are permanent. Because they are relatively rare in Caucasian infants, there have been unfortunate cases where Mongolian spots have been mistaken for actual bruises and the parents suspected of child abuse.

INFANT ACNE

You thought your child's zits wouldn't be a problem you'd need to confront for at least another 13 years, but since Baby's sweat glands are immature, up to 20 percent of newborns have a bad case of acne. It only lasts a short while, and it disappears without intervention in a few months. The spots can be red or they can be little whiteheads, usually in the nose and chin area.

SKIN PIGMENTATION CHANGE

"I wish he had known . . .
babies born to dark-skinned parents often start life fair skinned."

So complained a midwife after having to diffuse the commotion in her delivery room caused when an African American dad was confronted with his white baby. Babies are chameleons: hair can change color, eyes can change color, and skin can too. Pigmentation darkens over time, so a baby born to black parents can start life quite pale and gradually grow to look more like Mom and Dad.

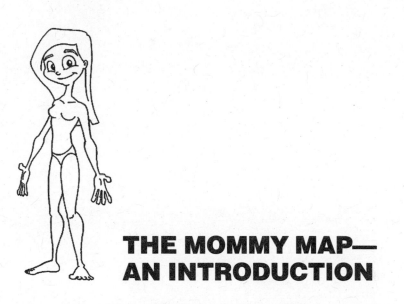

THE MOMMY MAP—
AN INTRODUCTION

Baby may be the most important thing in your life now and forever, and has undoubtedly stolen the limelight since her arrival,
but as postpartum moms we deserve some attention too. In fact,
we deserve equal billing. Look at all the hard work we did to get
Baby here, not to mention all the hard work we've done since her
arrival. We want to dedicate half of this guide to you, the rookie
mom. After all, a healthy, happy mom is a crucial component in
the upbringing of a healthy, happy baby.

The postpartum body you're faced with now is likely vastly different from your pre-pregnancy body—and we're not just talking
about the waistline. It's quite amazing how many things have changed
from your hair right down to your feet (yes, you may even have bigger
feet than you had before). So let's move on to ourselves and follow
the **Mommy Map** through the myriad physical and mental issues a
new mom might encounter in the first year postpartum.

CHAPTER 11

Mommy Map—Hair

HAIR LOSS

Did you notice that you had lustrous, full, thick tresses during pregnancy? Probably not, as you were too concerned with being the size of a whale and too consumed with aches and pains to notice a rare pregnancy benefit. But you surely notice now that your hair is shedding at an alarming rate. Don't worry; your hair is only returning to normal, although the transition can be quite sudden and distressing. You may lose clumps of hair at a time and have thin or even bald patches, especially at the temples—a state that is exacerbated by Baby's favorite pastime of tugging at your hair and yanking out fistfuls. There will be a ubiquitous hair either protruding from Baby's mouth or entwined around her fingers, wads of hair blocking the shower drain, a hairbrush that resembles a small pet, hairs on the pillow . . . in the dinner . . . Eurgh!

I remember being horrified when the prenatal fitness instructor, who was three months postpartum, gathered up enough hair in the shower after class to make Donald Trump a toupee, and matter-of-factly assured her bug-eyed students that this was perfectly normal.

Postpartum hair loss usually occurs one to five months after the birth. Everything should be back to normal by Baby's first birthday. We can blame those pesky hormones again, because it's the rise and fall of hormone levels that cause both the hair thickening during pregnancy and the compensation postpartum.

Hair has a three-phase cycle:

1. The growing phase lasts two to six years per hair. Normally 85 to 90 percent of your hair is in this stage.
2. The resting phase lasts approximately two weeks. This is when the follicle stops producing hair and its base moves up to the scalp surface.
3. The shedding phase, which takes about three months, is when the hair eventually falls out. Normally, you shed about 100 hairs a day.

During pregnancy, hormones prolong the growing stage, resulting in thicker hair. After birth, estrogen levels drop, hair suddenly exits the growing stage and consequently falls out all at once, giving you the impression that you are losing all your hair. As the re-growth starts, you may notice tufty patches and tentacles standing at right angles on top of your head, waving in the breeze. Some lucky moms don't notice any changes.

Comrades' Recommendations

- If you have long hair, the shedding will be more obvious simply due to the volume of hair you are picking up every day. For this reason, as well as the fact that there is no longer time to tend to your tresses each morning, many go for the shorter, more manageable "Mommy Cut" at this point.

- Try the celebrity mom look and buy a selection of baseball caps.
- Unless you are a Mr. Rooter shareholder, invest in a hair trap for the shower drain.

HAIR CHANGES

A less common and somewhat strange phenomenon is hair that undergoes a postpartum texture transformation. A few moms report previously straight hair developing a kink or a wave. Alternatively, some go from curly to wavy or straight hair. First time around, I developed a bit of a curl. This time, by five months postpartum, my hair resembles wire wool. It's a bit drastic to have another baby in the vain hope that I'll luck out third time around and end up with Jennifer Aniston tresses. It can get a bit annoying because your old hair style might not sit right any more, and even though you try your hardest to tease the hair into place, all you're left with is a do The Donald would be proud of. These changes are hormone related and likely happened during pregnancy. While some moms say their hair returned to normal about a year postpartum or after weaning, others say their new look was here to stay. Get a few more baseball caps.

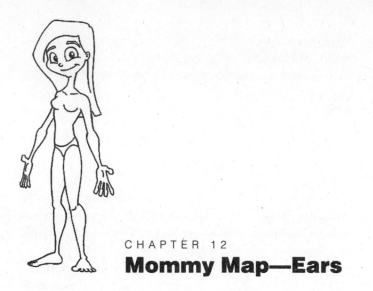

CHAPTER 12

Mommy Map—Ears

SUPER MOMMY HEARING

Remember the blissful nights of uninterrupted, exhausted sleep during pregnancy? What am I talking about? Okay, uninterrupted except for having to get up five times to pee and desperately trying to get comfy on that dead left hip. Well, you'll probably look back on those nights as blissful and uninterrupted once you have a baby in the house. As exhausted as a new mom is, sleep is hard to come by. All of a sudden you have the hearing of a bat, and you find yourself in a state of such heightened sensitivity that the flap of a butterfly wing in Baby's vicinity has you bolt upright and alert.

Meanwhile, through almost any level of Baby's distress, Dad slumbers on. After the fifth shove he might wake up and remember a few minutes later that he has a baby. A few more minutes will pass before he'll realize it was his turn to get up. By this time you will have reached the end of your short fuse, flounced out of bed and comforted the baby yourself. As you ease your weary body back under the duvet, Dad will stir and mumble something helpful like, "Shall I go to her?" immediately followed by a rattling snore, at which point you have to seriously restrain yourself from crowning him with the bedside lamp. If you're old enough, you may remember that it was the bionic woman who had the super hearing, not the bionic man!

My brother was born at home, as most babies were in early '70s England. As my mom was supposed to be on bed rest following the birth, my dad claimed the first night shift and stationed the bassinet on his side of the bed. Inevitably the baby woke and my dad didn't. My mom hoisted her weary, battered body out of bed and shuffled round to the baby in order to comfort him. To this day she blames her varicose veins on this episode.

We all have different sleep patterns, and some of us sleep more deeply than others, but you will likely find as a new mom you sleep very lightly. Your bonding hormones put you in tune with Baby's sleep patterns, so you start to "sleep like a baby"; in other words, you have short spells of fitful sleep. Dad is not naturally in tune with Baby like you are. If one of you is going to sleep through the baby's crying, I know who my money is on.

I didn't need a baby monitor. In fact, I often wished for an anti-monitor—one that would allow me to hear less of the baby's night-time shuffling, moaning, whimpering and grunting. I thought my daughter was a noisy sleeper until my son came along with his own bizarre nighttime cacophony. His specialty was a throat-clearing hawk every few minutes during light sleep after a feed. Why not wear earplugs? Oh no, then I couldn't hear my baby if I needed to, and I wouldn't be able to sleep at all.

When all the grunting and groaning subsides, you hear the most disturbing sound of all: silence. I guarantee this "sound" will have you at the crib side quicker than any cough or wheeze. After all, if he's silent, there must be something wrong.

Survival Secrets

- Get rid of the baby monitor. You and Baby will likely sleep better if you can hear less rather than more. If you must have it, turn it down so you can still hear distress, but not movement.
- Move the baby into his own room as soon as you feel comfortable doing so.

Joking aside, tuning out and getting much-needed rest is a challenge for some rookie moms. You get so used to having a broken night's sleep and listening for a waking baby that even once he has settled into a more considerate sleep cycle you still wake and have problems getting back to sleep. Many new moms, including me, suffer with insomnia. When I wake up I wonder what woke me, and I can almost feel my ears stretching out of my bed and creeping along the hall to the kids' rooms, straining to hear sounds of distress. If sleep deprivation is causing you problems and you aren't able to nap sufficiently in the day to pay off the sleep debt, talk to your doctor about possible remedies.

CHAPTER 13

Mommy Map—Boobs

BREASTFEEDING—OR NOT

There's no two ways about it: breastfeeding is magical. Here is this *free* food supply that can exclusively nourish a baby for six whole months. Breast milk alters to suit Baby's age and nourishment requirements, and the supply is based on demand.

Breastfeeding can be a very enjoyable experience for new moms. It creates a unique bond with Baby from skin-to-skin contact, and chemicals released in the mom's brain while feeding can make it relaxing and pleasurable. On top of this, there is no doubt it is super convenient; after all, your boobs are always with you and require no preparation or sterilization. If you ever get involved in the seemingly never-ending formula-feeding cycle of "wash, sterilize, prepare, warm," you'll realize how truly handy boobs are.

The long list of (mostly) pros and (a few) cons of breastfeeding has no doubt been drummed into you throughout pregnancy and you're sick of hearing it. I'm not going to repeat it all because at this point you will have already made your initial breast or bottle decision. Unless you have a health issue that will prevent you from breastfeeding, it will most likely be the option you have chosen for your baby because of all the health benefits. But you know what? It can be bloody hard work!

"I wish I had known . . .

how difficult breastfeeding can be. I thought it would just 'happen.' I didn't realize how much perseverance it would take to get it right."

Breastfeeding is the natural way to feed Baby, so it should come naturally, right? Not necessarily. In addition to being educated on all the benefits, a lot of moms wish they had been as well informed about how difficult breastfeeding can be. Not because they would have made a different choice, but they wouldn't have been left feeling incompetent when things got off to a bumpy start. If you are a lucky one-in-ten, you and Baby could take to it like ducks to water, but more likely you will encounter problems coming to grips with it in the early days. It takes some time to get the hang of latching; your nipples aren't used to so much chomping! They may get sore and cracked and even (curl toes, grit teeth) bleed.

The social pressure to breastfeed a baby is immense, and while you should be given every encouragement, sometimes well-meaning breastfeeding Nazis—oops, I mean advocates—can go a little far, and encouragement can become hectoring and even bullying. It is assumed in hospital that you will attempt to breastfeed, and you may feel a little pressured if things don't go according to plan. The maternity nurses are usually extremely supportive and will help you to find the methods and positions that work best for you (be prepared to have your boobs severely manhandled during this process), but occasionally their super-busy schedule doesn't allow them to concentrate on this one aspect of infant care. Besides, unless you have a longer hospital stay than most, you'll be home alone by the time the milk arrives, when you're more likely to encounter problems.

It doesn't take long before panic sets in if you can't satisfy a hungry baby. If things initially go wrong but you are intent on breastfeeding, persevere; most breastfeeding problems aren't insurmountable.

Tips from the Trenches

- You are the one with the boobs; therefore, the onus is on you to make it work. But you shouldn't feel like it's your responsibility alone. Dad and other family members should be there for you with help, encouragement and support to make the job as easy as possible.
- Contact a community health nurse or your doctor for help with your latch.
- If problems persist, you can be referred to a lactation consultant. Unlike the multitasking nurses and doctors, these no-nonsense

specialists only have one agenda: getting you to successfully breastfeed. "If you were doing it right, it wouldn't hurt" is their motto, but if anyone is going to show you how to do it right, it will be them. Be prepared to be chastised and bossed, and if you think you were manhandled by the maternity nurses, that was nothing; but remember they know their stuff. I am eternally grateful to the sergeant major—oops again, I mean lactation consultant—who helped me out. Truly, I am.

- It is perfectly reasonable to take some time off if your breasts are too sore and the whole new mommy thing overwhelms you. Stop, wait, and try again later when you are calmer and some of the pressure is off. You must pump in the meantime to maintain your milk supply; if you don't use it, you lose it.

- At the end of the day remember the choice is yours. For some moms, breastfeeding can be very hard. There is no point in plugging away at something that is seriously hurting or distressing you. It is more important for you to be a sane and happy mom than a cranky, depressed one who is doing something just because of other peoples' expectations.

Teething problems aside (who mentioned teeth? I'd rather not think about teeth alongside breastfeeding), what if you can't breastfeed? What if you just don't have the milk supply, Baby won't or can't breastfeed or isn't gaining enough weight, or for personal reasons you feel you really can't go ahead with it? If you were intent on breastfeeding from the get-go, it's quite natural to have feelings of guilt, failure and inadequacy and be worried you are letting Baby down. It's bound to be distressing, but if nature is just not taking its course for you, then move on to the next best thing and don't feel bad. Formula is a perfectly good substitute.

Breastfeeding my daughter had its challenges, but was mostly a pleasurable motherhood experience. However, breastfeeding my son was no fun at all, seemingly for either of us. He spent most feeding sessions pushing away from me, raking my chest with razor-like nails, whacking me with flailing arms and dragging my boob across the room as he habitually pulled away with the nipple still clamped in his jaws. It was a highly frustrating and depressing experience, and I only lasted six months before throwing in the burp cloth.

After reading all the breastfeeding propaganda, we start to imagine that we are doing a great disservice to our baby by not giving her breast milk. Will she be dumber, slower and sickly if we give her formula? I know a formula-fed kid, and it certainly didn't appear to hamper her development. She was the first of her peers to walk, talk and be potty trained. Okay, we would need a parallel universe to see if she would have fared even better on breast milk; maybe she would have had one less bout of diarrhea and one less cold, or maybe her mom would be filing her university application right now. But you know what? I was formula-fed; it was the trend for our baby generation. You were likely formula-fed too, and we're fine, aren't we?

MILK COMING IN

Milk arrives three or four days after the birth. There is no need for it prior to this as babies are not born hungry and we are sensibly programmed to supply on demand. Before then, babies will want to try out the feeding equipment from the get-go and get valuable antibodies from the colostrum that is available in the first few days. I remember my baby being a voracious feeder the first two nights in hospital. It was quite unsettling to be alone in the maternity suite with a baby who had wild, darting, slightly demonic eyes, and who would go for my boob like something possessed. I hardly got any sleep and was terrified this was the way it was going to be. I didn't even realize I had no milk at this point. "Oh yes, they will do that," said the nurse after I told her that my baby had been behaving like a wild animal and we were satisfied there was no mark of the beast on the back of her head. It turned out she was just taking the opportunity while my boobs were soft to learn how to latch properly and was putting in her orders for some future meals.

> ## "I wish I had known . . .
> there was no milk in the beginning. I could have had a nice celebratory glass of bubbly in the delivery room before hitting the wagon again for a year!"

One friend suggests taking the precaution of wearing breast pads and sleeping on towels for the first few nights at home, since her milk didn't so much come in as flood in. She woke in a soaked bed, and in her dazed state her first thought was that the waterbed had sprung a leak . . . shortly before remembering they didn't have a waterbed.

ENGORGEMENT

When the milk does arrive, your boobs will swell, feel tight and warm, and may be hard and painful. You may even get an associated fever. The swelling is not only due to the milk coming in but also to increased blood flow. Whether it will be excessive or painful will depend on your own body's reaction to the event. I really don't remember much about it so I guess I couldn't have suffered much. I think I would have noticed if my boobs felt like they had been filled with cement rather than milk, which is how one friend described it. Her boobs were so heavy in relation to her small frame that she could barely sit up by herself.

It is particularly unfortunate at this point, when you are just coming to grips with how to breastfeed, that suddenly Baby can't get a latch because the boob is hard and swollen. And boy, it hurts! But you have to bite the bullet, as laying off the feeding will not help the situation. Feed your baby regularly every two to three hours. Try to express some milk by hand or with a breast pump before you feed just to soften the boob enough to allow Baby to get a latch. If you're not planning to buy a pump, you can always rent an efficient electric one from a local pharmacy for the crucial period. Don't pump too much as this will send the "more milk required" signal to the boob kitchen, which will up production and make matters worse. Happily, engorgement is a temporary thing. Boobs will gradually settle over a few days as your body establishes how much milk your baby needs.

You could suffer bouts of engorgement later, but usually only in response to changes in your routine, like Baby starting to sleep through the night (yay!), or missing a couple of feeds if Baby is ill and off his food, or when you start to wean. These aren't likely to be as serious as the initial engorgement.

Comrades' Recommendations
- Take drugs! Stick to pain meds that are okay for breastfeeding moms, like acetaminophen and ibuprofen.
- You may find it more comfortable to support the weight of your boobs by wearing your nursing bra day and night, but don't wear a tight one as this will aggravate the pain.
- Take a warm shower with your back to the showerhead so that warm water flows over your boobs. This helps to get milk flowing so you can express a bit before trying to feed Baby.

- Use lightweight cold packs to relieve pain and swelling between feedings.
- Take the weight off those cement balls! Take a nice horizontal rest.
- Cabbage leaves? You've got to be desperate to consider draping your boobs with vegetables. There is mixed press about the success of using chilled cabbage leaves to alleviate suffering. Some reports say it works; others say it is not a proven remedy. If you're struggling to find relief, I say give it a go. You're supposed to wash and squash the leaves so that they can be molded into boob shape. Then cut a hole in the leaves for your nipples, put them inside your bra and remove them once they've wilted (after about 20 minutes, when you start to smell like a compost heap). Only do this two or three times a day while you are in pain as continued use can reduce your milk supply. Besides, I'd be a bit worried about anyone who stuffed veggies in their bra when not absolutely necessary.

- If you are prone to suffering, even though you are dying for an uninterrupted sleep, it might be best to wake a sleepy baby for feeds for the first couple of months to prevent engorgement.

DRYING UP MILK

Unfortunately, if you are not planning to breastfeed, there is no magic button to press that will immediately switch off milk production, so you're going to have to suffer through engorgement without the aid of feeding to relieve the pressure. If you're not nursing, your milk will take about a week to dry up. Follow the tips in the previous section for dealing with the pain. In addition, you can try drinking sage tea, which is known to slow down milk production.

Of course, if you are not nursing, you aren't restricted in your choice and strength of pain relievers and anti-inflammatory drugs. Try not to express milk, as this will signal that more should be produced, which will slow down the process. If you are really suffering, just express a little to take the edge off the pain.

BREAST CHANGES

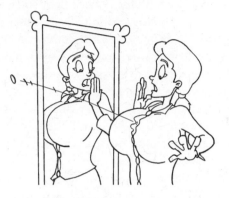

Don't be alarmed if you wake up one morning a few days after giving birth to discover your milk has "come in" and you've suddenly got two watermelons threatening to explode from under your straining PJs. Just when you'd gotten used to your grapefruit pregnancy boobs, things are on the move again—it's a volatile time for boobs right now. A week later they'll have settled down to cantaloupe size. Then you feed the baby from one side and you're left with one cantaloupe and one grapefruit . . . and on it goes. Like many things in pregnancy and childbirth, each new mom's experience will be different and the size of the fruit will vary from mom to mom. As long as your fruit analogies don't stretch to bananas or star fruit, you are perfectly okay. The size of your boobs doesn't affect how much milk you are producing for your baby.

You may be quite proud of your new larger boobs. Your man may be especially pleased, but he shouldn't get too excited as he probably won't get anywhere near them for quite some time. At this point your boobs take on a whole new role in life. No longer just decorative, they have become utilitarian, and this new function, plus the fact that they may be uncomfortably swollen, with sore nipples and leaking milk, may make you feel differently about your body.

Boobs will likely stay larger than normal for as long as you breast-feed, but will quickly settle down from the initial enlargement of the early days as you establish the required milk supply. Be prepared to have mismatched boobs if you've just fed from one; the empty one can be noticeably smaller. This can have its uses—no need to keep a feeding journal to remind you which breast you need to offer first at the next feeding.

NIPPLES

Nipples don't know what hit them when Baby starts to breastfeed, and they can get quite distressed initially. Because they are such a sensitive part of your body, your discomfort is intensified. Be prepared to have chafed, sore, cracked or even bleeding nipples for the first couple of weeks of nursing; three out of five women do. Luckily this is only a short-term problem, otherwise no one would carry on with breastfeeding no matter what the benefits. Nipples soon toughen up with use, so keep at it. Feeding less often or for shorter periods to save discomfort is not a good idea. At this point, most babies are going to take a while to feed, and if you meddle with the pace you will mess up the milk supply. You'll likely have painfully engorged boobs and a miserable, hungry baby on your hands to boot. "Is there no end to my misery and suffering?" I hear you cry.

Survival Secrets

- Your milk is a natural healer, so smear a little over and around your nipples at the end of a feeding. Let it dry before putting your bra back on.
- Lanolin-based ointments like Lansinoh are lifesavers. These are pretty gross when applied, but they work wonders. Despite what they look, smell and feel like, they are perfectly safe for Baby to ingest so there is no need to wash before a feed.
- When you do wash, you should use only water on your boobs because soap can be drying and cause cracked skin.
- Let your boobs breathe as much as possible. If you can bear to set them free of the support of the nursing bra, lose any inhibitions you have left and sit around airing your boobs while you rest. Don't suffocate them by wearing bras with synthetic material

in the cups or continuously wearing damp nursing pads where bacteria can breed.

- Nipple shields are not normally recommended because they force a baby to suck differently and reduce the amount of milk intake. They shouldn't be your first port in the storm; however, if the pain is too much to bear and using them is the only alternative to giving up breastfeeding, go for it. Be extra vigilant and make sure Baby has the expected number of wet diapers and is gaining enough weight.

If nipple soreness, cracking or bleeding continues beyond the first couple of weeks, it's an indication that something is wrong. It could be that Baby is not positioned right when feeding. It will put a huge strain on your nipples if Baby is just hanging on to the end of them and sucking for all she is worth. Baby needs to take a big mouthful of the breast to get the milk flowing properly. Ask your doctor or community health nurse to check your latch, or get a referral to a lactation consultant if you are still suffering. The professionals will immediately know if your latch is the culprit, and they will also be able to tell if there is an alternative reason for the nipple soreness, such as an infection.

BREASTFEEDING AILMENTS

I had a few difficulties with latching when breastfeeding my daughter, but when I began researching this section I was writing in a detached, "Ooh, that sounds nasty" manner because I never experienced any further complications. However, in order to be able to better empathize with my audience, while breastfeeding my son I managed to sample the entire range of infections. My boobs felt as if they had gone a few rounds with Tyson, with the knockout punch happening when Baby latched on.

Common breastfeeding ailments are plugged milk ducts, thrush and mastitis. If you notice a problem, you need to take action straight away to avoid it getting any worse. Luckily none of these complaints mean you have to stop breastfeeding. The ailments will not harm your baby, and often the process of feeding will help you heal. Try home remedies immediately if you notice a problem, but always consult your doctor if there is no improvement in 48 hours.

Plugged Ducts

If you've got a little sore lump or red area on your boob, it may be a blocked milk duct. They can get plugged by a pressure point: a tight bra, a baby carrier or your sleeping position, for example. Blocked ducts usually sort themselves out in a couple of days, but it's important to ensure the duct is cleared promptly as leaving it can lead to a more serious infection like mastitis.

Survival Secrets

- The best remedy is letting Baby feed from the affected breast, even though it is painful and even though he may not be too happy about this since the milk flow could be slower than normal.
- The most efficient milk removal happens when Baby's chin is pointing to the blocked area. This might require a bit of awkward positioning, which could further displease Baby. If Baby is not cooperating, just let him feed in his normal position—it is best that he feeds this way rather than not at all.
- Massage your breast from behind the plug towards the nipple.
- Use a warm shower or warm, wet cloth to help get the milk flowing before a feed.
- Sometimes a blister will be the outer indication of a blockage. Just pop the blister with a sterile needle.
- A doctor can give ultrasound treatment to remove the blockage if it persists.

Mastitis

A painful lump or red area on the boob is also the telltale sign of mastitis. It can be accompanied by feeling tired (a hard symptom to detect for a rookie mom) or achy like you have the flu with a fever. In this case, the inflammation is caused by infection. You are more likely to get mastitis in the first couple of months, before a regular feeding pattern has been established, and when you are more prone to engorgement if you aren't feeding or pumping regularly. Not emptying the breasts regularly can lead to plugged ducts or milk leaking into the breast tissue. A milk duct left blocked or breast tissue that's swollen can easily get infected. Also, in the early months, novice nursers who aren't getting a good latch are more prone to cracked skin on the nipple, which can be an entry point for bacteria.

Tips from the Trenches

- Get to your doctor, since mastitis needs antibiotic treatment.
- Meanwhile, Baby is the best aid in this situation as you need to keep emptying the breast to reduce the swelling and speed up recovery. If feeding is too painful, try pumping instead, but keep emptying the breast regularly.
- Use a warm shower or warm, wet cloth to help get the milk flowing before a feed.
- Rest as you would to combat any illness.
- Acetaminophen painkillers are okay to take when breastfeeding. Ibuprofen is also allowed to reduce swelling.
- Use lightweight cold packs to reduce swelling.

Thrush

You probably know of thrush as a vaginal problem, but since it is a fungal infection that loves moist, warm, dark spots, it can also thrive in the mouth and on nipples closeted under damp breast pads.

If you have red, itchy, burning nipples, you probably have a yeast infection. Shooting pain in the breast when Baby feeds is also a symptom. Other symptoms can show up in Baby, as it is nearly impossible not to pass it on. She can have white patches in the mouth or a yeasty diaper rash.

Tips from the Trenches

- See your doctor for an antifungal cream for your nipples. At the same time, Baby should be prescribed an antifungal swab for the mouth and cream for the diaper rash.
- Bite the bullet and keep nursing to avoid having full breasts that are more prone to deeper infection or other problems like mastitis. If feeding is too painful, try pumping instead, but keep emptying the breast regularly.
- Keep nipples as dry as possible. Allow them to dry before putting your bra back on after a feed. Change your breast pads if they are wet. A damp breast pad in a dark bra next to a warm breast is the yeast infection's utopia.

- Make sure you sterilize your breast pump properly after every use.
- Keep your nursing bras regularly laundered using water as hot as you possibly can without ruining or shrinking your bras. If you can line dry them in the sun, even better, since thrush hates sunlight.
- Because of the fungus's aversion to sunlight, topless sunbathing for a few minutes several times a day is a surefire remedy, but probably not a practical one, especially in winter.

Because it is so easy to pass back and forth from Baby to Mom, it can be hard to be completely rid of thrush. Once you have it, be sure to treat both of you even if Baby is not showing symptoms. Keep going with the full course of medication and continue to fight the nasty fungus by destroying its beloved habitat.

LEAKING

It can happen to anyone. A breastfeeding Pamela Anderson confessed to leaking through the famous red swimsuit on the set of *Baywatch*. Pammie wearing breast pads on set would likely have led to a dip in the ratings, but in the real world it's best to buy some, wear them and discard them if you find you don't need them, rather than finding out that you should have been wearing them thanks to embarrassing wet patches on your shirt or by soaking through a week's supply of T-shirts in one night. There's enough laundry to do right now without creating more.

Leaking happens when your breasts are so full they overflow. You'll feel a tingly tightening in your breast called "letdown," followed by a leakage of milk. Morning, when milk supply peaks, is the most likely time for it to happen. It can also happen as a reaction to all sorts of stimuli: around feeding time; when Baby cries; when another baby cries (for some women); and even when you see, hear or smell something you associate with breastfeeding. Or you may only leak through one breast while Baby is feeding from the other. Some moms never experience leaking. It's likely to lessen over time, and may only last a few weeks while you establish the right milk supply for your baby and get into the rhythm of breastfeeding. Although, you could continue to leak for months.

Comrades' Recommendations

- Wear breast pads. These pads sit inside your nursing bra. Oh great, the boobs look even bigger now! There are several brands of disposable pads on the market, but try to steer clear of pads that have plastic linings as these keep the dampness on the nipple, which can lead to soreness and fungal infection. You can also buy washable cloth nursing pads. Whichever pads you choose, you need to change them when they are damp to prevent health problems.
- If you're a really big leaker and go through several pads a day, carry a spare shirt or cover-up sweater or jacket when you are out in case of accidents.
- At home, save on breast pads by having a cloth handy for the leaking spare boob when Baby is feeding from the other. Sometimes when Baby pulls away, your milk continues to flow or even spray, so having a cloth on hand is wise.
- If you get that tingly feeling while you're out and about and not due to feed Baby, hug your arms around your chest to apply pressure to your boobs. Try to get somewhere where you can manually express a little milk to relieve the pressure.
- Don't get into the habit of pumping to stop leaking. This will only make your body think that Baby has a big appetite, and therefore you'll produce more milk and worsen the problem.
- Beware that leaking or even spraying can also happen during sex because the same hormones are racing about. So if you're already back on the horse, give Dad a heads-up for what might happen. Breastfeeding beforehand to relieve the pressure is a good idea. Plus, you are less likely to have your fun interrupted by a hungry baby.
- Watch out for a recurrence of leaking at weaning time. I'd happily relegated the breast pads to the back of the bathroom cabinet a couple of months into nursing, but when I weaned my son onto formula I found I leaked again for a week or so until the milk finally dried up.

NURSING BRAS

If you are planning to be breastfeeding your little one for at least a few months, then you should definitely invest some time and money into finding a decent nursing bra. Gone are the days of sexy, gel-padded Wonderbras for you—now is not the time for cleavage enhancement. You'll likely be spending your breastfeeding months trying to play down your fuller bosom. Practicality should now be the number one consideration on your bra selection list. Nursing bras allow you easy and discreet access to one boob at a time for no-nonsense feeding sessions, and provide extra support for your heavier chest. Modern nursing bras are getting more attractive, but are still likely more substantial and utilitarian than your regular bra, with wider shoulder straps and deeper back and side bands. It's worth sacrificing the satin and lace in favor of comfort, support and easy access for feeding.

There are four popular types of nursing bras:

1. Cups that open downwards and fasten with clips or hooks to the shoulder strap.
2. Cups that open to the side and fasten with snaps in the center.
3. Cups that have zips under them.
4. Stretchy material that you just move aside to feed.

Shopping for a nursing bra is difficult. Don't do what I did and grab the nearest one as you pass by the lingerie section en route to the more enticing merchandise in the baby department. The general advice is to buy them late on in pregnancy and buy one size bigger to allow for expansion when your milk comes in. However, there is no hard and fast rule as to how much bigger your boobs are going to be. Apart from being uncomfortable and putting pressure on already sore nipples, a bra that is too tight can cause a plugged duct, which could lead to infection or interfere with milk production. Try packing in a nursing pad and you've got even less room to play with.

A good suggestion is to find a store with a cooperative return policy and buy two or three bras: one in your expected size, one smaller and one bigger. Keep them boxed with the receipt handy. At about two weeks postpartum, when you're no longer engorged and the milk supply has been established, your boob size will have stabilized. Then you can decide which one fits and exchange the others for the same size. Alternatively, buy just one "test bra" late in pregnancy in what you think will be your correct size, and if by two weeks postpartum you like that style and the size is good, go ahead and stock up on more of the same. If not, get a proper fitting and choose another. Put the bad buy away—it might fit later during your breastfeeding months or come in handy in an emergency. In a pinch you can cope with two nursing bras, but they'll need frequent washing as they tend to get messy from leaks. Three is a good number—you wear one, wash one and have a reserve.

The type of bra that suits you best is a personal choice, but here are some tips.

Comrades' Recommendations:

- Choose one that you can fasten and unfasten easily one-handed and without looking while you hold Baby with the other arm.
- For maximum support and comfort, ensure the cup fits your whole boob and there is nothing spilling out or brimming over.
- A stretchy cup is a good bet since boobs change so much in size as they fill and empty. You also need expansion room to fit in breast pads if you need to wear them.
- Buy a bra that has several rows of hooks at the back to give you a bigger range of size options. It should fit you when fastened on the middle set of clasps—that way you have room for movement either way, to extend the chances of it fitting you throughout breastfeeding.
- Make sure the cup is made of breathable material. Bacteria thrive in damp conditions, so you'll be more at risk of an infection like thrush if you have a cup made of a synthetic fiber that traps moisture.
- Avoid underwire bras. They can constrict breast tissue and cause plugged ducts.

BREASTFEEDING IN PUBLIC

Through pregnancy and the birth of your baby you've probably had more people looking at the private parts of your body than ever before. (How many people were in your delivery room, for instance?) So by now you may have shed some inhibitions, and you'll be slightly more prepared for getting your boobs out in public to breastfeed. Some rookie moms will not be at all worried by the prospect of breastfeeding outside the privacy of their own homes; others will be uncomfortable or downright horrified by the idea. However, unless you are going to live like a hermit for the next few months, you're likely to need to give baby a few al fresco meals. Before we get all holier-than-thou about it now that we are in the ranks of breastfeeding moms, let's take a step back to the days before our boobs were functional. Unless you have a pop star's malfunctioning wardrobe or you frequent the beaches of Europe, boobs generally don't come out in public. When they do, they're fascinating to a lot of people. They don't become any less fascinating because a baby is attached. Let's be totally honest: it is genuinely hard not to look.

Once Baby is latched and contentedly feeding, your exposure is minimal, but getting him latched and staying that way can be difficult. A novice baby may take time and encouragement to latch. An older baby may flail around, play peek-a-boo with your cover blanket or just pull away to look around. You may find yourself chatting away to a friend, completely unaware that Baby has lost interest and is smiling at passersby while you sit with your boob on display.

Depending on your level of comfort, you may want to employ a blanket or a purpose-made nursing cover. This is like a large bib that fastens around you, and you can look down the neck of it to see underneath. Cover-ups can, however, make things more difficult because you have one more thing to worry about: trying to keep the cover in place. Baby may not like being in the "tent" and it may be difficult to see what you are doing underneath. Baby's distress at being hungry while you flap about with the cover-up may attract more attention than not bothering with one.

Button-down shirts are not the best idea, as you'll have to partly undress before you start. A pull-up shirt, T-shirt or purpose-made nursing shirt are the best options.

If you are nervous about it, practice your tactics for discreet feeding at home before you venture outdoors.

BREASTFEEDING AROUND FAMILY AND FRIENDS

It may make some family members or friends uncomfortable to see you breastfeed. I guess getting an eyeful of a strange woman's boob is less shocking than seeing the goods of your daughter, sister or best friend's wife. When my parents arrived from England to see their granddaughter for the first time, I greeted them and then said I had to finish feeding the baby. My dad shot off to the other end of the room as if I was sitting there naked. After that I felt compelled to go to the bedroom to breastfeed during their visit. I never bothered to establish whether he was uncomfortable or presumed I was uncomfortable with him being there. They were only with us for three weeks so the inconvenience was minimal, but as you're probably going to be breastfeeding for around a year, you should start as you mean to go on. Unless you want to be hiding yourself away every few hours, missing the conversation or the rest of the TV program, frequent visitors will have to learn to live with it.

For less frequent visitors, it's polite to establish if everyone is comfortable before you feed the baby. One of two things is likely to happen. Either eyes will be drawn to your boob as if under some kind of spell or the person will avoid looking at you altogether just in case he or she is caught glancing at your boob. Either way, it's kind of hard to carry on a conversation. Most other moms and dads probably won't bat an eyelid, being so used to it themselves, but friends without kids could be stuck not knowing where to look, especially the guys who still have decorative boobs in mind rather than the functional kind. It's often a good idea to adapt to suit your company and use a cover-up in these situations rather than make people squirm.

BREASTFEEDING DIET

You'll be relieved to know that you don't have to be as careful about what you eat now that you are breastfeeding as you did when you were pregnant. The makeup of your milk isn't dependent on what you eat. However, if your diet is really poor, your own resources will be stolen from you in order to make the milk, and your health could suffer as a result. You'll be even more relieved to know that breastfeeding can burn almost 500 calories per day, so you can eat a bit more without worrying which bulge or wobbly bit it might add to. You'll probably find you're ravenous and have no problem packing away a few extra snacks like a mid-morning sandwich or some fruit and a muffin.

Make sure you drink plenty of water to replenish all the liquids you're offloading. It will help you to remember to keep your intake up if you get into the habit of downing a glass while you feed. Carry a water bottle with you on all outings. Take a large sports bottle or a couple of glasses to bed for rehydration during night feeds. Initially I took just a glass, which would be drained by the third feed of the night, so I'd lie there parched, not daring to get a refill in case, heaven forbid, I disturbed the sleeping baby.

No-Nos

- **Smoking:** Just don't do it.
- **Drugs:** For pain relief, stick to acetaminophen. Ibuprofen in moderation is also allowed as very little makes it through to your baby. Check with your doctor before taking any other meds as some drugs can be harmful to Baby.
- **Vitamin overdose:** Postnatal vitamins are carefully balanced to give you everything you need, so limit yourself to these alone.

Be Careful with . . .

- **Alcohol:** Excessive alcohol can make Baby drowsy, reduce your milk supply and even slow Baby's development. But we're not talking about an occasional, lifesaving, stress-relieving glass of wine here. It's okay to have a little tipple if the mood takes you. It's even acceptable to chill out with a few drinks on a well-deserved night out, but you should plan your breastfeeding around this. Express some milk in advance for Baby's feed. Then before you feed the baby from the breast again, pump off the alcoholic stuff and throw it away.

  Not being able to overindulge on the alcohol front is really a blessing in disguise. While it may seem like a good idea, after a long period of abstention, to throw caution to the wind and join in the round of shooters, Baby will not be too sympathetic about your hangover. She'll likely wake earlier than usual as if she senses something is up. She won't stop pooping either, and will likely produce one of her messiest, smelliest offerings just to tip you over the edge. Trust me, you will regret it. This time when you moan, "Never again," you will mean it.
- **Caffeine:** While you desperately crave intravenous Starbucks to keep you going (or just conscious), it's not such a good idea to pass on the caffeine buzz to Baby. It might make her irritable, fussy and jittery, and might interfere with her sleep. You should be fine if

you limit your intake to one or two cups of caffeinated coffee or tea per day. I'd suggest switching to decaf, but what's the point? Don't forget to watch for the caffeine in soda pop too.

- **Strong flavors, spices and allergens:** While the actual nutritional makeup of breast milk isn't altered by what you eat, seasonings and strong flavors can filter through. The affect of this could be a positive one if Baby likes a good curry. Or it could be a bad reaction, ranging from Baby not liking the flavor to bad gas, a sore, red bottom or explosive poops. In rare cases an allergy to something like dairy or wheat can cause a more severe reaction like rash, dry skin or eczema, wheezing or asthma, runny nose, diarrhea, vomiting or blood or mucus in the baby's poop. Severe reactions are more common when there is a family history of food allergies.

Eat whatever you want and don't give it a second thought if everything is going okay. Baby's tastes might have been influenced by what you were eating when you were pregnant. However, if you've got an unhappy, fussy, gassy baby or one suffering from colic, the culprit could be something like gassy vegetables or garlic in your diet, giving your little one cause for complaint. Finding the culprit is difficult: a food takes two to six hours to affect your milk and it's not instantly removed from your system as soon as you stop eating it. Cow's milk protein, for example, can hang around in your body for a couple of weeks and for a similar time in Baby's system. It's best to keep a detailed list of everything you eat and drink alongside Baby's mood, and if you are distantly related to Sherlock Holmes you may have a chance of working it out some time before you wean. Just stop eating everything you enjoy and you should be okay. Only kidding, but unfortunately chocolate is on the list of most likely offenders. Here's the full list of foods that will potentially upset Baby.

- dairy products
- wheat
- eggs
- peanuts/nuts
- soy
- shellfish
- chicken
- beef
- chocolate
- beans

- citrus fruit
- vegetables (typically ones that give you gas like broccoli, cabbage, cauliflower, sprouts, green peppers, onions and tomatoes)
- garlic
- iron (vitamins containing iron can be the problem)
- caffeine (in coffee, tea, soda pop and chocolate)

For two to three weeks, eliminate the food from your diet that you suspect is causing the reaction and see if the symptoms subside, although you aren't likely to see an improvement for several days. If you believe you have found the offender, one way to double-check is to try eating it again, although of course this depends on how severe the original reaction was and whether you want to risk a repeat. The best course of action may be to simply avoid this food until you wean, and of course be cautious about feeding the same food to Baby when she starts solids. Most babies grow out of food sensitivities within the first year; others persist for the long term.

PUMPING AND STORING BREAST MILK

Without wanting to discourage anyone, I have to say I found pumping a highly unpleasant experience. Any magic behind breastfeeding is snuffed out in an instant by the sight of your nipple being stretched to incredible lengths until you're sure it's either going to detach and shoot off down the tube or else be 4 inches long for the rest of your life. Cows, udders and milking machines spring to mind. Being the milk provider is way more appealing when the mechanics are concealed inside the privacy of Baby's mouth.

Popping out a boob to feed direct is easy and convenient, but when you bring in the pump as the middle man, the process becomes way more complicated and time-consuming. Pumping, storing, washing, sterilizing, warming and feeding quickly becomes an endless cycle. A one-off pump for a night on the town isn't bad, but if you have to pump for extended periods it can be tedious.

Breast milk can be expressed by hand or pumped using a manual or electric pump into a sterile baby bottle, bottle liner or freezer bag. Sealed containers can be kept in the fridge for up to 48 hours or in the freezer for three weeks. Thaw frozen breast milk in the refrigerator or in a bowl of cool water and use it within 24 hours. You'll find the milk has separated into fatty hindmilk and watery foremilk, so it will need shaking before you serve it. Warm it to approximately body temperature by standing it in a bowl of warm water.

Tips from the Trenches

- Pump when your boobs are fullest (first thing in the morning is a good time). Pumping away for a pathetic return when your supply is low, such as last thing at night, can be discouraging and tiring.
- If you are pumping and not getting a satisfying stream, try repositioning the pump to get the seal right. If milk still isn't flowing well, leave it for a while and try again later when your milk may be more plentiful.
- If you are returning to work and unable to breastfeed exclusively, but are finding pumping too time-consuming, consider breast-feeding part-time and supplementing with formula the rest of the day. Your milk supply should adjust accordingly and Baby will continue getting the health benefits of breast milk.
- A warm towel around your boob may help to get the milk flowing to allow you to pump.
- If you only manage to express a small amount, your hard work doesn't have to go to waste—you can bag it, refrigerate or freeze it, and add it to another helping later. In fact, to avoid waste, it's best to store the milk in small portions (2 to 4 ounces or 60 to 120 milliliters) that can be added together if necessary to make up one feed.

WEANING FROM THE BREAST

Risking a visit from the La Leche League lynch mob, I have to say while I was happy to breastfeed a baby, the idea of breastfeeding a toddler disturbs me. If the kid can walk up to you, stick his head up your sweater and help himself, or if he has enough words to ask for it, for me it's time to stop. I know I'm not alone in this feeling, which is one reason a lot of babies are weaned at around a year. Some moms have no such issues and continue to breastfeed into the second or even third year, which is extremely beneficial for Baby's health. Other moms can't tolerate breastfeeding beyond a few months, and some end up weaning earlier than they'd like in order to return to work. Some babies wean themselves—they basically lose interest somewhere along the line. Mine did just before her first birthday.

Weaning a baby from the breast can trigger mixed emotions in a mom. If you've enjoyed the whole breastfeeding gig, you may feel a sense of loss at no longer providing your baby's nourishment. Even if you're relieved to get your body and some time back for yourself, you may still experience withdrawal symptoms. Weaning will trigger hormonal changes that could leave you feeling a bit depressed, irritable or moody. The act of breastfeeding actually triggers the release of pleasurable hormones, so weaning can even feel a bit like drug withdrawal.

Cold turkey is not a good plan of action for weaning—your boobs and emotions need time to adjust gradually. Knock out one feed at a time, starting with the feed that is least convenient to you or the least comforting to Baby. Aim to leave a week's gap before eliminating another feed, preferably at the opposite side of the clock to the first one so that your boobs will get more even relief. After a few weeks you may be left with just the early morning and bedtime feeds, for example. If you are weaning to return to work, it's possible to supplement with formula during the day and continue on one or two breast feedings once you are home for as long as you like—your breast milk supply will normally adapt to this schedule easily.

If you wean gradually as suggested, you shouldn't suffer with the type of sudden, agonizing engorgement that happens when your milk first arrives. However, it's possible your boobs will still be hard, lumpy and tender or painful as the stretches between feeds get longer, and for a week or two after you're done. It's surprising how long the milk sticks around—it's perfectly normal to see milk drops months after you've stopped feeding.

A gradual transition also gives Baby's digestive system a chance to adapt to the new input of formula or cow's milk (weaning to cow's milk should only be considered if Baby is over nine months old). Of course, if Baby has only ever had breast milk, you also have to overcome the hurdles of convincing him to accept the new drink as well as the new method of delivery. The **Bottle- and Formula-Feeding** section in the **Mouth** chapter of the **Baby Map** has Comrades' Recommendations on how to wage this particular battle.

Comrades' Recommendations

- Take painkillers, but remember if you are still breastfeeding Baby at all, stick to pain meds that are okay for breastfeeding moms like acetaminophen and ibuprofen.
- Wear a fairly firm supportive bra—maybe a sports bra over the top of your nursing bra—but don't bind yourself up too tightly as you're liable to get plugged ducts or an infection.

- Soothe your boobs with wrapped ice packs or cooled cabbage leaves (see **Engorgement** earlier in this chapter for details).
- Massage the boobs and gently express a little milk to iron out any lumps and relieve painful fullness, but don't express large quantities as this will just signal for more milk production. Relieving the fullness will reduce the chances of getting a plugged duct or infection.
- Wear breast pads as a precaution as your boobs are likely to start leaking once they become full and milk is not removed by feeding.

AND AFTERWARDS . . .

Most moms agree it's a huge relief to finally get their bodies back after weaning. However, the boobs you get back may not be the ones you remember. "Where did my boobs go?" or "What are they doing down there?" wonder many moms. If asked to describe my post-postpartum boobs in a nutshell, I'd have to say, "Not pretty." You've heard of the pencil test; I could carry a bumper pack of markers. And if we return to the fruit analogies, maybe bananas aren't so far off track after all. Although it's not breastfeeding itself that causes sagging or drooping of the boobs, it seems that way because it's when you stop breastfeeding that the changes become apparent. Once the milk is not bolstering the breasts they will be noticeably smaller, possibly smaller than they were pre-pregnancy, and sadly less perky. Your boobs have been under a lot of strain through pregnancy and the extra weight can take its toll.

Once you are done with breastfeeding, don't assume you are back to your pre-pregnancy size and shape. It's time to get a proper bra fitting and treat yourself to some new underwear. Indulge in a little retail therapy to help you get over the shock of losing a cup size—pick out something pretty after months of wearing those practical nursing bras.

CHAPTER 14

Mommy Map—Body

WEIGHT LOSS

The good news is that, as a rough guide, Baby + placenta + fluids =
12 pounds, all dropped at birth. Well, I hope no one dropped the
baby; they are slippery little suckers when they first come out. Another 4 pounds of accumulated fluids are lost in increased sweat
and pee in the first postpartum week. "Wait a minute, I put on
30 pounds during pregnancy," I hear you cry. Where is the rest and
when is it going? A bit more will disappear by four to six weeks
when your uterus has contracted to its normal size and weighs only
a couple of ounces instead of 2 pounds. That leaves Mrs. Average with
approximately 12 pounds to work on. If you only gained 25 pounds
during pregnancy, you're only dealing with a measly 7 pounds, so
stop complaining! If you gained 40 pounds, you do the math, and
let's just say you've got a bit more work on your hands.

The rest of the weight will take a while to drop off, but you can
reasonably expect to lose about 2 pounds per month. Once your
periods return and you stop breastfeeding, your body is finished
with the whole childbearing cycle and there is no longer any need
to keep stores of fat or fluids, so you could notice a more rapid return to
your normal shape and size. It's quite common for the last 5 to 10 pounds
to be the hardest to shed. You also have to be honest with yourself and
take into consideration your physical condition during pregnancy. You
know whether or not you were a pregnant couch potato who ate too
much chocolate and ballooned suddenly. If this sounds familiar, you

will find it harder to lose the pregnancy pounds than someone who kept fit, ate healthily and gained weight steadily (Little Miss Perfect!).

"I wish I had known . . .

how ravenous I was going to be while breastfeeding. I eat like a horse."

This is a common comment from new moms. One dedicated mom nursing twins confessed to dropping by the dining table and devouring half a chicken in minutes like some wild animal. The jury is still out on whether breastfeeding helps you actually lose weight. It's true that it burns about 500 calories a day, but it's also true that you are prone to pigging out while breastfeeding. And rightly so, since you need the extra input to give you the energy to continue breastfeeding. Nursing does stimulate contractions of the uterus, which helps it to shrink to its normal size more quickly. Don't break into a sweat at the mention of contractions; these ones are a piece of cake after everything you've been through.

GETTING BACK INTO SHAPE

Argh, what a drag! Let's not bother. You want to? Okay, I suppose we should.

I found this section the most challenging to write, not only because I loathe exercise, but because the feedback we got on the subject was so mixed. On one hand, moms complained of feeling pressured by themselves, advice manuals and society in general to get their figures back ASAP, so I am tempted to take the "accept our mommy body and let nature take its course" approach. On the other hand, I heard disturbing stories of moms who wished they had known the importance of specific exercises early on so they could have saved themselves hard work and difficulties later, which makes me lean towards being a drill sergeant and telling you to get on with it.

The conclusion I came to is that, up to a point, nature will take its course and your body will take its own sweet time to get back to anything resembling normal to you. It is sensible to remember that it took you nine(ish) months of growing to get to your D-day size, and some experts say it takes at least as long to shrink back down. The decision to exercise, the way I think of it—involving gym equipment, jogging or aerobics classes—is your call. Listen to your mind and body signals, heed the warnings given below and if you want to, go ahead. If not, relax and don't feel pressured, but keep in mind that except for a few lucky women, pregnancy pounds aren't just going to magically melt away without some effort on your part. And regardless of how we feel about true exercise, there is some gentle repair work that it makes sense to do to ensure our bodies don't start to disintegrate in the near future (see the **Body Repairs** section later in this chapter).

Getting back into shape after giving birth is not something to obsess about and certainly nothing to even consider for the first six weeks. At this time you need all your energy to recuperate after labor. Initially you're far too busy with aches and pains and "everything baby" to give a bit of extra girth a second thought. I don't imagine there are too many of you brimming with energy and anxious to get back into Lycra at six weeks. Your ideas prior to childbirth about how soon you would be springing back into action are likely to change once you hit the realities of coping with your postpartum condition. You shouldn't exercise when you are exhausted—and if what you are feeling now isn't exhaustion, I don't know what is.

Give yourself time; trying and failing to find time and energy to exercise on top of all the upheaval will only give you one more thing to be miserable about not achieving. Odds are you are going to want to get back to your pre-pregnancy weight and size one day—if only so you can pack away the maternity duds and fit back into your old clothes—so you'll need to start easing back into exercise eventually, but do so slowly. Baby achieves an important milestone somewhere around three months: he reaches stage one of becoming a reasonable human being. At this point, if you're lucky, you should start getting more sleep and feeling less like a zombie and a bit more energetic. Your war wounds are pretty much healed by this juncture too, so you might feel a little encouraged to start some exercise.

"I wish I had known . . .
my body shape was going to be completely altered by having a baby."

Maybe "getting back into shape" is a misnomer, since for some women pregnancy and childbirth can alter the shape of their bodies. Wider hips are common, as are a thicker midriff and unfamiliar boobs: bigger; smaller; (sadly) droopier. I was quite amazed to find that after 15 years of being a size 12, I actually had slimmer hips after having my first baby, and that it was a difference in bone structure rather than in padding. So it's important to keep in mind that what we are striving for may not be attainable. We should aim to get fitter and healthier rather than trying to regain the shape and size we used to be.

BODY REPAIRS

Just when you thought you were off the hook for six weeks, there are some very gentle movements (let's not call them exercises) you can and should do before the six-week watershed to help your body recover from its ordeal. They are easy and you can do them lying on the floor—that part at least must sound appealing. Note that if you had a C-section, your rules are different. See **C-section Recovery** later in this chapter.

Kegels

The sooner you start these, the better. While there is a lot of conflicting advice on other exercises that we should concentrate on postpartum, every expert stresses the importance of pelvic floor strengthening from day one. Some would have you doing them as the obstetrician ties off his last stitch. There are numerous benefits to pelvic floor exercises, including assisting perineal recovery, strengthening your core and steering clear of peeing your pants every time you sneeze. We've covered Kegel exercises in detail in the **Nether Regions** chapter under **Bladder Control**.

Gentle Tummy Contractions

After a week, you can start to strengthen the core tummy muscles. It is quite common for your abs to have separated during pregnancy—a condition called diastasis recti. Sounds icky, doesn't it? Think of it as your six-pack being split into two three-packs by the expanding uterus when the central band of connective tissue gets softened by hormones. Sounds even ickier now, doesn't it? Sometimes the separation closes by itself within a few months; sometimes not. If you have a separation, you will want to try and correct it and take extra care not to widen it. Sit-ups and crunches should be avoided at all costs. Good, a perfect excuse to never do another crunch! Who wants to exercise anyway? Move on to the next chapter. Unfortunately diastasis recti is not something we should ignore as it will only get worse over time if not corrected, especially with subsequent pregnancies. Your core will be weak and your posture and back will suffer in the long term. More seriously, for the first six weeks postpartum while the central band of tissue is still loose, you are prone to herniation if you stress your stomach (by crunching up suddenly out of bed, for example). Once the connective tissue hardens up, you are no longer in danger of hernia, but if the gap isn't closed it adds to a wider waistline.

To check if you have a separation, lie on your back and breathe out as you lift your head and shoulders off the floor, and clench your tummy muscles. You should be able to feel two strips of muscle running down your abdomen. With fingers pointing down towards your pubic bone, feel just below your belly button for a gap. If you can fit more than two fingers in this gap, you probably do have a separation. Your best bet is to get the community health nurse or doctor to check your self-diagnosis and consult a postpartum exercise instructor for the best way to deal with it.

The following are some exercises that you can do to help close the gap to an acceptable one- or two-finger width. Even if you do not think you have a separation, these exercises are a good way to start. If you are positive you do not have a separation, you can do the same exercises but without the assistance of hands to hold your two sides together.

Assisted Head Lifts	
<ul><li>Lie on your back with knees bent as shown.</li><li>Place your hands flat on your tummy on either side of your belly button with fingers pointing down to your pubic bone.</li><li>Exhale and lift your head off the floor while pulling your belly button towards your spine and using your hands to help push the muscles toward your belly button. Lower head and relax.</li><li>Repeat 5 to 10 times, several sets per day.</li></ul>	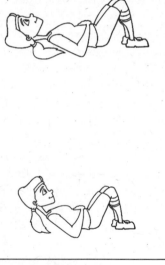
	**Single Leg Slides**<ul><li>Lie on your back with knees bent as for *Assisted Head Lifts*.</li><li>Exhale and slide one foot away from your butt along the floor as shown.</li><li>Inhale as you slide it back. Repeat with the other leg.</li><li>Repeat 5 to 10 times, several sets per day.</li></ul>

Suck It In

- Lie on your back as for *Assisted Head Lifts* or sit as shown.
- Exhale and slowly pull your belly button back towards your spine as if you were trying to suck in your tummy to look thinner.
- Hold for a count of 10, then slowly let your belly out again.
- It is easy to forget to breathe when doing this exercise. Try to remember you are sucking in your muscles, not sucking in your breath and holding it. You will only be able to breathe lightly through the contraction.
- Repeat 5 to 10 times, several sets per day.

Assisted Pelvic Tilt

- Lie on your back with knees bent as shown.
- Cross your arms over your tummy at belly button level and give yourself a hug, pulling your sides towards your middle. Exhale as you pull your belly button down to your spine, and tilt your pelvis toward your belly button.
- Inhale as you release.
- Repeat 5 to 10 times, several sets per day.

Diastisis recti can be a lasting problem for some. While it is usually improved by exercise, in some cases a severe separation may persist and leave you with a hard protrusion, giving you the look of a four-months-pregnant stomach. More than just the appearance, it is the long-term health considerations, such as back issues and intestinal troubles, that make it necessary for a small minority of women to have surgery to reattach the muscles. If you are concerned, consult your doctor, and if it is truly a risk to your long-term health he or she will likely suggest surgery once you are sure you've finished having children.

Walking

It is also recommended that we start shuffling about as soon as possible. Never undervalue the benefits of walking: it improves circulation, which speeds up healing; gets our bowels moving; and boosts our energy levels. Start with a 5-minute amble around the maternity block and build up to a brisker 30-minute walk every other day for the first few weeks.

EXERCISE FOR REAL

We have a gym in our apartment building, so I had grand visions of my postpartum fitness routine: me pacing on the stepper with Baby parked alongside in the stroller sleeping peacefully. This happened once. Once or twice I got to the gym and the cessation of stroller motion woke the baby after minutes. I did consider rigging the stroller to the treadmill to maintain the motion and jogging alongside. I also considered rigging the stroller to the treadmill to maintain the motion and sitting down to read a magazine and eat some chocolate. The rest of the time I didn't even make it to the gym in the first place. So I settled for walking. Okay, I admit I was a lucky one and only gained the minimum in pregnancy, but I can vouch for 60- to 90-minute walks being excellent for losing a few pounds. I'm not talking about an amble to the first park bench where we stop to breastfeed Baby, drink a coffee and then head home. It has to be a brisk walk, pushing the stroller or toting Baby in the carrier to expend extra effort. Baby will likely enjoy the motion and take a nap. If nothing else, walks at least hold at bay any additional pounds waiting to attach themselves—the pounds that would accumulate fast if the alternative to an afternoon stroll was sitting watching TV and eating cookies. I know my butt has expanded a couple of inches in the months I've been working on this book because my afternoon walks have been shelved in favor of sitting and typing. I guess my fingers are fit.

The following types of exercise are considered safe bets for postpartum women. Choose those that appeal to you most. Failing that, choose the one you find the least repellent.

- brisk walking
- swimming
- aquarobics
- yoga
- Pilates
- low-impact aerobic workouts
- cycling
- strength training, with dumbbells, body ball or resistance band

However you feel, from extremely reluctant to raring to go, it makes sense to initially attend a postpartum exercise class for several reasons. First, their focus will be your problem areas. More importantly, they won't be doing any exercises that are going to jeopardize your recovery. Second, you get to meet other rookie moms battling the bulge, and you won't feel intimidated by having to work out next to some skinny-minny. If you can't manage a full course, try and get to one or two sessions and use what you learn from their guidance in your own exercise routine. If you can't or really don't want to go to the class, some postpartum exercise specialists will come to your home, which is obviously a pricey option, but worth the expense to ensure you aren't doing yourself any damage. There are many postpartum body conditioning DVDs and books available too, but you can't ask questions, and no one will be able to check that you are getting the movements right, so to be safe it's best to catch the live show.

No time to exercise? No time to have sex? Why not kill two birds with one stone and tone up your relationship at the same time as your muscles? Sex is an excellent burner of calories.

Once your baby is nearing one year, you can consider taking her along on a bike ride in a bicycle trailer. These are not safe for younger babies, however, because of the impact from bouncing along without proper support.

Still not keen? Surely you're dying to be dubbed a "yummy mummy"? No? Okay, I'll try to sell it another way. Exercise has so many other benefits: it boosts your energy level, helps you to sleep better, helps you deal with stress and depression, generally makes you feel less of a dozy lump and, most importantly, allows you to eat more chocolate. Sold!

Comrades' Recommendations

- Wait the recommended six weeks before starting. Most women will see their doctor at this time for a postpartum checkup, so it's a good time to check that you are ready to launch into action.
- Oops, hold on there—no launching; start small and work up. Even if you feel great, don't dive straight in to a workout you would have done before pregnancy. You need to take it easy and give your body a chance to let you discover any new limitations.
- Make sure your tender boobs are well supported for exercise.
- Exercise after breastfeeding so boobs aren't heavy and full.
- If you join an exercise class, however gentle the activity, tell the instructor you are postpartum. There may be some exercises not recommended for postpartum women and the instructor may have an adaptation for you or, even better, let you sit it out.
- Joints and ligaments are still softened for about three months and are prone to damage from high-impact exercise or vigorous stretching.
- Drink plenty of water before, during and after exercise.
- Pair cardio exercise with some strength training to maximize the benefits of your postpartum exercise routine.
- Tons of moms are turning to Wii Fit and EA Active video "games" as a fun and effective way to exercise in the comfort of their own home when taking care of Baby doesn't give them the time or opportunity to do much else on the fitness front. As an added incentive, I bet Junior will find Mommy's Wii antics highly entertaining.

BELLY BULGE

"I wish I had known . . .

my maternity clothes would still be needed for weeks after having the baby. I wasn't naive enough to pack my skinny jeans, but I did expect to be able to come home from the hospital in a regular pair of sweats."

Many rookie moms are crestfallen at how big their guts still are when they leave hospital. It's such a kick in the teeth when someone tactlessly asks, "When's the baby due?" and you have to admit it's already out. I had the sneaking suspicion that there was another baby in there, one they hadn't noticed on all the ultrasounds. It wasn't long ago you couldn't see your feet over your rotund baby bulge—what did you think was going to happen to that expanse once the baby was out? That it was going to magically snap back into place? Some of the tummy bulge is due to stretched abs and skin, and the only way to tighten up the saggy, flabby, wobbly bits is to tone them up. Although you are keeping active around the house doing chores and lifting Baby, this isn't enough to stop your stomach from looking like a waterbed that has sprung a leak.

When we have very little time and even less energy, knowing the right kind of exercise to do is a huge advantage. Why and how do you think all the celebrity moms get their figures back so quickly? It's because they have specialist postpartum personal trainers telling them the right way to do things for the best results. (Their entourage also includes a nanny so they can spend hours working out, and there's probably a chef on hand to rustle them up a healthy, balanced meal whenever required. They also have the added motivation of knowing the paparazzi are lurking in the bushes to pounce if they risk leaving the house with the merest hint of a mummy tummy.)

A sit-up or crunch may be the furthest thing from your mind now, and it should stay that way—seriously. The traditional exercises most of us think of for toning the tummy can actually do more harm than good to the postpartum waistline. Typically we amateur exercisers will leave it a few months, then after trying and failing miserably again to get the zipper done up on our favorite jeans, drag ourselves to the gym, grab a body ball and launch into sit-ups and frantic knee-to-elbow cycling. What is likely happening when we do this is that our abs are bunching and bulging out with the effort. They might firm up, but they are going to do so in this protruded formation, leaving you with a bigger potbelly than before you started. Sure, this one will be firm instead of wobbly, but it will still be a potbelly.

We have four layers of abdominal muscles and it is the inner layer of these that holds everything in. When toned, they give you a nice flat tummy. It is important for new moms to work on these *transverse abdominis* muscles to get a strong core. When exercising, keep it in your head to pull your belly button towards your spine so that your abdomen remains flat. Correct yourself if at any time while you are exercising you notice your stomach bulging out.

We aren't trying to write a fitness book. Would you buy exercise advice written by a self-confessed exercise-phobe? There are tons of classes, books and DVDs out there focusing on postpartum fitness, and if you want more than a few basic tips, go check them out. The belly is the main bugbear of most rookie moms, but only one of the potential problem areas you might want to trim down or strengthen up right now. (For example, it's a good time to work on push-ups for arm strength to prepare for all the lifting and carrying you will be doing.) Here are some suggestions for tummy flatteners you can add to the movements you did for body repairs, assuming you are beyond any abdominal separation by now.

Double Leg Slides	
• Lie on the floor with knees bent as shown. • Press your lower back to the floor in a small pelvic tilt. • Exhale, and using your abdominal muscles to keep your back flat, slide both heels away from your bum along the floor. • Only go as far as you can without arching your back before sliding your feet back towards your bum. • Repeat 5 to 10 times, several times per day.	
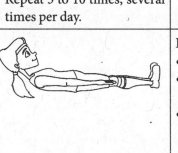	**Head and Shoulder Lifts** • Lie flat on the floor. • Pull your belly button down towards your spine. • Exhale, and keeping your chin tucked in, reach forward with your arms parallel to the floor past your thighs to lift your head and shoulder blades off the floor as shown. • Hold for a few seconds, then inhale as you lower. • Repeat 10 times per session.

Plank

- Lie face down on the floor and contract your tummy muscles.
- Push up on your toes and rest on your elbows as shown, keeping your back flat, like a plank.
- Take care to hold your stomach in rather than letting it sag down, and make sure your butt isn't sticking up in the air.
- Hold this position for 20 seconds, remembering to breathe, then lower and rest.
- Repeat 3 to 5 times.

Don't expect any instant results from your exercise; it takes at least a few months to see improvement. Allow a full year to achieve your goal and you shouldn't be disappointed. Little but often is the key. Going mad in the gym once a fortnight isn't going to get you there, but consistent half-hour sessions three times a week at home will.

Oh, and one last tip while we're on the subject of belly bulge. Please don't expose your post-childbirth midriff between a crop top and hipster jeans unless you are positive it doesn't look like the flabby skin of an 80-year-old elephant or a deflated beach ball. No one wants to see that. Meeoow!

EXTRA BELLY SKIN

It really isn't fair, but some moms can work like crazy to achieve a toned stomach and still have an overhang that won't disappear. Because it is skin: skin that's lost its twang and has nowhere to go, so it just sits and peeks over the waistband of your jeans. Lovingly termed a "pooch" by those who have come to terms with it; dismissed as a wrinkled flap by those who haven't.

Wrinkled skin after pregnancy is more common if you had a particularly big bump compared with your normal body size; for a multiple birth, for example—we all shuddered at the sight of Kate

Gosselin's post-sextuplet stomach. There is nothing we can do to tone up skin that has lost its elasticity. Any creams you see claiming to help are a waste of money. If you really can't make friends with your new body part, the only thing to do is take the pretty drastic and expensive step of going under the knife for a tummy tuck once you are sure you've finished having babies. And if you have your own reality TV show, you may be lucky enough to get the procedure done for free.

DIETING

We shouldn't panic postpartum and dive into dieting. We may have gained 30 pounds, but it isn't the disaster it would be had we gained the same amount without the end result of a baby. Take a look at the **Weight Loss** section earlier in the chapter and you'll see that a lot of the extra pounds will be gone by week six.

While dieting isn't something you should consider off the bat, healthy eating is. If diet to you means cutting back on the chocolate and cookies, then yes, you should diet postpartum. If, on the other hand, dieting means eating two crackers and a bag of carrot sticks per day, no you shouldn't. After childbirth, we need to eat healthily and regularly to help our bodies recover and give us the energy to deal with the demands of the new job. Breastfeeding moms especially shouldn't skimp on the calories since about 500 hundred a day are burned breastfeeding. Hungry breastfeeding moms can happily eat a couple of extra healthy snacks a day, with the emphasis on healthy. If we eat junk while producing milk, our own body's resources will be tapped for Baby's needs.

Healthy eating is very easy to preach, but very hard to practice at this time of upheaval. You haven't got the time to think of the nutrition going into a meal, and maybe a trip to the grocery store for the fresh ingredients is too much of an expedition with Baby in tow. You are more likely to be ordering take-out again or nuking another portion of Aunty Betty's lasagna that is overflowing from your freezer. It's very easy to eat scrappily, graze and fail to eat regular meals while we put Baby first and ourselves last.

If you've got a lot of pounds to lose, dieting might realistically be the only way you are going to do it. As long as exercise is your first line of defense, cutting back after six weeks is okay, but only in moderation. No crash diets—you shouldn't lose more than a pound a week.

Tips from the Trenches

- If we're feeling a little run-down, blue or stir-crazy, what better than a comfort snack of a nice sugary muffin? Unfortunately most of the quick and easy sugary comfort foods are the culprits of both extra calories and bloating. In your heart you know all the bad stuff that should be avoided like soda pop, chips, cookies and family-size bars of chocolate. If you have problems with temptation, make sure there are none of the offending articles in the house.
- Try cereal bars, a bowl of cereal or fruit salad for a sweet treat to curb cravings.
- Be sure to drink lots of water to keep your digestion going.
- Take the time to sit and eat at least three regular meals a day. It's easy to spend all your time tending to Baby's demands and realize at 5 p.m. that you've only eaten a bowl of cereal today (oh, and that family-size bar of chocolate when you got the shakes at 3 p.m.).
- Eat healthily with your baby once he's on solids. Okay, so this advice isn't going to come into play for a while—no one wants to eat that mush he's saddled with for the first couple of months—but towards the end of the year when you are concentrating on providing him with healthy, balanced meals, practice what you preach and prep a little more of the same for yourself.

C-SECTION RECOVERY

You should have been sent home from hospital with strict instructions on how to take care of yourself after your C-section surgery. Exercise and lifting anything heavier than Baby are out of bounds for about six to eight weeks. You must get the go-ahead from your doctor before embarking on any body reconditioning; however, walking is a good activity to get your blood flowing and speed up the healing process.

Once you are healed, the key to getting a flat tummy is the same as for women who had vaginal deliveries (see **Body Repairs** earlier in this chapter). You need to work the same deepest layer of muscles first, but you have the added complication and frustration of numbness and muscles "not working" in the area of the incision, which can last for a year or more. Exercising might be uncomfortable or even painful if you have a tingling or pulling sensation. It's not very pleasant, but perfectly normal to feel this when you are stretching your scar tissue. If abdominal exercises are hurting you too much, try massaging along your scar and wait a while before trying again, and the discomfort will get better over time. If you have decreased sensation in the area, unfortunately it might take patience and dedication to retrain the muscles and see results.

CHAPTER 15

Mommy Map—Back

BACKACHE

I have to admit that my back is shot. As I sit here writing this, I am in the worst pain I've experienced in my life (aside from labor). So it's my turn to say:

> ## "I wish I had known . . .
> how much parenting can wreak havoc on your back and how important it is to heed advice on postpartum back care."

Your back is very vulnerable right now. The pelvis and the spine joints take time to return to normal after being softened by hormones for childbirth. Also, the stomach muscles (don't worry, they are still there . . . somewhere) that usually help take some of the strain off of the back are weak. All of this, coupled with the strain put on the back by a pregnancy bump and the bruising of the tailbone that can occur during labor, means it will take months to heal. Labor is done (thank heavens) and the bump is gone (mostly), but the potential cause of a chronic backache, namely Baby, is here to stay and getting bigger and heavier every day.

Daily life with a new baby can be compared to starting a new form of exercise program—you will become acutely aware of muscles and parts of your body you never knew you had. Postpartum, your back will be stressed by pushing a stroller, toting Baby around town in a carrier or sling and lifting random baby paraphernalia, like the stroller in and out of the car. Oh, and you may also need to lift the baby from time to time. The 8-pound newborn may not be a strain, but all too soon you'll be hefting 30 pounds about, so it is best not to get into bad habits where lifting is concerned. Also, consider all the additional bending and bobbing to retrieve chucked Cheerios, propelled pasta shapes, tossed toys and spat-out soothers.

I've been there: propped contortionist-style in a chair with a cricked neck and one dead arm, hardly daring to breathe let alone reposition myself because Baby has finally, *finally* dropped off. You might doze in cramped positions on the couch because Baby is balanced on your chest and it's the only way to get him back to sleep between 5 a.m. and a respectable time for getting up. Add to this the strain of the tense, hunched posture of an inexperienced breastfeeding mom and you are setting yourself up for a lot of back pain.

It's very easy to dismiss or forget this kind of advice when you're frazzled and rushing and you just want to get the job done. As a new mom, you're always thinking of Baby's well-being, but you should try really hard to give a thought to your own well-being too. You're worth it, and besides, you'll be little use to Baby if you're half crippled with back pain.

Tips from the Trenches
- Get comfortable before you nurse. Ensure you sit in a supportive chair. A footstool is also useful to help your posture.
- Use a nursing pillow or as many regular pillows as it takes to bring Baby up to boob level; don't hunch over to take the boob to Baby.

- Try to relax while feeding rather than being stiff and tense.
- Make sure your stroller handles are the right height for you. They should be at waist level so that your back is straight and your elbows are slightly bent as you push.
- Make sure your changing table is also at waist level.
- Lift with your legs. Bend your knees into a crouch, keeping your back straight, and then use your leg muscles to lift yourself into a standing position. I admit it's not very graceful squatting with legs akimbo to lift, but then neither is walking like you've pooped your pants when your back has gone into muscle spasm.
- Try going down on one knee instead of bending at the waist to do things such as lift Baby from the stroller.
- Hold Baby close to you when lifting.
- Try not to twist as you lift.
- Limit the use of your baby carrier or sling. Once you've wrestled yourself into the contraption and mastered the tricky task of getting baby safely fastened into it the right way up and facing the way you intended, you may be reluctant to take it off again— or possibly unable to take it off again until someone comes to your aid.

    We are assured that toting Baby round in the carrier or sling all day won't spoil him, but it will spoil your back. Forget all the baloney about bonding with Baby through contact and closeness. You won't be able to do much bonding if you are confined to lying flat on the floor for six weeks with a busted back. If you start to feel your muscles complaining, put Baby down indoors or move him to the stroller outside.
- Getting the baby in and out of the car seat without stressing your back is virtually impossible. I am not sure what to suggest other than to leave it to Dad.

Exercise will help you to strengthen your core abdominal muscles and shed the extra pregnancy pounds that put additional strain on your back. (See the **Body** chapter for suggested core-strengthening exercises.) Strengthen your arm muscles too so you can lift using these muscles rather than your back.

CHAPTER 16

Mommy Map—Nether Regions

PERINEAL DISCOMFORT

They'll probably tell you in the hospital to expect some degree of pain or discomfort in the perineum for about 10 days. In my view they are trying to pretty it up a bit here. It all depends on how much trauma the area went through during labor, but I would set the expectations more realistically at feeling uncomfortable for up to a month.

If you had a vaginal delivery, your already sensitive perineum has been bruised, stretched and (curl the toes; sorry to remind you) possibly torn or cut to assist delivery. Your vagina is also swollen and bruised from being stretched. Think of your body like a kid's toy at Christmas: all expertly packaged and sealed, but once it's been ripped open and the toy yanked out, what sort of mess are you left with? Right now the packaging is all bent out of shape and busted. Good thing you don't want to put the toy back in! If you had stitches, they will dissolve after five or six days. The swelling will go down in a few days as your muscle tone returns, and the vagina will continue to contract over a few weeks, although it will never be as tight as it was before you were pregnant.

Each maternity nurse brought her own talents to my experience in the hospital. Most were sweet, jovial and intent on making sure Baby was doing well, but there was one stern, no-nonsense gal that dealt with Mom's nitty-gritty undercarriage stuff. I will forever be grateful to her for the lifesaving items she sent me home with: a plastic squirty bottle and a little container of soothing witch hazel. They may not seem like much, but as far as I was concerned these were priceless gifts that got me through the next few days of unpleasantness and stopped me from going out of my mind.

To be honest, I was "aware" of that part of my body for months afterwards. I would liken it to how your mouth feels after a rigorous scrape and clean at the dentist. Your teeth are all pulled out of alignment and you kind of know they are there for some time afterwards. Vaginal discomfort and dryness can be a problem for months for breastfeeding moms, even if their delivery was by C-section, due to abnormal hormone levels. This lack of natural lubrication can cause chafing and itchiness.

Comrades' Recommendations

- Take the drugs! The hospital sends you home armed with some heavy-duty painkillers like Tylenol 3 to get you through the early days.
- Get a squirty bottle full of warm water and spray this on your perineum as you pee to reduce the stinging sensation.
- Soak a pad in soothing witch hazel and wear it for a few minutes.
- Changing your pads regularly keeps the area from becoming damp and creating the ideal breeding ground for infections.
- Have frequent but short warm baths.
- Start your Kegel exercises as soon as you can possibly bear it. This will improve circulation in the area and speed up recovery. (For more information on the benefits of these exercises, see the **Bladder Control** section later in this chapter.)
- If sitting is really painful, you can invest in a doughnut pillow. As the name suggests, this is a ring that prevents you from putting your weight on the traumatized area.
- Unless you are a fan of the *Saw* movies, don't look at the damage. Ignorance may not be bliss in this case, but it can certainly make you feel a little faint to come face-to-face with the disaster zone.

POSTPARTUM BLEEDING

With any luck you were sent home from the hospital well-informed on what to expect in the way of postpartum bleeding. While you should anticipate a fair amount of bleeding, it is important to know how much is too much as a postpartum hemorrhage is extremely dangerous and needs to be treated immediately.

It will normally take two to three weeks for your body to completely clear out after the birth, although some form of bleeding can continue for up to six weeks. It's essentially a long, heavy period that starts with bright red blood for about four days, then gradually fades and lessens to brownish or pinkish, and then tapers off to a yellow/white discharge. Initially you may see blood clots, which can be alarming, but it's perfectly normal as long as they aren't bigger than the size of a grape. Other messy tissue debris from the uterus lining will also be flushed out.

In the hospital you kind of just sit or lie around bleeding on things. It's shocking at first, and you try to keep clean, but you soon realize it's a losing battle and just let nature take its course. What the heck, they're used to gore; besides, the sheets get boiled when washed. As for your attire, what's to spoil? The tie-at-the-back nightie or those bizarre net knickers? What is the idea behind these odd undergarments? Are they cost-effective on fabric, designed for maximum airflow or an eco-friendly option to create less waste for the landfills? I found them mystifying. At the hospital, everything gets sterilized or disposed of, but you aren't going to want to treat your sofa cushions the same way, so once you're at home, it's best to take precautions. Sit on towels for the time being and don't wear anything you don't want to ruin. You should be over the worst by the time you leave the hospital, but getting up after a long time sitting can cause a gush that even an industrial-strength maxi pad can't contain. You'll need to stock up on pads for heavy flow. You shouldn't use tampons for about six weeks, as you are prone to infection at this point.

It's not normal for the heavy bright-red bleeding to continue beyond a week, nor should you expect to soak pads in less than an hour or pass golf ball–sized clots. Other warning signs of a problem are having foul-smelling discharge or feeling faint. If you experience any of these symptoms, call the community health nurse or see your doctor straight away.

BLADDER CONTROL

It takes one honest, brave friend to admit to something like peeing her pants. A mortified new mommy friend admitted to a group of us she'd rejoined her running club but had to drop out half way on the first run because she was leaking pee. Hearing this actually made me happy, not because I'm evil, but because I was relieved to hear I wasn't the only one. I had experienced the same thing walking home from a Christmas party where I'd enjoyed my first few alcoholic drinks after having Baby. I was too busy concentrating on aching feet from wearing high heels for the first time in ages, and alcohol numbs the senses. Lucky for me I was wearing black pants, and I hope to goodness the babysitter didn't notice. I was so embarrassed, I didn't even tell my husband.

One-quarter of postpartum women suffer with "stress incontinence" caused by pressure on your pelvic floor during pregnancy and labor. Maybe you experienced a loss of bladder control during pregnancy—for example, when you coughed or sneezed—but at the time you were likely not doing much vigorous exercise so the effects were limited. If you are suffering after delivery, my advice would be to avoid jumping jacks for the time being.

Tips from the Trenches

- Be prepared: when you go to exercise for the first time after having Baby, wear a pad just in case anything embarrassing happens.
- Avoid caffeine and alcohol.
- Steer clear of trampolines.

Did anyone mention Kegels to you at some point in the last year? Good for you if you took notice and were diligently tightening these muscles throughout pregnancy; you can probably skip this section! On the other hand, you could be thinking, "Hmmm, sounds familiar. Was it covered in prenatal classes; at the hospital; did the community health nurse mention it; is it a type of breakfast cereal?" If you had any idea what they were talking about, it probably didn't make much sense or seem very important at the time. After your undercarriage is stretched all out of proportion during labor, you may suddenly find out the hard way that these little muscles are really pretty useful. They are the ones that play a big part in bladder control and the ones you'll want to tone up ASAP. It's a complicated little exercise: a squeeze and lift of the pelvic floor. It's always billed as a discreet exercise you can do anywhere: in the gym on a body ball; while watching TV; even in the queue at the grocery store. Personally I found it more than a little tricky to locate and isolate these muscles. Even now I can only do so giving it my full concentration sitting on a body ball, and by my facial contortions anyone observing would be led to think I had a bad case of gas.

Try it: I bet you're also sucking in your stomach, squeezing your thighs or your buttocks, or all three. It feels like you're doing something, but are you doing anything with the right muscles? Try to lift and squeeze just the pelvic floor. Got it? Ah, but are you holding your breath? Apparently that's not allowed either. Aim to hold the contraction for eight seconds, rest for four, contract for eight, etc. You need to build up to doing about 120 a day. To ensure you've identified the correct muscles, try stopping yourself peeing when you are on the toilet.

You probably will only do your Kegels sporadically unless you set yourself a serious target. Are you really going to take time to do them before you fall exhausted into bed at night? My tip would be to do a set with each of Baby's feeding sessions. This timetable ensures you do several sets a day, and the baby's great big noggin right there in front of you will serve as a good reminder to do them.

If bladder control doesn't improve over time as your body heals and exercise tones up your muscles, ask your doctor for help. He can refer you to physiotherapists who will teach you the proper way to do Kegels (you're probably not contracting them effectively) and other exercises to help tone up the pelvic floor muscles.

CONSTIPATION

Women are often frightened to have a poop after the birth, and no wonder. Aside from perineal pain, there is also the fear of everything "down there" bursting open if you've got stitches. The thought of wiping isn't too appealing either. It's quite normal for your digestive system to be on a bit of a go-slow at this time due to a combination of hormones and muscle relaxation in pregnancy. Often it's a while before you need to—or dare—go. So quite often you end up suffering from constipation.

Survival Secrets

- Up the fiber in your diet. Eat whole grain bread and pasta and lots of fruit 'n' veg. Gone are the days when chewing on the cereal box was preferable to trying to get through a bowl of bran for breakfast. There is now a big selection of palatable high fiber cereals. Sprouted grain bread is also worth trying. It might be a bit chewy as sandwich bread, but is quite tasty toasted.
- Prunes, figs, prune juice: you might not like them, but they help.
- Drink lots of water. If you are nursing you should be doing this anyway, but aim for eight to ten glasses a day. Nursing moms are typically dehydrated.
- Get your feet moving with a brisk walk and it might help get other things moving too.
- Don't hold on to a bowel movement—brave it and go as soon as you feel the need.
- Try to avoid laxatives or stool softeners taken orally if you are breastfeeding as the effects could be passed on to Baby through your milk. 'Nuff said.

HEMORRHOIDS

Another unmentionable, but again you are not alone if you are suffering. These ghastly little things (or not-so-little things) are common in postpartum women after the pushing of labor—the baby wasn't the only thing that popped out! They are varicose veins of the rectum that resemble little bunches of grapes. They can be painful—and even bleed, especially when you are trying to poop—and can be itchy and uncomfortable all the time. If you suffered with piles before or during pregnancy, they are likely to show up again postpartum.

It's a vicious circle because constipation after birth aggravates piles, and the more you hold back from bowel movements because of the pain, the worse the constipation gets.

Survival Secrets

- Follow the guidelines above for avoiding and curing constipation, and this pain in the butt should soon leave.
- To ease the discomfort, take warm baths.

- If wiping with toilet paper is painful or irritating, use unscented wet wipes instead, or wash after a poop.
- Witch hazel on a pad can be very soothing.
- Kegel exercises also help as they increase healing blood flow to the area.
- There are many ointments, like the delightfully named Anusol, for treatment and easing discomfort of hemorrhoids. If you had tearing or episiotomy during labor, you should avoid using these before getting the okay from your doctor.

RETURN OF PERIODS

There is no sensible answer to the question of when your periods will return after having a baby. There are all sorts of factors that can affect the arrival time, and even if I bothered to list them it's still impossible to predict when it might happen to you. Like so many other postpartum issues it is an individual response. Here are some ballpark figures.

- If you aren't breastfeeding, expect your period to return between four and twelve weeks after the birth.
- It's true that breastfeeding usually delays the return of menstruation. Nursing moms get their period on average after four to six months, but the range can be anywhere from six weeks to eighteen months.

It can take a while for your cycle to regulate. Periods can be erratic at first. They can return with a vengeance, or they may start with spotting and gradually build up to more regular periods over a few months. They won't necessarily be as you remember them either. They might be heavier, longer, lighter, shorter and more or less painful than they used to be.

If you are still breastfeeding when your period returns, it is possible that the event will not go unnoticed by Baby. The hormonal changes can cause a drop in milk supply, and Baby might react to the change to her meal by fussing at the breast.

RETURN TO SEX

Resuming sexual relations has to be the most discussed topic in mommy circles. It seems fairly common for there to be both physical hurdles and mental challenges involved. The authors of the very funny book *How Not to Completely Suck as a New Parent* had a very short chapter dedicated to "Resuming Sexual Relations After the Birth of Your Child." It consisted of just two words: "As if."

Let's start off being optimistic and assume you and Dad are relatively issue-free and eager to know when you can finally get close without that great bump in between you. The official medical okay for new parents to have sex is around six weeks after delivery. You may feel ready for sex before this, or you may not feel ready for weeks or even months. You should listen to your body, and if the perineal pain and discomfort are a dim and distant memory and you feel emotionally ready, then go for it. The recommendation for getting back to exercise is also six weeks, so this is a pretty good indication that it's best not to push the envelope before this. All forms of exercise should be taken slowly and the effort increased gradually. Sex is a pretty vigorous workout, so take it easy. It might be better to choose a position where Mom is in the driver's seat as she can then control the depth of penetration. It's also a good idea to plan ahead and purchase some lubricant, since you are likely to be dryer after giving birth, especially if you are breastfeeding. It's best to feed Baby before you head for the bedroom for a couple of reasons: first, it gives you a maximum window of opportunity before the next meal demand (if you're lucky); second, since the same hormones are rushing about during sex as during breastfeeding, you may experience some leaking or spraying of milk, which will be worse if your boobs are full. Don't be put off if you have pain or discomfort the first time. Give yourself some more time to heal before trying again. With all the stretching of vaginal births, you might also find the experience somewhat lacking in satisfaction. I once heard postpartum sex described as "throwing a hot dog down a hallway." Enter the Kegel exercises again to tighten those muscles.

If you read this section and laughed, or even cried, because that six-week mark came and went ages ago and sex is still not something you want to contemplate, be assured you aren't alone. There are many reasons why you can be feeling unsexy. Take a look at **The Mind** chapter for some more information and tips on getting the fires going again.

CONTRACEPTION

As soon as you are "back on the horse," or rather before you saddle up, you need to consider contraception. Since there is no hard and fast rule as to when you start ovulating again, it is impossible to tell whether you are fertile. Just because your period hasn't returned yet doesn't mean you can't fall pregnant again. Unless you are mad enough to want—sorry; I mean, "unless you are ready"—to hear the patter of another pair of tiny feet soon, then you should take precautions.

Don't just grab a pack from a leftover birth-control-pill stash and resume taking them; it's quite possible they passed their expiry date. Also, if you are breastfeeding, some pills, contraceptive rings or patches are not suitable as they can reduce milk supply. Condoms are, of course, a safe bet until you can get to your doctor to discuss options.

CHAPTER 17

Mommy Map—Legs and Feet

VARICOSE VEINS

I had a summer baby and a winter baby, and I have to say it is far more convenient to have a baby in the winter months when you can take liberties with unshaved legs under long pants. Rookie moms barely have time to shower, let alone groom. When you do finally get around to shaving your legs a month (who am I kidding?—a few months) after having the baby, you might not like what you find. Ugly varicose veins may have emerged. They could have actually made an appearance during pregnancy when blood pressure in the leg veins increased under the weight of your expanding uterus. You are more likely to suffer if varicose veins run in the family or if you are overweight.

There are degrees of unpleasantness with varicose veins, from blue lines under the skin to more unsightly bulges. They can be itchy or a bit achy or painful, but are rarely a threat to your health. The only real danger from varicose veins is if you develop a blood clot. This only happens to a small percentage of people. If you find a red, tender area on the vein, go to the doctor to have it assessed.

The good news: Varicose veins tend to improve after pregnancy once the extra pressure is gone.

The bad news: At three to four months postpartum, if they are still visible, they probably aren't going to improve on their own.

More bad news: It's too late to take any prevention or minimization advice (avoid too much pressure on your legs during pregnancy by putting your feet up; exercise to improve circulation; sleep on your left side; wear support tights (sexy!); don't stand for long periods; don't cross your legs when sitting).

The good news: You can consider these tips next pregnancy.

The bad news: Once you have them, they tend to get worse with each pregnancy.

The good news: They are surgically correctable with laser treatment.

The bad news: This is fairly expensive if not covered through insurance.

So, if you can't live with them, save your pennies while you complete your family, and once all the damage has been done, splurge on the surgery. In fact, as my left calf resembles a relief map of the Rockies, when all the royalties come flooding in from this book I'm going to get mine fixed up. Thanks for the donation!

BIGGER FEET?

Oh, I've heard it all now. It's understandable that having a baby might stretch your private parts a tad and stretch your stomach skin a bit more than a tad. But come on, stretched feet? Apparently yes, you can end up with bigger feet.

Feet tend to swell during pregnancy due to fluid retention and weight gain, and will return to normal a month or so postpartum. However, the body also produces a hormone called *relaxin*, which is "relaxin' " your pelvis joints to make it possible to let the baby out. This hormone also causes ligament stretching in the feet. The bones are less tightly held together, so they spread out, making the feet grow bigger and making them stay bigger. Some moms will notice their postpartum feet have "grown" a half or a whole shoe size. Luckily the feet don't grow a further size with each pregnancy, so if you are planning a big family, don't worry: you won't end up having to shop for clown shoes.

CHAPTER 18

Mommy Map—Skin

STRETCH MARKS

"Be proud of your stretch marks," they try to convince us, "they are symbols of the wonderful experience of pregnancy and childbearing." Phooey! Let's face it; even if you dub them "badges of honor," stretch marks are still ugly. No one wants them, but over 75 percent of women will get them. The red, purple and brown lines are caused by inflammation, which occurs when the flexible components of your skin have been stretched beyond their limits and finally split. Stretch marks will fade to silvery scars but will not disappear. On any part of your body where you put on weight rapidly, you may notice stretch marks once things get back to a more normal size. This means not only your tummy, but also your hips, thighs, butt and even boobs.

Don't waste money on creams that promise magic. The only way to reduce the appearance of stretch marks is through laser therapy, and this is a pricey patch-up rather than a fix.

PERSPIRATION

For a couple of weeks after giving birth you may find yourself perspiring profusely. You probably thought that it was the stress of getting Baby into the car seat for the ride home from the hospital that got you all hot under the collar. Or was it the pain of trying to shuffle from the car into the house that made you break out in a sweat? While these are valid causes for getting a bit hot and bothered, it was probably the first of many hot flashes you could experience for the initial couple of weeks.

They are caused by hormones instructing your body to get rid of stored fluids, which is really good news because it will reduce your weight by a couple of pounds.

Survival Secrets

- The excessive perspiration is more common at night, so sleep on towels to avoid adding sheets and pillow slips to the ever-growing laundry mountain. In the first few nights you can be excreting all over the place: bleeding down there, sweating like a pig, and soon enough, your milk comes in and adds to the deluge. Forget the bed; it may be best to sleep in a kids' wading pool.
- Make sure you drink lots of water so you don't dehydrate, especially if you are breastfeeding.
- Wear 100 percent cotton garments, particularly to bed, and you will be more comfortable.

THE BEAT-UP LOOK

They told you not to push with your face. "Push DOWN HERE," they yelled. As if you could do anything to order at that time. The result of extreme strain in your upper body during labor could result in red or purple marks on your face and chest, and bloodshot or black eyes. These are caused by tiny blood capillaries that burst under the increased pressure. You don't need to do anything; just wait for a few days to a couple of weeks for the evidence of your ordeal to disappear.

ACNE

"I wish I had known . . .

my complexion would be worse than it was when I was a teenager. I am one mess of spots and blotches. I really don't want to be in the baby photos at all."

Bloody hormones! Here they are causing trouble again. Fluctuating hormone levels mean that for two or three months you may find yourself with bad skin. It may be oilier than you are used to, or in some cases, drier. Typical new mom issues like lack of sleep, stress, bad nutrition and dehydration can increase the chances of complexion problems. Plus, although meticulous attention is given to caring for Baby's skin down to the last pinkie, I doubt you've been spending much time on your own daily skin-care routine since her arrival.

Survival Secrets

- Eat well. Make time for nutritious meals and snacks. Ensure you are getting your daily servings of fruit 'n' veg.
- Take a postpartum multivitamin.
- Drink eight to ten glasses of water a day to stay hydrated.
- Try to make time for a daily cleanse and moisturize, and stick to plain, unscented, oil-free, non-comedogenic cleansers and moisturizers.
- If you're breastfeeding, don't slap on acne treatments without consulting your doctor first. Chemicals could be absorbed into breast milk and make it through to Baby.
- You may have developed a postpartum thyroid problem if your skin is unusually dry and you are suffering from other related symptoms (see **Fatigue** in **The Mind** chapter). Mention it to your doctor.

PREGNANCY MASK

If you suffered during pregnancy with dark pigmentation patches on your face, commonly known as a pregnancy mask, don't expect them to disappear immediately after Baby is born. It will usually take a few months for these to fade as your hormone levels gradually return to normal. If you are breastfeeding, it may not happen until you wean. There isn't much you can do besides waiting it out and buying another tube of your favorite concealer. Protecting yourself from the sun is advised, as sun exposure will exacerbate the condition. Some moms do have permanent or recurring darkening (especially if they return to using a contraceptive pill, ring or patch that contains estrogen) and should consult a doctor or dermatologist if it bothers them.

CHAPTER 19

Mommy Map—The Mind

FATIGUE

Be prepared to be tired. "Oh, come on," I'm sure you're snorting
scornfully, "tell me something I don't already know." If you didn't
even know that, where have you been for the last nine months?
Did you even know you were pregnant? My bet is that during
your pregnancy several old hand parents laughed knowingly
and smugly warned you that once the baby arrives you'll never
have a decent night's sleep again. You didn't really believe them;
at least you didn't want to. I'm here to tell you that you won't be
tired at all. You will be TIRED, burned-out, out of it, wrecked,
wretched, disoriented, discombobulated, exhausted and TIRED.
In this first year a new mom can expect to lose, on average, 700
hours of sleep.

"I wish I had known . . .

how lousy sleep deprivation would make me feel. All I wanted to do
was go to a hotel for a night and *sleep.*"

Your sleep is rationed; your sleep is broken. You're physically
drained and emotionally run-down. You're learning new skills and,
if breastfeeding, using up precious energy producing milk. Your eyes
feel like they are full of sand. I used to have the "gray meanies" in my
head: giant cell formations dancing on my closed eyelids. You move
around like a zombie, like you've got the worst hangover.

Over the years you've probably burned the candle at both ends, worked long hours and partied long hours, but it didn't go on incessantly. You could drop out at any time, throw a "sickie," go home and get some sleep. A baby doesn't let you do that. Your instincts won't let you do that. Now you have the hangover without having done the partying—that's a real kick in the teeth.

Don't worry; this extreme fatigue will only last about three months while the baby is settling in and your body is recovering. Then you should settle down to moderate exhaustion. Soon you'll be discontinuing night feeds, and you'll get to sleep through for one blissful night and think you've got it cracked—but oh no. You still have those freaky bat ears waking you at every stirring, and the little imp will soon find another reason to disturb you in the middle of the night: teething; a cold or cough; change in seasons; daylight savings time; lost soother. That should get you through the first year. In the years to follow (as a little enticement to read our sequel), you can look forward to: nightmares; separation anxiety; lost teddy; too hot/cold/light/dark; thirsty; toilet trained and needing a pee; sort of toilet trained and peed the bed; in a big boy's bed from which he can climb out or fall. If you're lucky, you might get a week of uninterrupted sleep before the next crisis hits, and all too soon you'll be lying awake waiting for the sound of the key in the door.

It's easy to imagine that you once had some pool of life force inside you and the baby soaked it up while in the womb and grabbed the remaining energy on the way out. It's why a baby greets the new day with a beam and an up-and-at-'em attitude, while your first thought is, "Oh crap, get me a coffee." Over the next few years you will likely explain away your baby's fussiness, your toddler's tantrum and your little kid's crankiness by saying, "Oh, he's just tired." Think about yourself. You are super tired; no wonder you feel like having a meltdown.

Survival Secrets

- There's really nothing you can do about it. You just have to live with the suitcases under your eyes until the kid is old enough to be sent to boarding school.
- You know the drill: sleep when the baby sleeps. It is sage advice. Even if there are a million other things to do, it's important for you to get sleep when you can.

- If you are a breastfeeding mom reaching the end of your tether, express milk so Dad can take over a night feed.
- Stop feeling sluggish by taking a daily walk in the fresh air.

If we prepare you for the worst and it doesn't feel that bad to you (you're only exhausted, not the living dead) then you should be extremely relieved. I've scanned popular parenting website FAQs and not once have I seen, "I heard I would be exhausted with a new baby, but I feel chipper. Is there anything wrong with me?" My advice to that mom would be, "No, you're fine and lucky, but if you repeat that comment in mommy circles, you may not be fine for long."

If extreme fatigue persists into the second half of the year, it is possible that you are suffering from postpartum thyroiditis; up to 10 percent of new moms do. It's hard to detect simply because the symptoms are all par for the course for a postpartum mom. In addition to feeling TIRED, you are gaining weight or not losing pregnancy pounds as you'd hoped, have dry skin, are experiencing worrying hair loss, have a mind like a sieve, are feeling cold, are suffering with constipation or are feeling depressed or highly emotional. It's worth mentioning these symptoms to your doctor because a simple blood test can confirm if you have a thyroid problem. It is not serious and will probably right itself in time—usually a few months—but it can also be treated.

EMOTIONAL ROLLER COASTER

Have you turned into a big softy? Do you burst into tears at the drop of a hat? You're not alone. Many rookie moms admit to crying at things they thought they'd long since gotten over, like Dumbo being separated from his mommy. I get watery eyed now over someone massacring the national anthem at a hockey game, and it's not even my national anthem and I don't even like hockey. Pregnancy hormones and the birth of a baby often unleash an emotional side you may not have had before. Reports of sick or deprived kids can particularly pull at the heartstrings and have you reaching for the tissues. Motherhood changes the way you see the world. Maybe it's because you can't afford to be as selfish any more, if you ever were. I think it makes you a better person, even if it's a sappy better person.

MOMMY BRAIN

In the space of one week I left my purse at the checkout, a bag of goods at the gift shop . . . and there was a third mishap, but I've forgotten what it was. Does it exist or not? What were we talking about? Oh yes, mommy brain. It's hard to find concrete medical evidence for mommy brain, but there are thousands of postings on the web from moms vehemently agreeing that motherhood turns your brain to mush. I'm sure you're doing some vigorous nodding in agreement right now. Be careful, all that nodding is shaking the last few brain cells loose. You know the sort of thing: you forget the basics like brushing your teeth or you leave the washing in the machine for hours, noting that it needs to come out every time you walk past it en route to some other task, then "poof," the thought vaporizes. I lost count of the number of times I found myself standing in a room with no clue as to why I was there. Short-term memory loss; general memory loss (some call it "Momnesia"); doing silly things; doing downright stupid things; lacking concentration; being unable to finish a conversation; being unable to finish a sente . . . You used to be a together, capable, intelligent woman who could write a shopping list, remember to take it and her purse to the store, remember to bring the groceries and her purse back home, and even put the cold things in the fridge, not the cereal cupboard.

Sufferers of mommy brain may not be surprised to hear that our brains actually shrink during pregnancy and don't return to normal size until six months postpartum. Your brain is altered by childbirth because different parts of it are required to be on full alert to nurture the baby. Rather than suggesting you have lost intelligence, let's just say it is being channeled elsewhere—it's a time of learning. Your life now is full of new responsibility, and you are consumed with your new world. You're drained by constantly thinking of Baby's needs and performing mundane tasks.

Sleep deprivation has to be the primary suspect. It's a fact that you function better on a good night's sleep. A good night's sleep is not just defined by the duration of sleep, but also by whether it's uninterrupted. Remember one of those? Mommy brain or not, you must remember that. The experts say you remember things better if you sleep on them. Stress is another contributor to memory function. On top of all that, breastfeeding keeps us drugged with hormones, making us less focused and unable to concentrate. Yes, rookie moms are doomed.

Mommy brain serves one useful purpose. A year down the line, you won't recall the pain of labor or the most hellish days of new motherhood, and you'll decide to go through it again. Mommy brain ensures the survival of our species. On the flip side, if you want to remember anything about bringing up this baby to help you with later additions, start a diary now. I guarantee in a couple of years' time you won't remember a thing.

Comrades' Recommendations

- Write it all down. For example, when the pediatrician gives you important advice, record it. The act of writing ensures you are paying attention and establishes information in the brain, so you may not even need to refer to your notes when Dad asks how things went at the doc's. You can come back with an intelligent synopsis of the visit, instead of "Huh?"
- Get napping. Like you need an excuse. A decent hour's nap is a good reviver for both mind and body. Handily, babies tend to nap for this amount of time. If yours isn't cooperating or you aren't a good napper, get to bed early. So life is dull and you're in bed every night by 9 p.m.; it won't be forever.
- Eat regularly and nutritiously.
- If you are apt to forget things when in a rush, prep your bag well in advance, such as the night before when you have time to think and remember the 1,001 baby essentials that need to be taken whenever you venture out.
- Ask your doctor about a multivitamin and mineral supplement suitable for postpartum women. Fish oils can help your brain function, iron in particular helps your memory, and calcium and B vitamins can help you sleep.
- Buy an intravenous coffee drip, now available in the gift section at Starbucks.

Don't worry; when you return to work you won't find yourself relegated to making the coffee (unless you work in a Starbucks; then you probably will find yourself making the coffee—or selling the intravenous coffee drips). I have it on good authority that returning to work is a good brain boost. The daily mundane baby-grind is someone else's job right now, leaving you with more mental capacity to concentrate on your job. Carry a toothbrush in your purse, just in case you have a relapse and forget to brush your teeth . . . again.

CONSTANT WORRY

A common complaint we've heard from new moms is that they didn't enjoy early motherhood because they were constantly worried: about being a good mom, about keeping their relationship on an even keel, but first and foremost, about the baby.

These kinds of worries and many, many others probably flip through your mind a hundred times a day. Of course they do. I haven't met a parent who doesn't worry, and old hands will tell you the worry never stops, even when your baby is old enough to have his or her own babies. When motherhood is all so new and your seemingly helpless little mite is reliant on you for everything, the worry can become overwhelming. It is natural to be anxious, but remind yourself that worrying about something beyond your control doesn't actually help; it doesn't change the outcome. I know; telling a worrier not to worry is pointless. If worrying were a competitive event, I'd have to invest in a cabinet to house my trophy collection.

Aim to live each day without anticipating what tomorrow will bring. It's easy to get caught up worrying that every day will be like today; every night like this one. Baby might not eat today, but will probably be hungry tomorrow. On a rough night when Baby has woken five times, don't assume that you won't get any sleep tomorrow night either. Try not to think of a bad day as the new norm—wait and see what tomorrow brings.

I know firsthand that it's easy to get caught in a trap of making it all more difficult than it needs to be. Rather than over-complicating matters, try to do what you want to do rather than what you feel you should do. Relax and enjoy! Keep reminding yourself that generations of parents have successfully survived year one of parenthood and all that lies in wait after that. Did our grandparents read any parenting advice manuals? I doubt it. Did our parents have the web to surf for advice on nutritious infant feeding? No. Heck, does a mommy lion need help getting her wee one to finish up his wildebeest leg? No. (Hang on, maybe she does—it could be a gap in the market. Contact the publisher!) Put this dumb book back on the shelf and trust your instincts. Right now your instincts tell you that this is a great book, so get it back off the shelf and carry on reading.

BABY BLUES

Fifty to eighty percent of new moms will suffer from a short period of emotional instability known as "the baby blues," which can strike suddenly a few days after giving birth. This phase of tearfulness, fatigue, irritability and anxiety is not serious and is not an illness, and it disappears without treatment after about 10 days.

Do you remember being on a high immediately after the birth despite the hard work of labor and lack of sleep? I was buzzing like I'd had a triple espresso. I phoned people I hadn't spoken to in years and regaled them with my heroic tale of childbirth. That was hormones playing games again. A few hours later, hormone levels drop suddenly and rapid changes take place in your body. These physical changes, linked with exhaustion and emotional factors such as anxiety over your new responsibilities, can contribute to the blues. During this blue period, try to rest when you can. Even a quick 10-minute nap can perk you up. Accept all offers of help and support from family and friends.

You should soon feel brighter; still unbelievably tired, but brighter. However, if there is no improvement in how you feel after a few weeks or if depression descends on you later during the first year of motherhood, you could be suffering from postpartum depression, a more serious condition for which you will need to seek help.

POSTPARTUM DEPRESSION

So, that gorgeous baby that you've been excitedly planning for and looking forward to has arrived. You're out of the rat race, and glorious months of mat leave stretch in front of you. You are so lucky; you couldn't be happier—or could you? You knew becoming a mom was going to be a change of lifestyle and a lot of hard work, and—unless you were in denial—you guessed it would be tiring. But you also expected being a new parent to be a fulfilling, joyous period in your life. It can come as a bit of a shock, a huge disappointment and can ultimately be very worrisome when, instead of being full of joy, you are filled with despair. You may feel various negative emotions such as confusion, irritability, anxiety or anger, or you may just feel downright miserable and not even be able to get out of bed. If so, you could be suffering from postpartum depression (PPD).

You are not alone. As many as one in five moms are struck with some degree of PPD soon after the birth of their baby, or later through the child's toddlerhood. My mom suffered when I was a small colicky baby. She would be fine on weekends when my dad was around, then cry uncontrollably when he tried to leave for work on Monday mornings. I suffered later; not severely, but I knew something was wrong when my waking thought would be, "When can I get back into bed?" I finally mustered courage to consult a doctor when my baby was almost one, but the symptoms had been slowly creeping up on me for about six months by then.

PMS sufferers will be familiar with the horrible, irrational mood settling in and the realization dawning on you that a month has gone around again. There is nothing you can do to control it; it just creeps up and plagues you for a day or two and then is gone. PPD is like a long, drawn-out bout of PMS that hangs around indefinitely.

The severity scale is quite broad, ranging from feeling mildly depressed, overwhelmed and anxious, to extreme cases in which anger and frustration reach worrying levels and Mom wishes fervently that the baby hadn't been born. All the while, she is guilt-ridden for feeling this way. If you are ever worried that you might hurt baby in your rage, walk away and leave her—go to another room so you can't hear the cries. My mom was advised by her doctor to park my stroller at the end of the yard whenever I was screaming my head off and it was getting to her. I hope it was summer. Hey, wait a minute—I was born in September. That was kind of mean.

Because PPD is a mental condition, it's hard to diagnose and hard for you to be sure you are suffering from it. You might wonder if you are imagining it, making it up or just being weak and feeble. You might wonder if you are going crazy. But probably not if you are suffering from a mix of the following:

- trouble sleeping
- lack of energy
- hobbies and interests no longer appealing
- loss of appetite or eating too much
- excessive crying

- irritability
- bouts of anger and frustration
- feeling sad and worthless
- feelings of helplessness, uselessness or inadequacy
- emotional numbness
- loss of sexual desire
- physical symptoms such as headaches, stomachaches and muscle aches
- having unloving, scary or violent thoughts towards your baby
- having nightmares about something happening to you or your family
- panic attacks or just constantly feeling anxious (For example, an everyday activity like grocery shopping makes you agitated; you feel the need to abandon the task and get home, or you feel unable to make simple choices.)

Why Are You Feeling This Way?

Hormones play a part, of course, but there are many factors besides a chemical imbalance that can contribute to PPD. Just a few are listed here. You will probably spot one or two that apply to you, but there are no hard and fast rules. Just because none of these sound familiar doesn't mean you aren't suffering from PPD.

- You lack a support network.
- You lack structure during the day.
- You feel let down that you aren't living the dream of motherhood.
- There is an unequal division of child care and domestic duties in your household.
- You have anxiety over Baby.

- You have extra challenges associated with a sick or high-maintenance baby such as a colic sufferer.
- You are a bit of a perfectionist.
- You are self-critical.
- Your mom suffered from PPD.
- You or members of your family have a history of depression.
- You have had upheaval in your life recently, such as moving, relationship changes or the loss of a loved one.
- You are particularly sensitive to changes in your life.

What Can Help?
You need to find ways to get back in tune with your old self. Remember, you are still an individual and a capable woman, the only difference being that now you are also a mom. Someone once calculated that if you had to pay employees to do all the work a housewife/mother does, you would be out of pocket about $100,000 a year. Yet a mom earns no base salary, no overtime for those (frequent) all-nighters, no bonus for pulling off a difficult task like potty training and no holiday allowance. Heck, she doesn't even get a lunch break. On top of this, there is little social recognition of how much work is involved. You often hear a stay-at-home mom referred to as "just a housewife." You may feel this way yourself or be reluctant to say that's what you do. There is no "just" about being a mom. Give yourself credit for what you do. Mothering is a complex and challenging job.

Here are some DIY therapies to help you regain your sense of self worth.

Comrades' Recommendations

- Make sure you eat regular nutritious meals and sit down to eat them. Irregular meals and junk food will make you feel more sluggish.
- Catch up on sleep by napping or resting when Baby is napping.
- Accept help when it is offered by your partner, family or friends.
- Try to shower, brush your teeth, do your hair and put on makeup before your partner heads off to work. If you look more like your old self, you will feel more like your old self.

- Take time out to have a leisurely bath and pamper yourself.
- Arrange a weekly "night off" or regular time to yourself on the weekend when your partner is around to look after the baby. Get away from Baby so you're not tempted to help out or get involved if there is a problem, even if this means just locking yourself away in a different room with some music on. Try hard to think about something else other than Baby—don't spend your time off worrying. Don't use this time to catch up on chores, even if you think that will make you feel better. Be frivolous and do something you used to enjoy doing before Baby came along.
- If your man isn't available to relieve you of your duties, consider hiring a babysitter just to give you a break now and then.
- Exercise or try some form of relaxation like meditation or yoga. Physical exercise may not be appealing when you are tired, but it will actually make you feel less drowsy. Exercise is now thought to be as effective as antidepressant medication in some cases.
- Go for a walk instead of staying cooped up indoors. Walking is good exercise, and even if you are feeling tired, a walk in the fresh air can pep you up.
- Talk to someone about your feelings. Tell your partner rather than bottle it up.
- Write about your feelings. Get it all out on paper, have a good vent and relieve any remaining stress by ripping it up after. Or keep it as a journal to track your feelings day by day.
- Have a good cry. Sometimes shedding the tears helps to release emotions and relieve stress.
- Get angry. Thump a pillow or scream behind a closed door—vent your frustration in a controlled way.
- Get out and meet some other moms. If you don't even feel like getting out of bed in the morning it will be a struggle, but ultimately you'll feel better than hiding away indoors with only Baby for company. Keep busy. Joining a mommy group or some mom and baby activities will give your week some structure; encourage you to get washed, dressed and brush your teeth; and most importantly give you grown-ups to talk to (providing you have washed, dressed and brushed your teeth, that is). PPD sufferers are often dying for company but, unfortunately, don't want to talk to anyone. They want visitors, but if people come round it means they can't sleep, which is constantly on their minds.

- Chat with other moms. On the surface it may look as though all the other moms are coping, relaxed and happy, but once you start an honest chat you are likely to find others are struggling too. It's a huge relief to know you're not the only one.
- Enlist a comrade. You know how it works when you start an exercise regime with a buddy; it gives you incentive to go. Find a pal (if possible, a forceful personality) who will put pressure on you to get out of the house for walks, fresh air and company.

How Can Dad Help?

He's probably noticed that something is not quite right by the number of times you've bitten his head off, unless you're hiding it really well. Seriously, you should tell your partner exactly how you are feeling and let him know that you need his support. Only if he understands the condition can he know how to act and best help you through it. Research suggests recovery is speedier if your partner is supportive. Let him read any literature you have about the condition. If you are finding it hard to broach the subject, leave this book lying around open at this page. The word **SEX** will likely draw his attention. It will be a relief to Dad to know that you are not undergoing an unpleasant character transformation, but that you are suffering from an illness, and that he can help. The typical guy thing to do is to come up with solutions, and encourage you to "snap out of it" or tough it out. Unfortunately, this positive, gung-ho-attitude approach doesn't help with PPD.

Here are some tips for Dad:

- Listen, listen and listen some more. Even if you've heard the same tearful complaints a hundred times, listen and be sympathetic. Show that you are trying to understand.
- Encourage Mom that she is doing a good job.
- Volunteer to take over baby care and housework while Mom takes a relaxing break.
- Suggest you do the grocery shopping or bring home take-out for dinner. Volunteering to do something goes so much further than being asked, nagged or pleaded with. Despite popular belief, women do not enjoy nagging.
- Help Mom get sleep if at all possible. This is difficult with breast-fed babies, but even one night a week of uninterrupted sleep

will be extremely welcome if you can get Baby to take a bottle of expressed milk.

- Take Baby out for a walk periodically to force Mom not to respond if Baby cries.
- If Mom's PPD is severe and you can afford it, hire some temporary assistance like a babysitter or cleaner. Make sure you broach the subject carefully so as not to make Mom feel even more worthless.
- Don't expect or push for sex. Be patient and affectionate and make do with cuddles and snuggles for the time being and tell her you love her. Mom is probably feeling lonely and undesirable right now and may have fears that because she is not meeting your sexual needs, you are going to pack your bags.
- Support Mom if she decides to seek help from a doctor, therapist or support group. Get involved in the treatment if at all possible.

We mustn't forget that Dad has experienced a big upheaval recently too. There is a chance that he too may suffer from depression, especially if the brunt of the baby care and household chores have fallen to him while you are ill. Your condition means you are not there to support him and be his partner like you used to be. He's not likely getting much affection from you and even less likely any sex. It's difficult for him not to take this personally.

The therapies suggested to Mom also apply to Dad. Both parents need nurturing breaks away from the baby, sometimes alone and sometimes together. On the bright side, if you help each other through this tough period, you can emerge with a stronger relationship.

Who Else Can Help?

The subject of PPD can be somewhat taboo, as it's often associated with the stigma of being a failure as a mother. Far worse, you fear your baby could be taken into care if you admit to any unloving or violent thoughts toward her. Most moms suffering with PPD have similar feelings of guilt and shame; as a result the topic is not openly discussed and sufferers feel isolated. The first important step towards recovery is finding out that you are not alone. The next big hurdle to overcome is actually admitting to someone that you think you have a problem with PPD.

The severity of your depression will dictate the level of help you need. Help is not always that easy to find, but this illness is not likely to go away on its own. You may have to push quite a bit to get help at a time when you're not feeling like being assertive. First, try your family doctor. For starters, the doctor will probably send you for some blood work to rule out postpartum thyroiditis. Five to ten percent of new moms develop thyroid problems postpartum, and the symptoms of the condition are very similar to those of someone suffering from PPD. If blood tests rule out other conditions, the doctor may refer you to a therapist or psychiatrist, or suggest antidepressant medication. Some doctors are more receptive than others. If your doctor is not sympathetic, you might have better luck talking to a community health nurse. She can put you in touch with excellent local support groups that offer different levels of therapy. It may help you just to read the group's literature and to discover the reasons why you might be feeling depressed. It gave me great relief and encouragement just to talk to others who felt the same. Understanding the contributing factors and symptoms is a step on the path to recovery. Support groups hold regular meetings run by a facilitator who has suffered through and recovered from PPD. Support groups often hold information sessions for partners too. Or you may prefer confidential telephone counseling to help you through the bad days.

When Will I Recover?
There is no instant cure for PPD. The healing process is generally a gradual one and often described as a "roller-coaster recovery," since a good day can be followed by a down day. If you are prescribed medication, it may take a month before you notice the effect. PPD can last a few weeks to several months, and some symptoms may linger.

Further down the line, you could notice some of the old, bad feelings are starting to creep back in. This is a signal to stop and take stock. Have the good practices you set up, such as a weekly night off, lapsed since your recovery? Probably, so slow down and take some time for yourself.

What really helped me feel better was writing this book. It gave me something to think about besides my baby. Okay, I was still thinking about babies, but in a constructive way instead of worrying and obsessing. I felt useful, creative and employed. I was tired each day because ideas would pop into my head at night and I'd have to get them written down. But I wouldn't mind feeling tired because there was a good reason behind it, rather than when I used to get further depressed over not having a good reason to be tired. I had to find time to write, and found there was time after all—time I'd previously spent watching reruns on TV or trying to nap because I was so tired from not doing anything . . .

RELATIONSHIP CHANGES

The most important thing in your life is now your baby. He's your new love, project, job and hobby all rolled into one. Other people who were used to being the focus of your affections and your time now have to take a back seat, at least while you get used to your new role and come to grips with how to juggle your priorities. Number one on this list is your man, but there are also changes ahead in your relationships with other members of the family, like the grandparents, and also with your friends.

RELATIONSHIP ISSUES—DAD

Show me a couple who managed to sail along happily in their same established relationship after the arrival of their first baby, and I'll give them a medal—after I've finished chanting "Liar, liar, pants on fire," that is.

I'm not suggesting that your relationship is about to fall apart or be less happy than it was before, but there are bound to be some ups and downs and big changes ahead while you adjust to being a family. Most moms admit that relationship issues and arguments with their partner increased once the new baby was around, and those who considered themselves to be in a very happy relationship showed their first signs of discord. There are many reasons why Baby's arrival can test a couple.

Attention Focus

Suddenly you are infatuated with a new love. Right now, and possibly always, you love your baby more than your man. Okay, so the love is different, but you don't have the time or the inclination to analyze it at the moment. You are wrapped up in your new love and nothing else matters.

As a couple, your partner was the focus of your affections. Without being too cavewoman about it, pre-baby there was probably some part of you that used to enjoy "looking after" your man. Once Baby is on the scene, your mothering instincts shift into gear. Your undivided attention moves to Baby, and suddenly it's no longer possible or appealing to tend to Dad. Maybe you used to enjoy spoiling him and took pride in cooking nice meals and caring for the house. But now you don't have time for any of this and feel he should be taking care of himself, looking after you and pitching in to help with Baby and the house to boot. While it's true that Dad should help out and most will be happy to do so, it's likely that Dad's paternity leave was a measly week or two, so he's probably had to return to work. The sudden change in home life and how you treat him will be a shock to his system, on top of coming to terms with being a father and having to function at work on new-parent sleep rations. So don't expect instant changes and an immediately harmonious new family life. You need to work together to establish a new routine and lifestyle for your family.

Changes in Sex Drive

A big stumbling block in a lot of new parents' relationships is getting some sort of sex life back. The medical sign-off to resume sexual relations is about six weeks after giving birth, but this is purely based on when you'll be physically ready to have sex without excruciating pain. It doesn't take into consideration a raft of other potential setbacks. So, what really happens?

It's a popular discussion topic in mommy circles once babies are about three months old. At least it is once the brave one has broached the subject; then it all comes flooding out. Who has and who hasn't? One tried it once and it hurt—isn't going back there for a while. Another hasn't been near hubby yet. One couple isn't even sleeping in the same bed; Baby has Dad's spot, and Dad's in the spare room with earplugs. One allows hubby to do it, but doesn't enjoy it and tells him to hurry up! One was semi-seriously hoping her man would go off and have an affair to get her off the hook. One friend held out her hands in a scale and told her hubby one end was desire and the other murder. Because he had just given her a foot massage he had inched out of the murder zone, but if he kept going on about having sex he'd be right back where he started. On a positive note, one friend has two daughters 12 months apart— you do the math!

We all know men have stronger sex drives than us, and there is no time when this is more apparent than after the arrival of Baby. Come on: unless you are some sort of sex goddess, the man is starved right now. Whatever rations you doled out to Dad in that short window between puking at the slightest movement and having too much bulk to heft into position (does anyone look at the pregnancy manual for third-trimester sexual positions except for a laugh?), they were likely unadventurous and, let's face it, a long time ago.

Conversely, women often experience a lack of desire after childbirth. Besides their hormones being all out of whack, it's not too hard to see why if you think about it.

- Top of the list: You're TOO TIRED! An early night is now just that. You fall into bed exhausted as early as possible after you've eaten dinner, washed up, put in the last load of washing and given the baby her 10 p.m. feed, knowing that in an unbearably short time you'll be up again giving the baby her 2 a.m. feed . . . then her 6 a.m. feed . . .
- Finding time for sex is hard. If there is a time during the day when you're not doing something with the baby and you're not too tired, you're doing well. Just because the time is available, are you in the mood? It also helps if Dad is there when this blue moon comes around. Once you do have a window of opportunity, is Baby going to sleep long enough to let you finish?
- You might not be too happy about your body right now. You're still trying to lose the extra padding; you've got stretch marks; a lot has happened to you "down there" and you imagine it must be a horrible mess; you just don't feel very glamorous, desirable or sexy.
- If you're breastfeeding, your boobs could be both a physically and emotionally sensitive body part. Besides potentially having sore nipples, they've taken on a new role: they are functional now and you don't feel like they have any part to play in sex. You may feel uncomfortable about the switch from Baby using your boobs to breastfeed immediately after or before using your body sexually.
- Although it's a different kind of love, a lot of your emotional focus has now shifted to Baby, and you may be feeling distant from Dad while you adjust to your new role as a mom.

Personally, I think there should be a sex talk scheduled for dads at the hospital while the moms are busy bleeding all over the place. At this information session, a little (okay, big) white lie should be told: he shouldn't expect his wife to be ready for sex until Baby's first birthday. That sets nice, comfortable expectations, and if it happens any time before, you'll be seen as an eager-beaver sex goddess.

How to Rekindle the Desire

Here's a big tip for the guys: doing household chores could be a new and effective form of foreplay! Amongst all this new relationship turbulence, what used to work might not work any longer. After all, there's not much chance you'll be able to enjoy an intimate, romantic meal and a couple of bottles—er, glasses—of wine any time soon. Helping out with mundane tasks will cast you in a whole new light in the eyes of a very tired, stressed-out mom. She is likely to feel gratitude, which can translate to closeness, respect and, if you're lucky (and the moon is blue), desire. Conversely, if you come home from work, put your feet up on the sofa and tune in to the TV, Mom's going to start to feel resentful that she's got to finish the day's chores. A cheesed-off mom is not going to suddenly transform into a woman who wants to rip your clothes off at bedtime. She'll more likely rip your head off.

Remember that communication is key. You may suddenly feel sexy again in a few weeks; then again, the situation might be 10 times worse as Dad gets more frustrated and feels rejection and neglect while you feel stressed, pressured and guilty. Nothing is going to magically change unless you put your cards on the table. It may be hard to express your feelings, especially if you don't really know why you're feeling this way. But if the answer is something simple, like dissatisfaction at the unfair division of duties, explain how you feel. It may not be obvious to a dad, who feels he's done his share at work for the day. Talking also puts you in a situation of intimacy with Dad when you otherwise don't have much time for each other, so it's a step in the right direction.

Survival Secrets

- Don't put your sexual relationship at the back of the queue. Admittedly there are lots of new demands on your time now, but some things can be put off. The house doesn't have to be in perfect order before sex gets a turn.
- Take it slowly. Rekindle the desire on a low, slow simmer rather than a fast boil. Pretend you're in the early days of dating, and purposely be close and "make out" without having sex. Remember how much you wanted him at the end of an evening in those days?
- Don't be pressured or put yourself under pressure to want sex. Trying desperately to get in the mood won't help. It's a bit of a catch-22 situation: worrying about it tenses you up and puts you further away from your goal. You probably feel guilty that you are rejecting your man's advances and worried that it's going to drive you apart.
- Take time out from Baby. If you're having trouble getting together, take away interruptions by getting someone to babysit— preferably somewhere you're not—and have a night together at home or away. But don't build it up too much by labeling it a "dirty weekend." You shouldn't spend your time together with sex being the expected conclusion. Focus on each other and romance, and the sex will eventually follow of its own accord.
- Take time at the end of the day to wind down. Easier said than done, but women often have trouble swapping roles from mother to lover. Dropping the last dirty diaper in the bin and immediately stripping off the spit up–stained T-shirt for sex isn't an easy transition. See if Dad can finish off the day's chores while you relax in a warm bath, have a glass of wine or read a magazine.
- Give it a go. Maybe in this case you need a little matter over mind. You can spend so much time over-thinking the issue and fearing the consequences. Start with a bit of kissing, and you might find the mental barriers melting away as you get into it.

It Can Happen to Dad Too . . .

It is possible, but a lot less common, for new dads to experience a lack of desire. It's a good thing if this is the case for the first six weeks because then no one's going to be frustrated. And there's nothing to worry about if it continues for a while after. Dad is also going through a highly stressful period and is trying to cope with big life changes. The sleepless nights and preoccupation with all things baby affect you both. He could be worried that sex will hurt you. He may be a little put off by seeing the functional side of your body after witnessing the birth.

Neither of us had any intention of my husband being at the business end of the proceedings on D-day, but as soon as it was all systems go, the nurse had him forcing my leg up to my ear. Unless he closed his eyes, it was all right there, up close and very personal for him to see. It wouldn't surprise me if this horror flick puts some men off for a wee while; I think it would even put me off my chocolate. Similarly, a boob man might be suffering because his major turn-on is out of bounds right now. He may have issues with the whole function-versus-decoration issue after seeing you breastfeed.

The main thing is not to stress that he has gone off you because of your extra pregnancy pounds and wobbly bits. Be assured that he's way less concerned about your shape than you are.

Sharing Duties

The simple truth is that Mom is programmed to take care of the baby and Dad is not. A few generations ago this didn't present a problem. A crying baby was Mom's domain, or for the wealthy, the nanny's; Dad wouldn't dream of interfering and wasn't expected to. Nothing has changed biologically, but now a dad who takes a Victorian hands-off approach is risking the wrath of a rookie mom. I don't think many dads really want to sit back and let Mom do all or most of the work, but because Mother Nature has wired Mom with a stronger physical and emotional connection to Baby, it's harder for Dad to react and equally hard for Mom to sit back and let him at it. Dad simply finds it easier to continue with life as it was.

He's not being unhelpful on purpose; he's just not tuned in to the baby channel 24/7 like you are. Mom's nerves are tensed and strung like a laser security web around Baby. Her fuse is short. Ten seconds of crying seems like an eternity and it is all she can stand before leaping into action. Dad is able to watch the sports replay or the last five minutes of the game before he goes to Baby's aid. At a friend's house, Mom will be checking her watch every few minutes as Baby's bedtime approaches and making noises about getting things together and leaving, whereas Dad can likely carry on the conversation, start a new conversation and accept another beer. It won't occur to Dad that it's no longer practical to go on an unannounced bathroom break for upwards of 20 minutes (depending on the length of the magazine article he's currently reading) when Baby's bath time is imminent. You, on the other hand, will be lucky to get a 30-second pee in peace. And unless you can retrain your digestive system to function only between 9 p.m. and 7 a.m., don't expect to be able to empty your bowels without the door swinging wide to admit an inquisitive, "Are you having a poop, Mommy?" face for the next five years.

Putting nature aside, we have to try to find that happy medium and share parenting. While the nurturing instinct will always be with you, the desire to do everything for the baby will wane as the hormones settle down. It works better for everyone if Dad has been given a chance to bond with Baby early on, learned how to take care of Baby's needs and built an awareness of what goes on in Baby World. Moms are great martyrs, and it is easy to get into the habit of doing everything until you lose it—usually because Baby is being particularly unreasonable—and Dad has to salvage the situation. It's not fair that you tend to 99 percent of Baby's needs. Nor is it fair that Dad gets the shitty end of the stick and only gets to tend to the bad-mood baby.

Tips from the Trenches

- Short periods of letting Dad go solo from the early days are a good way to start. Mom gets a break; Dad gets bonding time and deals with anything that crops up in that period without prompting. It should help Mom to realize she's not the only capable one and to chill out a bit. Mom feels good about Dad; Mom feels good about herself.
- Later, do the same thing for longer periods. Don't limit the solo stints to Baby's nap times. Dad is the other parent, not the babysitter, so let him cover a whole day to see how challenging it is. We can all be much more appreciative of each other if we understand the other's world.
- Be careful to let Dad do as he thinks when he's dealing with Baby. Don't hover over his shoulder and immediately criticize his methods—your way may not be the best. Back off, bite your lip, and you'll find you both have different parenting strengths. Okay, so Dad definitely isn't going to be any good at breastfeeding, but where do his strengths lie? My guess is his specialties would be

gas- and sleep-related tasks like burping the baby and getting him off to sleep. Sure, it's hard to stop yourself from just marching in and taking over, but if you do it gives Dad the excuse to claim that he doesn't know how or that you do it better. An older baby will soon learn Mommy usually does a particular task and kick up a fuss when Daddy tries to do it instead.

- If you can't tune out, go out. Busy yourself so you're not worrying about what is going on at home. Are we scared they will steal our job? No danger of that.

Take a Break

A change is as good as a rest—never were truer words spoken. Dad is likely working five days a week, and while his job may be tiring and stressful, he does at least get a change of scenery on his days off. No such luck for Mom. The tedium of the same old tasks is draining, and it can take a toll on your emotions and your relationship. You don't have to be suffering from depression to feel cheesed off with the monotony and desperately crave a break. You deserve one. In fact, you should make sure you get one regularly. It doesn't mean you should expect to hand over Baby on a Friday night and skip off to the spa every weekend—after all, Dad needs some down time too—but do try to get away from the usual routine. Take a couple of hours off to go and do something on your own: shop; get a haircut; have coffee with a friend. Maybe you agree to expressing milk and Dad taking over the night feeds when he doesn't have to work the next day. Mom then gets at least one night of replenishing, uninterrupted sleep. In theory this is a great idea, but unfortunately it doesn't work out for all moms. It shouldn't present a problem if you miss the night feed once in a while; however, if you do it regularly your milk supply will soon adjust accordingly and you'll be left not having enough. Also, if you are prone to engorgement, sleeping through with overflowing boobs might be a challenge. Getting up to pump milk in the middle of the night kind of defeats the purpose.

Sleep

Sharing duties and taking breaks from the night feeds are sensible, but be realistic about getting sleep the rest of the time. If Dad has to go to work and wants to be able to function effectively at his job, he does need to be rested. There is no sense in you both being awake at night. I'm sure you don't need moral support (well, maybe only on special occasions, like when Baby cries all night instead of only half the night), so let Dad sleep if tomorrow is a work day. If you're lucky, you can grab a nap during the day when Baby naps, whereas it's not so advisable for Dad to nap on the job, especially if he's a pilot. This plan might mean investing in earplugs or using a spare bedroom or the couch for a spell. As suggested above, you can have your turn at a good night's sleep on the weekends.

RELATIONSHIP ISSUES—GRANDPARENTS

If you are lucky enough to have parents around to make into proud grandparents, enjoy it. It is the greatest feeling to see your parents dote over their new grandchild. My parents always claimed they weren't particularly bothered about having grandchildren before the event. You should see them now, clucking, cooing and spoiling with the best of them. The wider family dynamic changes once you have a baby, and it's common to feel closer to your parents than before. It's like the baby has brought with her a whole bunch of love to share around.

In the early weeks, grandparents provide invaluable support. It feels good to just have them around making a fuss over the baby, but they can help with more practical things too, like cooking you a decent meal or taking baby for a walk so you can catch up on some sleep. Make the most of it. Take them up on their offers of help while you recover, adjust to your new role and gain confidence in what you are doing. Most grandparents love to babysit, so when you're ready for a night out, let them loose!

However, it's also common to have troubles—actually, "troubles" may be a little harsh; let's call them niggles and gripes—with grandparents, particularly in-laws, and it can be hard to broach these issues without upsetting them or living with the problems and upsetting yourself. Just be aware of the following little aggravations that might crop up.

There are the **over-zealous grandparents** who offer too much advice and expect you to do things as they did. It's true: they are older and more experienced parents than you, but not always wiser. You may find yourself biting your tongue when they throw in a comment like, "She could do with missing a meal or two," in reference to your angel's chubby cheeks. While you may be able to take comments like this from your own mom, it's likely to grate more coming from ma-in-law unless you are lucky to share a close relationship. Don't get into family squabbles. Be polite but firm, and just let them know that you have your way of doing things and that's the way it's going to be. Also consider that sometimes they might be right!

Local grandparents can overstay their welcome by popping in too much. Be careful that they are not taking over, and particularly that Dad isn't getting pushed out of opportunities to bond with his child. He's going to be left with slim pickings after you and grandma have each done your share. You need time to build your own little family unit and establish your new routine.

If Baby is lucky enough to have two sets of grandparents, you may have the problem of **competing grandparents** vying to spend the most time with Baby and trying to outdo each other with presents. Of course it is a grandparent's perogative to spoil Baby, especially a first grandchild. I think it appears on the job description. A bit of spoiling and more toys than you know what to do with or have room for? Admittedly, it's not tragic. I suspect there are many people out there who would love to have such "problems." Rotate the toys, suggest the grandparents keep some at their places for Baby to play with when you visit, and rent a storage space.

While insisting that I was potty trained at 18 months and sitting impeccably behaved and feeding myself soup from a spoon around the same time, my mom becomes less informative when I ask for advice on how to pull off these amazing parenting feats. I put her in the category of **memory-impaired grandparents**. Her parenting advice is as vague as her cooking advice: "Put a bit of this in . . . I don't know exactly, till it looks right, then cook it on a medium heat till it's done." Great, thanks Mom.

RELATIONSHIP ISSUES—FRIENDS

Do you remember griping about other couples who had just become new parents? Did you ever utter the complaint, "All she has to talk about now is babies," when a good friend of yours became a mom and you were still just half of a twosome? As a late bloomer in motherhood, I know from experience how irritating it is when your best friend is suddenly unable to finish a phone conversation with you, or breaks off every fifth sentence to tell you the baby has just farted or some equally mind-bending, groundbreaking piece of baby news. Maybe now that you are a newly obsessed mom you can see it from the other side. I had one childless friend left when I had my baby, and it only took about 18 months of my baby-talk emails (and I was trying to be restrained) to drive her away.

At this turning point in your life it's easy to grow distant from childless friends. For a start, you are hideously busy, and it's likely that you will suddenly be doing very different things. They will still have the freedom to pop out to a bar or restaurant on the weekend; go for a spur-of-the-moment coffee; embark on a whirlwind shopping spree. From here on in, you'll need to plan ahead for all these activities or do them with a baby in tow, which might not be quite as enjoyable an experience (especially for the friend, whose pace through the mall is hampered by you stopping every few minutes to feed, clean spit up and change diapers).

Childless friends will not be overly interested in "talking Baby." This is rather unfortunate, since it's your new favorite subject. And, if you are at home with Baby full-time, it could be your only conversation topic for a while. While we're on the subject of "talking Baby," remember that only grandparents are truly interested in Baby's milestone achievements and funny antics. A baby rolling over for the first time is not remotely fascinating to a childless friend; even people with kids are only vaguely interested. Grandparents can be relied upon to provide enough ooohing and aaahing for the rest of your social circle.

While you may have moved on to a new part of your life, old friends are precious, and you should never underestimate the power of a good friendship. There might be tough times ahead that only your best friend can get you through. If you don't want to lose touch with your friends or make them feel alienated or replaced, you should make a conscious effort to make time for them. Don't bombard them with baby talk and photos when you do see them, and be sure to save the descriptions of the latest diaper contents for your mommy friends.

On the plus side, you may grow closer to friends who have kids. Just as in the past you have bonded with people who have similar interests, once you have a baby you will naturally gravitate towards other couples with kids. You can all not be able to go anywhere together!

If your social circle needs widening, it's also a great time for striking up new friendships as you meet other parents at prenatal classes and mommy groups. I was lucky enough to click with a few moms I met at prenatal class. Their friendship over the first year was a lifesaver as we shared zombie-like days, funny moments, emotional times, accomplishments and, most importantly, husband-bashing sessions.

My husband has a rule that he doesn't socialize with people when the only thing they have in common is a baby. This is a bit harsh, and I'm the one left dodging invitations for get-togethers, but in principal I agree. It's easy to suddenly find yourself spending precious weekend time with acquaintances you know nothing about beyond their child's name and the brand of diapers they prefer. As one friend says, "I have enough friends I don't have time to see without adding more." Enjoy your new friends, but cherish your old friends and remember who is most important to you.

RELATIONSHIP WITH BABY

Did you ever worry that you wouldn't love your baby? Some parents-to-be have no doubts and love the little ball of cells from conception straight off the bat, and others fall in love instantly at the birth. However, not everyone is an Earth Mother. I have to be honest and admit I never really liked kids. Consequently, I was anxious about how I would feel when my baby arrived. I was kind of holding out for that bonding business I'd heard about—wasn't there supposed to be a sudden rush of maternal instinct the first time I held her? I can't say there was. She was a strange creature to me with her own agenda, and I didn't feel instantly like a mom. If you're in the same boat, don't worry; the mothering instinct will creep up on you soon enough.

New babies really aren't much fun. In fact, if I had to rate them on a fun scale out of 10, I'd give my daughter a generous 2 and my son a 0.5 if it had to be a positive number. Sounds harsh? Then I assume you are either reading this prior to having your baby or you are simply kidding yourself. If new parents are completely honest, they'll admit I'm right—the first three months might as well be written off to somewhere between unpleasant and downright miserable. Until your baby starts to smile, interact and look a bit less like E.T., you may feel a tad distant. However, as soon as he starts to develop a little character beyond being a wailing, crapping, nursing machine, parenting becomes more palatable.

The magical three-to-four-month mark is generally seen as a pivotal point when things start to fall into place. Then he will get cuter at every stage until you will think he can't possibly get any more lovable, but of course the very next day he pushes the envelope. I still don't like kids much, yet I love my own with all my heart and then some. In fact, it's quite likely that I've worn a dent in the top of my baby son's head because whenever he's near I'm compelled to plant a kiss (or six) on him.

Oh sure, we can still have off days. It's okay and quite normal to dislike your baby at times. Babies are highly unreasonable, selfish beings. He has no thought for his poor old mom beyond where her boobs are at meal times. He is happy to take all your adoration but he isn't giving much back beyond bodily excretions. It's fine to feel desperate to get away from Baby once in a while. The great thing is you'll find you're equally desperate to get back after the shortest separation. I'm a grudge-holder, known to simmer for days before a fight with my husband and sulk for days after. The excellent thing with babies is that exasperation passes in an instant and is just as quickly replaced by that rush of heart-exploding love. He can have kept you awake all night and pushed you to the end of your tether, but just go and look at his cherubic sleeping face now and your heart melts.

RETURNING TO WORK?

All too soon maternity leave will be drawing to a close, and you'll need to make the decision of whether you will return to work. Yes, yes, I know being a mom is work, but I mean a proper job. Yes, yes,

I know being a mom is a proper job; I'm trying to think of a way to describe it. Let's call it paid employment—that should avoid all confusion. I have to say that I am shocked to learn that in the US (at the time of writing) there is really no such thing as mat leave; only 12 weeks of job-protected leave at best. So I expect the decision making comes a lot sooner for US mommies than for we lucky Canadians with our subsidized year off (sorry to rub it in).

Maybe the decision has been made for you because finances dictate that you start earning again as soon as possible. Perhaps you feel that you'd like to return to work just for the time being, until you have a second child. (Okay, so the real reason is so you can squeeze as much maternity pay out of your employer as possible.) Maybe your career is important to you and you are keen to pick it up again. Even if you are dying to get back into the thick of it and have something more challenging in your day than reading *The Hungry Caterpillar* again or being able to plan a meeting with six colleagues instead of a "play date" with six nine-month-olds, you're probably dreading the day when you actually have to start relying on someone else to regularly take care of your child.

Full-Time or Part-Time?

From polling all my mommy friends, the optimum seems to be returning to work part-time; preferably for a three-day week. Moms who go back full-time often find the weekend is not long enough to catch up on all the chores and spend family time together. They feel they are missing out on milestones in their child's development, and would like to be able to join in more activities with the little one. Moms who stay at home full-time sometimes have issues with keeping their minds stimulated, feeling useful and keeping their child occupied.

Of course, you have to do what suits your family financially and fits your employer's needs, but most importantly you have to do what fits your own needs. Some moms find they are just not cut out for being at home. It can make you feel horribly guilty if this is the way things turn out for you, but it happens and you need to make the best of the situation. By making the choice that works best for you, you are still being a good parent. A happy mom pursuing a career is way better than a depressed, struggling mom who feels trapped yet forces herself to continue with full-time child care.

Take care not to take on too much with reduced hours. It's fairly typical to end up trying to do a full week's work in three days. You tell yourself you are going to stick to the rules, but before long get caught up and burden yourself. Beware—it is easy to forget any agreements about working reduced or specific hours when you are faced with a deadline. Sometimes it is the boss or your colleagues who expect more from you; sometimes you get caught up in the urgency and find it hard to keep to the agreed hours. Remember, you've got plenty of work waiting for you at home, so don't take on more than you can handle and exhaust yourself.

FINDING THE RIGHT CHILD CARE

Your budget and needs will determine which type of child care is best for you. I hope you are not reading this chapter two weeks before you are due back at work because finding suitable child care can be a stressful and time-consuming experience. It's not a decision you want to make in a hurry, and you don't want that dreaded first morning back to work to be made worse by doubts that your child will be safe and happy.

Mommy and Daddy Day Care

Most people will be comfortable with someone in their immediate family taking care of their child. Who better than yourself and Dad? Now that a lot of jobs have flexible hours and working from home is an option, some couples are lucky enough to be able to juggle child-minding between them while they both pursue careers. Just to be clear, you juggle the child-minding, not the child—that can be dangerous.

I almost forgot: there's nothing to stop Dad from staying at home full-time if you are the chief breadwinner or get precious health and dental benefits that it might be prudent to keep. I have seen a few out there. I almost feel guilty saying this, and I apologize to the one or two Super Dads reading this, but I feel I should warn you that looking after the baby is probably all he will manage. Cleaning beyond baby's mouth and hands after lunch won't be part of the deal, nor will doing the laundry, grocery shopping or evening meal prep. Sorry if I am stereotyping; you know your man and what you can realistically expect.

Although it might seem like the perfect solution, be warned that working from home really doesn't work too well if you don't have a babysitter. If all you needed to do was feed the baby and let her sleep peacefully for a couple of hours, it might be feasible, but we all know this isn't the case. As Baby gets older and demands more attention, it will only get harder. You won't be able to ignore Baby's demands sufficiently to concentrate for any length of time, nor should you. Likely you won't get much done beyond a few emails.

Sibling or Grandparent Day Care

You may consider local siblings, friends and grandparents to take care of Baby for you. Sisters or "sisters" who are stay-at-home moms might be glad to help you out and take on another child for some extra cash. Or if they are working part-time, you can consider doing the same and "job sharing" on the child-minding front.

Grandparents are also a popular choice. After all, look what a fantastic job they did of raising you! However, there are a few things to consider before you assume they can step in. First, their age: there is a good reason why the natural and popular childbearing age-range is the twenties and thirties. After this you start to run out of gas. I'm an older mom and I know I have considerably less energy than when I was in my twenties. Heck, I used to manage four consecutive nights a week clubbing in those days. Suddenly, when I hit 30, I started falling asleep on the sofa in the evening, and that was long before my offspring came along to wear me out. If you are exhausted running around after your little one, think how the next generation will feel.

Second, just because they dote on their grandchild, you shouldn't assume grandparents want to become parents again and take on your child full-time. They finished their parenting stint years ago and are likely enjoying the grandparent role; it's much more fun.

Part-time care—one or two days a week—is probably more than enough for the oldies. Make sure they really want to do it and aren't just saying yes because they can't refuse. If they insist on taking on the day care on a full-time basis or if finances mean you have to rely on them, assess the situation frequently to make sure they are coping and still happy. Look for signs of stress, tiredness and ill health. If it's clearly a strain on them, it's time to rethink your arrangement.

Other Child Care Options
If you aren't lucky enough to be able to keep it in the family or amongst friends, you'll have to take the big step of finding a stranger you can trust. It is a daunting task, but one that will be made easier if you plan ahead, start the process in a reasonable amount of time and don't panic! Options include group settings like center-based group day cares and family day cares, or personalized care such as babysitters and nannies.

There are pros and cons for group establishments versus one-on-one care. You might prefer a group setting so that your child will get to mix with other kids in preparation for school life. Be aware, though, that mixing with others also means mixing with their germs. You will notice a sudden bombardment of colds and seasonal ailments, but it has to happen at some stage—if not now, then when your child goes to preschool or school—and the experts tell us that we need this exposure in order to develop our immune systems. You may prefer that your child have individual care in your own home. If you are lucky, a trusted friend may recommend a caregiver. You should still check out that the level of care provided meets your expectations, but it will save you a lot of hunting.

Group Day Care
Group day cares are those run by schools, churches, universities, employers and organizations like the YMCA. Depending on where you live, unless you enrolled your child in the popular group day cares immediately after peeing on the stick, this option could already be closed to you. In busy towns and cities, group day care waiting lists can be years long. It may seem hopeless if you are number 101 on the list, but places can open up since most moms sign up early for several day cares to increase their chances of obtaining a spot. Popularity is usually a good sign, of course, and this type of day care is almost always licensed or registered, but you should make sure that the organization meets the local care standards. Here are a few considerations to keep in mind when choosing.

- Location, location, location: just as it is with house purchasing, this has to be one of the top considerations when choosing a child care center. Close to home, close to your work or somewhere in between on the regular journey are optimal choices. The most fabulous day care that adds 30 miles a day to your commute is not a good choice as you are eating into precious family time, which will soon become an annoyance. Remember, if you are going to be sharing drop-off and pick-up with Dad, it's best to pick a location that is on both your routes. Being close to day care is also an advantage in case, heaven forbid, there is an emergency.

- Ensure that the day care can accommodate your intended working hours and check their policy for late pick-ups. Some day cares will charge overtime rates, and if you often get caught up at work, this could soon add up to more than you budgeted for.

- Be warned that day cares often charge a weekly rate to secure a place, even if you only need your baby to be there part-time.

- Common sense, personal tastes and standards indicate whether a child care center is right for you, but here are a few suggestions of what to consider:
  - Visit when the center is in full swing so you can see firsthand what goes on.
  - Do the babies and toddlers seem content?
  - Are the caregivers warm, friendly and, most importantly, enjoying their work?
  - Is it too noisy and completely chaotic, or is it strangely quiet and no one is having any fun?
  - Are the kids constructively busy? You should expect a good range of activities to be planned for each day, such as reading, crafts, physical activity and music.
  - What play facilities do they have? For example, if it is important to you that your child spends part of the day outside, do they have an outdoor play area or take the children to one nearby?

Some of these may not seem very important if your baby isn't even crawling yet, but presumably you don't want to repeat this search in a few months' time. You'll want a place that can provide for your toddler as well as your baby.

Family Day Care
A family day care is care in someone else's home, and is often operated by a stay-at-home mom who is opening her house to other children.

There are plenty of good ones, but of course there are also some that are not so good. If you aren't lucky enough to have a recommendation from a friend, talking to the parents of the other children at the day care is a good idea. The quality of care can vary quite a bit. You should check out lots of them before making a decision to get an idea of the range of options. First impressions count for a lot. You will probably be able to tell immediately whether you can short-list a day care. Here are some things to think about before you make your choice.

- Are you happy with the space? Is it big enough, warm enough and airy—not a gloomy basement?
- Find out what activities the caregiver intends to do on a normal day.
- Do the children have an outdoor space to play in or will they take trips to the local play area?
- What provisions do they have for naps and meals?
- What other infants or children are in the home? There are legal limits to how many children one caregiver can take on, especially if there are babies in the home. Assuming they are keeping within these limits, are you happy that one person can properly meet the needs of all the little ones attending?
- Are there pets? If so, are you happy with animals being around?
- Is it clean and safe? Everyone has their own comfort level when it comes to cleanliness, and we all get a bit picky when it comes to hygiene around our baby. I am a bit fanatical, to be honest, but even I had to laugh when I was researching this part of the book. The official recommendations for choosing a day care suggest you check whether a toy is sanitized between one infant putting it in his mouth and another picking it up. The list of times when caregivers should wash their hands is so long that, if followed, there would be no time to look after the kids: they'd permanently have their hands under the faucet. Of course, the toys should not be broken or covered in grime and spit up, but do you really douse all your kid's toys in bleach at the end of every play date? Be realistic. If you're too picky, you're not going to find any care.

Even if you have looked at a day care during a scheduled visit, drop in unannounced before you decide. A scheduled visit gives a bad day care time to disguise its faults. You might pop in to find children lined up in front of the TV. Okay, not too serious a crime, but in straightjackets?

Babysitter

There is no doubt that having a babysitter come to you, instead of having to arrange drop-off and pick-up as part of your busy schedule, is very convenient. Having a babysitter in your own home means you don't have to worry about any of the environmental issues as you do when the caregiver is in a different setting. But you do need to be really sure that you have the right person, so effective interviewing is critical, and you'll need to be organized. Interviewing and hiring can take months. Be prepared for setbacks if your first choice turns you down or has already been snapped up. Chances are, if you think they are worth hiring, so will other parents. I don't think it's ethical to poach.

Comrades' Recommendations

- Take care when budgeting. Babysitters charge by the hour, and once you've factored in the time from when you leave for work until you get home, you have a lot more than the average working day to pay for. This option works better financially if you and Dad can stagger your work hours so that one can leave later and one arrives home early.
- Rather than interviewing every applicant, you can cut to a shortlist by doing an initial screening on the phone. This weeds out obviously unsuitable candidates and people who cannot accommodate your working hours.
- For the interviews, prepare a list of questions and make sure you ask the same questions of all applicants or you'll never be able to compare candidates. When you ask questions, record the responses; otherwise you'll forget who said what.
- A huge plus has to be a person who loves kids. Qualifications are one thing, but unless it is obvious that a babysitter wants to be with children and enjoys the job, don't consider her. If a candidate has potential, interview her at home where she can meet the baby. You will see from her reaction to the baby whether she is a warm and caring person.
- Find out what the sitters would do in a typical day. This gives you an idea of how organized and creative they are.
- Issues like discipline and meal choices are not for the babysitter to decide; they're for you to suggest. You should discuss these topics, but maybe not use them as interview questions.

- Check that they can deal with medical emergencies and basic first aid.
- As with any job interview, you'll want to know about their experience and why they left their last employer. Often when babysitters don't work out, it's because their experience is with a different age group. They may be fine with babies, but not experienced at handling toddlers; they may have looked after older kids before and have glowing references, but not have the first idea what to do with a baby.

Nanny

Surprisingly, hiring a live-in nanny can work out cheaper than day care or a babysitter since the provision of room and board is part of the salary. This is a good option to consider if you have room to accommodate an extra person and won't find it an intrusion on your family life. Some nannies will also prepare you an evening meal and do basic housecleaning, which is a huge benefit when you are working full-time and want to spend all the free time possible with your family rather than doing chores. Don't forget she is primarily a nanny, so looking after Baby should be her first priority. The fact that she can rustle up a fabulous pot roast should be considered a bonus rather than counted as a qualification for minding your baby.

Tips from the Trenches

- Unless you are lucky enough to inherit a nanny from a friend (remember, no poaching), your best bet for finding a reliable nanny is through an agency. But first you need to find a reputable agency. You will have to pay a placement fee (which can be up to a month's salary), but a good agency has already done the lion's share of the work of ensuring its employees are suitably qualified, and they offer other assurances like a replacement nanny if your first choice doesn't work out. Be aware that there are bad agencies out there that have not vetted applicants and are just running an online matching service. If the agency doesn't deal with the difficult things like police checks and immigration, they are probably not worth the money.

- Just because the agency has given the nanny a clean bill of health doesn't mean you should trust its judgment. You need to be sure that your nanny is affectionate and warm, loves being with children and enjoys her work. Trust your gut reaction in deciding who is right for the job, and back it up with interview questions like those suggested above for hiring a babysitter.
- Find out how long they want to commit to the job and indicate how long you anticipate you'll want a nanny.
- Once you have found the ideal person and are ready to offer her a position, lay out all your expectations to ensure you are both on the same page. Draw up a contract once you have agreed upon duties, hours and holidays. If you have hired through an agency, they will deal with this.
- Have the nanny come by a week early, if possible, so you can introduce her to your child, allow her to familiarize herself with the new surroundings and make sure you're happy with your decision.
  - Show her where everything is in your home, especially things she might need in an emergency. Don't leave her to flounder on day one and call you 15 times at work. You'll break out in a sweat every time she calls and assume some dreadful accident has befallen your child, when in fact she is only trying to locate the can opener or fathom how to operate the Diaper Genie.
  - Make sure she knows the surrounding area and where to go for any activities you want your baby to participate in.
  - Introduce her to your friends.
  - Jot down your baby's food likes and dislikes and what kind of appetite she has. Most importantly, if your child has allergies or a special diet, be sure the nanny knows.
- Don't forget a backup plan. If your caregiver is sick, what will you do? Group day cares should have enough staff to deal with caregiver illness, but if your nanny, babysitter or family day care provider is sick, you need an alternative. You probably don't need reminding that the little ones get sick a lot, especially if they are around a bunch of other kids at day care. They also like to share their germs with the family when they get home, so you could find yourself using up your sickness allocation at work if you have to take a sick day every time your child or caregiver is sick.

Mixed

A lot of people opt for a mix of some of the above options, such as grandparents two days a week and day care for the remainder.

Monitoring Your Child's Care

Talking to the caregiver every day is a bit of a tall order, but you should make sure you are chatting once a week to ensure your baby is happy, the arrangement is working and you keep in touch with what is going on in Baby's world. This gives both you and the caregiver a chance to air any grievances.

While not suggesting you "spy" on your child-minder, for peace of mind and your child's well-being you should not be completely out of touch.

Occasionally come home early or visit during the day. Talk with your friends who see your caregiver out and about with your child to get feedback. My personal test of a good nanny or babysitter is one you mistake for the child's mom, because they obviously care very much for the little one and seem relaxed and happy. I've been caught a couple of times chatting with an assumed "mom" and was really surprised to be told they are the nanny. Some are obviously not the child's mom. They are wary of the child, and hold back from discipline, love and encouragement. Of course, who will make an excellent nanny is hard to ascertain in an interview. It's when you see them working with the children that it becomes obvious, and that usually means they have already been snapped up by someone else. If there are any problems or misunderstandings, make sure you deal with them promptly. In most cases your nanny or babysitter becomes more of a family friend than an employee.

Full-Time Mom

Of course, let's not forget that extremely important commodity: the stay-at-home mom. Had we been writing this book in the 1950s, there would have been no need to write this section as it was almost unheard of for a woman to have a second job beyond the mothering/housekeeping combination. Then again, in the 1950s we would have been too busy laundering and line drying our cloth diapers, baking apple pies, knitting sweaters and pinning and curling our hair to write this book in the first place. Now the tables have turned, and we assume every new mom came from an alternative job and considers going back. But for some women there is no question of going back to work when they are financially able to stay away from paid employment.

Maybe I move in the wrong circles, but there don't seem to be many of us left. As one of this dying breed I feel I should sing the job's praises, but I have to admit it presents challenges. I feel lucky to be able to take this time to be with my little one and wouldn't have missed it for the world, but it's surprisingly hard to keep both a baby and yourself entertained for a whole day on a full-time basis. The little ones have pretty short attention spans, and let's face it, when it comes to the sort of activities they are able to participate in, we also get bored pretty quickly. Unless you are unusually imaginative and creative, thinking of new entertainment is quite tough. The section that follows contains some tips for keeping the tedium at bay.

LIFESTYLE CHANGES

Almost all of the emotional issues you'll deal with in the first year come down to the fact that life has changed for you in a big way. Of course, there's a little hormonal activity thrown in for good measure, just in case you weren't messed up enough.

There is a strange conflict of interest when you're a rookie mom. You have no time to do anything, and yet quite often you are bored. It sounds ridiculous, I know, but it can happen. After all, a small baby really doesn't do much. Of course she eats a lot; she needs lots of diaper changes; she sleeps quite a lot. But after that the activity is limited. She'll mostly just cry—which means it's time for one of the previously mentioned activities—or she'll just sit there chewing on something, which means you can do something exciting like tackle the laundry mountain. It's not exactly rocket science, is it? And you don't have to be on mat leave from NASA for these mundane tasks to leave life feeling a little empty. You're not doing anything constructive, and you're convinced at times you can hear the tumbleweed rolling across the wasteland that was once your brain. The short stretches of free time through the day aren't long enough to get involved in anything challenging, even if you're not using them to nap. By the evening, once the tyke has gone to bed, any energy you had in the morning has dissipated, and instead of doing something constructive you are left vegging in front of the TV. At this point you might be wondering if you can stand to stay at home with Baby full-time. You can love her to bits, but it doesn't mean she is stimulating company.

There is light at the end of the tunnel. Around six months Baby will get mobile and things will liven up somewhat. She'll be sitting, crawling or rolling; at least it's a change of pace. She'll start to treat you less like a milk dispenser and start giving back some love. Around one she'll be walking; soon after, talking; soon after, talking and talking and talking. She'll be able to participate in more activities and interact with friends, and her favorite pastime will be goofing around to entertain you, closely followed by making life difficult for you. You'll be looking fondly back on the first six months as the good old days when things were easy and you had time on your hands to think about being bored.

"I wish I had known . . .

how much I would mourn the loss of my old life and self. Not sure I've completely adjusted to that one yet."

Motherhood officially changes your brain. It may feel like you are out of touch with your old self, and that is because you aren't the same person. Some moms are at ease with their new role as primary caregiver; others struggle to reconcile their old life with the new one. For those who struggle with the loss of independence (and relaxation), it may help to know that you can control to some extent how much Baby rules the roost. Rather than give up on your old life, try to include Baby in as much of it as you can. Whenever Mommy World gets tedious, it helps to have an outlet.

According to a survey, the first year of motherhood can be the loneliest in a woman's life. Being suddenly cut off from work colleagues and a social life can lead to feelings of isolation. The family support and neighborhood network that existed 40 years ago is now much less common, with families living far apart and the village lifestyle becoming increasingly rare. Meanwhile, after a week or two of paternity leave, Dad is back to his old routine: going to work; interacting and conversing with adults; lunching with friends. It can leave you feeling a tad resentful of your new lot. This is why comrades are vital to new moms. When we can't fit in with "normal" life, we have to build our own new mommy community to keep ourselves sane.

Survival Secrets

- Join in local activities. Life will seem less empty if you embrace the new lifestyle. Your local community center will probably have lots of mommy and baby groups and activities for you to join. Things like story time at the library, baby music circles, baby massage, mommy and baby exercise classes, and playtime where they can toddle, drool and roll while you chat and drink coffee—and supervise, of course.
- Have friends over under the guise of a "play date." At this point the babies will be having more of a drool date or a joint breastfeeding session, but you get some vital adult company. Try to think of them more as mommy dates, where the babies just come along for the ride. You don't have to discuss all things baby with a group of like-minded women.
- If you're really ambitious, start your own group doing something you like; for example, a running group or a book club.
- Get out daily for fresh air and a walk.
- It may sound silly, but on your night off, try something new and fun. Take up salsa dancing or learn a language. Learning something new will give you a boost and clear out some of the cobwebs.
- Go on outings. Stretch yourself, be brave and get out there to the museum, zoo or art gallery, either alone or with your mommy friends. There's a lot you can do with a baby in tow when you're not on a strict timetable. The baby may not be too interested in van Gogh just yet, but you might.
- Include Baby in as many of your activities as you can. Exercise with her, or try taking her to restaurants.
- If the restaurant thing doesn't work out, bring the restaurant to you. Invite some of your fellow new-parent friends over for a nice meal or take-out.

Lighten up. Look at this "time off" positively instead of hankering for what you no longer have. Throw yourself into your new role with gusto. Did you really enjoy work that much? All too soon the kids will be at school and you could find yourself back at your desk for, what, another 20 years? Isn't that enough?

"I wish I had known . . .
what a total and complete joy it all is—there is absolutely nothing sweeter than this."

Fast Facts Survival Sheet: Quick Answers to Mom's Everyday Questions

EATING

- A newborn will feed as many as 10 to 12 times in 24 hours. (p. 51)
- A breastfed baby's diet needs to be supplemented with 400 IU infant Vitamin D drops per day. (p. 52)
- The rule of thumb for formula intake is 2.5 to 2.7 oz per pound of body weight in a 24-hour period. (p. 55)
- Sterilize feeding equipment for at least the first four months. (p. 57)
- Trust your baby when it comes to how much and how frequently he wants to eat. (p. 55)
- A baby may have growth spurts, during which he will want to feed more often. These commonly happen at two to three weeks of age, six weeks, three months and six months. (p. 86)
- Solid foods can be introduced at six months, starting with iron-fortified infant cereal mixed to a liquid consistency. (p. 87)
- Food consistencies: Move from pureed to mashed around seven to eight months; minced around nine months; diced around 10 months. (p. 89)
- Finger foods can be introduced at seven to eight months. (p. 89)
- Do not introduce cow's milk to Baby's diet until at least nine months of age. (p. 62)
- Do not give a baby egg whites, honey, shellfish or peanuts. (p. 96)

SLEEPING

- Make sure your baby sleeps on her back. (p. 27)
- A newborn will sleep about 15 hours out of 24. (p. 26)
- Ideal room temperature for your sleeping baby is 65–68° F (18–20° C). (p. 135)
- Use lightweight blankets. Never put a pillow, duvet or thick blanket in the crib with your baby. (p. 136)
- Do not let your baby fall asleep with a bottle. (p. 70)
- New babies should not sleep through the night because they need regular nourishment. Don't expect Baby to sleep for more than three hours at a stretch until she's at least two months old. (p. 34)
- A baby may have periodic sleep regressions, particularly at four and eight months of age. (p. 42)

HEALTH

- A baby's normal body temperature is 98.6° F (37° C). (p. 134)
- A fever is a temperature of 100.4° F (38° C) and above. (p. 134)
- All fevers in babies six months and younger should be reported to your doctor and a temperature above 102° F (39° C) in babies over six months should also be checked. (p. 134)
- Febrile seizures involving convulsions and a possible brief loss of consciousness are a fairly common reaction to a sudden spike in body temperature. They are worrying to witness, but should be brief and are not serious. (p. 135)
- Expected weight gain:
  - Month 1: 4–7 oz (110–200 g) per week
  - Months 2–5: 1–2 lb (450–910 g) per month
  - Months 6–12: around 1 lb (450 g) per month (p. 85)
- Less than four wet diapers a day is a sign that your baby is not drinking enough. A noticeably sunken fontanel indicates severe dehydration. (p. 52)
- Colic can be recognized using the "rule of threes": prolonged unexplained crying lasting at least three hours per day for more than three days per week, beginning around three weeks of age and continuing for at least three weeks' time. (p. 22)
- Don't give cough medicines to a baby or young child. (p. 47)
- Only medicate a cold under a doctor's instruction. (p. 47)
- To test if Baby is hot or cold, feel the back of his neck or tummy. (p. 134)

SAFETY

- Choke hazards are anything that fits into a toilet roll tube. (p. 66)
- A choking baby will not necessarily be coughing; he may have difficulty breathing, flail his arms and legs or turn blue around the mouth. If you think Baby is choking, summon emergency help immediately. (p. 67)
- Heating milk and food in a microwave is not recommended. Take great care if using the microwave—always stir thoroughly and check the temperature before serving. (p. 55)
- Avoid using bumper pads in the crib during the first three months. (p. 29)
- Don't attach a soother to Baby's garments or to the crib with a ribbon or cord because this could cause strangulation. (p. 65)

Bibliography

The majority of the tips and advice that *The Survival Guide for Rookie Moms* offers were provided by fellow moms or learned during our own experiences surviving the first year of motherhood. However, there were times when we needed to turn to other kinds of experts for facts and figures. Here are the sources of our reference and inspiration, which all make very interesting reading—if you have the time!

FOR FACTS

BC Ministry of Health. *Baby's Best Chance*, revised sixth edition. Open School BC, 2006.

BC Ministry of Health. *Toddler's First Steps: A Best Chance Guide to Parenting Your Six-Month to Three-Year-Old*. Macmillan Canada, 2002.

Louann Brizendine, M.D. *The Female Brain*. Broadway Books, 2007.

Ann Douglas. *The Mother of All Baby Books: An All-Canadian Guide to Baby's First Year*. John Wiley & Sons Canada, Ltd., 2001.

Heidi Murkoff, Arlene Eisenburg and Sandee Hathaway. *What to Expect the First Year*. Workman Publishing Company, Inc., 2003.

Elizabeth Pantley. *The No-Cry Sleep Solution: Gentle Ways to Help Your Baby Sleep Through the Night*. Contemporary Books, 2002.

Benjamin Spock, M.D., and Steven J. Parker, M.D. *Dr. Spock's Baby and Child Care*. Pocket Books, 1998.

Hetty Vanderijt and Franz Plooij. *The Wonder Weeks: How to Turn Your Baby's 8 Great Fussy Phases into Magical Leaps*. Kiddy World Promotions B.V., 2008.

FOR FUN

Scott Feschuk and Paul Mather. *How Not to Completely Suck as a New Parent*. McClelland and Stewart, 2004.

Muffy Mead-Ferro. *Confessions of a Slacker Mom*. Da Capo Press, 2004.

Christie Mellor. *The Three-Martini Playdate: A Practical Guide to Happy Parenting*. Chronicle Books, 2004.

MAGAZINES

BabyStages, www.babystages.ca

BC Parent, www.bcparent.ca

Nestlé Baby Magazine, www.nestle-baby.ca

Parents Canada, www.parentscanada.com

Tesco Baby & Toddler Club Magazine, www.tesco.com/babyclub

Today's Parent, www.todaysparent.com/baby

Urbanbaby & Toddler, www.urbanbaby.ca

ONLINE

AskDrSears.com, www.askdrsears.com

Ask Moxie, www.moxie.blogs.com/askmoxie

BabyCentre, www.babycenter.ca; www.babycentre.co.uk

BBC Health, www.bbc.co.uk/health

BeFit-Mom, www.befitmom.com

Berkeley Parents Network, http://parents.berkeley.edu/advice/babies

Blush for the Modern Mother Magazine, www.blushmom.com

Breastfeeding.com, www.breastfeeding.com

Dial-a-Dietitian, www.dialadietitian.org

DrGreene.com, www.drgreene.com

Dunstan Baby Language, www.dunstanbaby.com

Kellymom Breastfeeding and Parenting, www.kellymom.com

MayoClinic.com, www.mayoclinic.com

Pacific Post Partum Support Society, www.postpartum.org

Parenting.com, www.parenting.com

Tiny Love, www.tinylove.com

Vancouver Coastal Health Authority (health education materials), http://vch.eduhealth.ca

Wikipedia, the Free Encyclopedia, www.wikipedia.org/wiki/Child_development

Bios

ERICA WELLS

A mother, wife and businesswoman, Erica Wells lives in beautiful Vancouver, British Columbia with her husband and two children. Erica graduated from university with her Bachelor of Business Administration and has held numerous senior sales and marketing roles throughout her career in telecommunications and information technology.

Once Erica gave birth to her two treasured children she decided to take a break from the corporate life and spend time writing about her wonderful experiences with her children. Erica is now the coauthor and cofounder of *The Survival Guide for Rookie Moms*. Erica is passionate about motherhood and a champion for women's growth and development within our society.

LORRAINE REGEL

Resting on the laurels of winning second prize in a school novel writing competition at age 10, Lorraine took a break from her writing career; a long 28-year break. In 2006, inspired by her toddler's voracious appetite for a good story and spurred on by the glut of dire picture books she encountered, she decided she could do better and began work on a children's picture book. This book is still a work in progress, but has moved to the back burner since the conception of *The Survival Guide for Rookie Moms*. So, Lorraine cannot boast an illustrious writing career, but even J.K. Rowling's author bio must have been fairly thin at one time.

Lorraine was born and raised in Essex, England. After a fairly unremarkable 30 years of schooling, art college and a career in banking, she changed gears in 1999 and in a busy decade moved to Vancouver, Canada, got engaged in Alaska, was married in Las Vegas, had two babies and, while coming to grips with her new career as stay-at-home-mom, wrote this book.

Lorraine doesn't claim to be a parenting expert in any way, but she has one important credential: she admits to excelling at being a clueless new mom. Having recently worked her way through the trials and tribulations of the first year of motherhood, she describes it as easily the biggest upheaval of her life, and knows firsthand the importance of support, friendship and comradeship during this period.

Postscript

Erica would like everyone to know that it is Lorraine who gets the five o'clock shadow on her legs.

Erica would like everyone to know that it is Lorraine who peed her pants on the way home from the Christmas party.

Erica would like everyone to know that it is Lorraine who admits to not liking kids much.

Erica would like everyone to know that it is Lorraine who has week-old pieces of dried-up ham under the dining table.

Erica would like everyone to know that it is Lorraine who can hold a bumper pack of markers under her boobs.

Erica's husband would like everyone to know that it is Lorraine's husband who has only changed a handful of diapers and who makes ridiculous noises in his sleep.

Index